The Geographies
of War

The Geographies of War

Jeremy Black

Pen & Sword
MILITARY

First published in Great Britain in 2022 by
Pen & Sword Military
An imprint of
Pen & Sword Books Ltd
Yorkshire – Philadelphia

Copyright © Jeremy Black 2022

ISBN 978 1 39901 591 2

A CIP catalogue record for this book is
available from the British Library.

Typeset by Mac Style
Printed and bound in the UK by CPI Group (UK) Ltd,
Croydon, CR0 4YY.

Pen & Sword Books Limited incorporates the imprints of Atlas,
Archaeology, Aviation, Discovery, Family History, Fiction, History,
Maritime, Military, Military Classics, Politics, Select, Transport,
True Crime, Air World, Frontline Publishing, Leo Cooper, Remember
When, Seaforth Publishing, The Praetorian Press, Wharncliffe
Local History, Wharncliffe Transport, Wharncliffe True Crime
and White Owl.

For a complete list of Pen & Sword titles please contact

PEN & SWORD BOOKS LIMITED
47 Church Street, Barnsley, South Yorkshire, S70 2AS, England
E-mail: enquiries@pen-and-sword.co.uk
Website: www.pen-and-sword.co.uk

Or

PEN AND SWORD BOOKS
1950 Lawrence Rd, Havertown, PA 19083, USA
E-mail: Uspen-and-sword@casematepublishers.com
Website: www.penandswordbooks.com

Contents

Preface

Conflict occurs in time and space, and each impose their disciplines. The spatial dimension, the subject of this book, is the key setting of war, the setting that provides for the geopolitics that determines tasks, the strategies through which they are pursued, and the operational and tactical methods and results. At every level, and in each sphere, land, sea and air, geography and geographical factors provide opportunities and problems for combatants. These are our topics.

The book rests on a lifetime of teaching and researching military history, and of visiting sites from Hastings to Guadalcanal, Gettysburg to Normandy. Principally, however, it rests on childhood interests in both geography and history. The onetime small boy who made a *papier maché* motte-and-bailey castle, played little soldiers, read from the local library R.R. Sellman's *Medieval English Warfare*, and drew maps, became an adult with a long-standing determination to bring geography and history together.

I have also benefited from the company, in person or through their writings, of a range of historians, academic and public. I owe them all a debt. In writing this book, I would particularly like to thank Leopold Auer, John Abbatiello, Ian Beckett, Lane Callaway, Stan Carpenter, Kevin Chapman, Charles Esdaile, John France, Howard Fuller, Roger Kain, Alan Rooney, Edward Rose, Kaushik Roy and Ulf Sundberg who commented on all or part of earlier drafts, and Ted Cook, Bob Higham, Andrew Holland, Mike Leggiere, and Philip Mansel who provided information on specific points. As I do not wish to repeat what I have presented elsewhere, I would like to draw attention to maps reproduced at a generous scale and extensively captioned in my *Mapping War, Mapping Naval Warfare, Forts,* and *The Second World War in 100 Maps*.

It is a great pleasure to dedicate this book to Andy Kerr with thanks for his friendship.

Abbreviations

Add   Additional Manuscripts
AWM   Canberra, Australian War Memorial
BL   London, British Library
JMH   *Journal of Military History*
LH   London, King's College, Liddell Hart archive
NA   London, National Archives
SP   State Papers
WO   War Office Papers

Unless otherwise stated, all books were published in London.

Chapter 1

Introduction

Geography frames conflict and accompanies war. It does so always, but notably so for tactical grasp, operational purposes, strategic planning, geopolitical consideration, news reporting, and propaganda. For the different stages of conflict, preparation, planning, initiation, waging, outcome, and retrospect, geography helps set the parameters, experience and perception of war at various scales. And it does so to very different audiences, from strategists to tacticians, from the military to the public, from those who were present to those who were distant in space and time. Moreover, geographical understandings developed in peacetime were used in wartime; while the map, the key tool, beyond the senses, notably sight, of human engagement with geography, was very much developed for, in, and through, war.

War occurs as a spatial process, across territory in all its forms, on land, at sea and in the air; but also with differing characteristics and to very varying degrees of intensity. These variations reflect a range of geographical, political, cultural and military factors. Separately, at the tactical, operational and strategic levels, collapsing the constraints (and, alternatively, seeking protection against this process) of space to get at the enemy, and to control territory, has always been a theme in warfare. Overcoming these constraints has been a continual factor, from the most local conflicts upwards, and, as with the range of the horsed societies of Inner Asia discussed in Chapter 5, is far from a novel aspect of mechanised society.

In turn, as considered in Chapter 10, overcoming geographical limits, has been differently seen, and with greater possibilities since the mid-nineteenth century, as the prospects for doing so increased thanks largely to technological change. Steam-transport, on land and at sea, was followed by the use of oil, and subsequently by the transformative addition of airpower and, later, rocketry. Indeed, the world as an isotropic surface – equal in all respects – appeared increasingly the case militarily in the

2010s and 2020s, as research and development in space weaponry and surveillance intensified, and as the potential of air power and rocketry to shrink the globe, and thereby project power, appeared ever more possible.

These ideas had been advanced from the outset of aircraft in the 1900s, were accentuated with the introduction of jet aircraft in the 1940s, and came to the fore with the 1980s' American concept of the Strategic Defense Initiative (SDI), and, subsequently, in the 1990s, with the so-called Revolution in Military Affairs, another American concept. Moreover, these concepts appeared taken into war-winning tactical and operational capability, and notably so with the targeting and communications employed by the Americans and their coalition allies to victorious effect in the Gulf Wars of 1991 and 2003 with Iraq. In the face of this capability, geography and its impact apparently were, at least to politicians and political commentators, of little consequence, apart from to place the non-West as clearly vulnerable in comparison to a supposedly superior 'Western Way of War.' This, however, was a highly misleading view that underlay much of the approach and that affected its application.[1]

That set of assumptions might then be seen as a case of American hubris about military 'transformation' by the 'hyper-power', in turn brought low in the 2000s by the subsequent difficulties of counter-insurgency conflict in Afghanistan and Iraq. These difficulties, particularly in the shape of Improvised Explosive Devices and ambushes, made the specificities of a roadside or a garden a basis for death and, separately, led to much talk in the United States of the 'return of geography'. In practice, as military professionals were well aware, geography had never gone away for others, nor, indeed, for the United States, and in both war and peace.

Yet, in the 2010s and early 2020s, these technological ideas revived in the context of deteriorating international relations, especially tensions between the United States on one side, and China and Russia on the other. A renewed air race saw expensive new long-range technology, notably hypersonic weaponry, as well as a greater interest in both space and cyber-warfare, both offensive and defensive. Again, geography appeared banished, and with more states able to seek to do so, a process compounded at the tactical level by drones, and their very rapid development to operate in a number of environments.

In this book, I want to argue that the approach suggesting a geography that has been overcome is limited, both in terms of the present-day situation, and with regard to the idea that such a development sets the clear pattern for the past. I have a formidable task as I wish to cover the different levels of conflict, contrasting types of war, and particular geographical, political and military environments. Key factors include reachability (getting there), transportability (moving around there), survivability (living there), and fightability (terrain, reach for weaponry), although each of these factors was, in part, shaped, or at least, in practice, its impact was shaped, by both perception and the operational and strategic tasking of militaries. Changes to all of these factors were important to the waging of war even if particular terrain corridors and key terrain might ensure that the spatial pattern appears constant. To argue that the location of battles occurs in similar places over time, and, therefore, that making military operations more or differently efficient was not a geographic factor is not a helpful way to consider the interactions of geography and war.

Separately, battles, campaigns, and wars are each very difficult to summarise and explain, let alone to assess their interaction, geographically and chronologically. Indeed, even battles that are frequently mentioned are often open to debate because the surviving sources contain discrepancies, as with Pavia (1525) and Waterloo (1815). Participants could be confused due to poor visibility, as with those two, and also Belgrade (1717), Inkerman (1854), and many other battles. Each of those battles cited were, in addition, to a significant degree, a matter of small-unit engagements, often poorly coordinated. These latter two factors were also true of many battles, including Ceresole (1544) and Adua (1896), due to the hilly topography that divided the battlespace. At sea, battles were difficult to coordinate beyond individual ship-to-ship clashes.

For many important battles, including the siege of Troy (date unknown), Lake Trasimene (217 BCE), Teutoburger Wald (9 CE), Brunanburh (937), and Bosworth (1485), there has been significant debate over the very location of the fight and the related terrain factors, let alone the course of events. Uncertainty also frequently relates to the numbers involved, which obviously affected the formation frontage.[2] Battlefield archaeology can play a major role in understanding the battles that can be located,[3] but much still often remains uncertain. Indeed, the narrative of battles is often far more unclear than is suggested by many accounts, and this includes the topography.[4] There are more general questions about the nature of our contemporary knowledge and understanding of the past, the partiality and compatibility of different types of sources, the silences in the historical record, and the objectives of those charged with accounting for military engagements.

In his *Battling the Elements* (1998), Harold Winters delivered the 'overarching message ... that, despite the evolving technology in warfare, physical geography has a continuous, powerful and profound effect on the nature and course of combat'.[5] That conclusion is valid, although Winters' study, like much of the literature on the subject, suffered from the extent to which the problems posed by alien environments were considered solely in terms of Western forces. More generally, there is a need to widen the geographical scope to include the human environment alongside the physical one. Doing so further leads to a stress on variety, as well as on human agency, and, as such, emphasises the degree to which both war, and writing about war, have to address these elements.

War itself is a protean phenomenon, one that you might think you know when you see it; but, in practice, war has varied definitions and different meanings to those involved in, and experiencing, collective violence. And so also with the geographies of war, for as the definitions of war vary, so do the geographies. This is most obviously so in terms of the conceptual and linguistic slippage, as in 'wars' on terror, crime, drugs, poverty, cancer, climate change, covid, and others, a process, moreover, that can be readily expanded in terms of differing languages, cultures and ideologies. War on 'crime' is possibly the most significant of these 'wars' in terms of this book, not least once it is also appreciated that disagreement in many states is regarded as a political crime, and that there can be a continuum between civil conflict and large-scale criminal activity. Moreover, police forces can serve as paramilitaries.

All these 'wars' are spatially variable, and thus significant in terms of geography, and notably so as they interact with the very detailed local geography of households and communities. Thus, with the 'war on crime', the wall, the gate, the fence, each a ubiquitous form, are central to the definition of space and its protection against a threatening outside. So also with the long-standing use of a narrow stairway to an upper floor (above a windowless ground floor) which is where the residential quarters are.

In turn, in terms of the military, there is an attempt to understand, reduce and shape, by means of doctrine, strategy, training, experience, weaponry and surveillance,[6] and through the use of force, control and fortification, the variety of war and its environments; a variety in practice seen in time and space. However, the resulting challenges in planning for, and fighting, war across many environments are very different, as well as difficult; and the responses of the military therefore have to adapt.

So also with the need by commentators to offer variety in exposition about war, not least breaking from misleading unitary arguments about its nature that in fact tie together disparate military events, settings, and cultures, into a coherent, but dubious, theme. In practice, the experience of geography, both physical and human, saps any such coherence, with distance and other geographical features acting as a constraint on unitary phenomena and also a setting for diversity.

My objective presents problems, and all readers will be able to feel that more should have been covered on topic x, or covered differently. Just so, for no book is definitive. And also with the classification adopted that provides the basis for the chapter organisation, and, indeed, the order of the chapters, and notably putting tactics and the experience of fighting in a given environment, before the strategy and geopolitics that help ensure the significance of particular areas. Debate over elements is welcome, and, to that end, this book provides an introduction to an important context and aspect of war, and also a key instance of the interaction of geography and history.[7]

Throughout, it is necessary to remember that what might seem 'academic' relates to the suffering, loss and fear of real people, as is always the case with war. There is also the savage strain of war on the physical and human landscape, one seen from deforestation in Antiquity to the more modern inroads of industrial warfare, including the vast amount of concrete fortifications left after the Second World War. On 20 October 1918, travelling the Bapaume Road, close to the Western Front of the First World War, Edward Heron-Allen, a visiting civilian, wrote in his diary: 'The whole landscape seen on either side ... was a scene of complete desolation. As far as one can see to the horizon, blasted woods and ruined villages.' Two days later, he reached Ypres, the site of three epic battles in 1914–17:

'I thought I had seen absolute devastation and ruin at Bapaume and Peronne [on the Somme], but Ypres by comparison is as the Sahara to a sand dune. I could not realise that we were approaching – much less in – the outskirts of Ypres…. Even the streets are obliterated…. The whole landscape is ploughed up into "hummocks" like pack ice in the Arctic floe - mounds and crevasses of blackened earth, dotted about with English and German graves, the entrances to dug-outs leading apparently into the bowels of the earth.'[8]

Chapter 2

Tactics

Geopolitics provides a context for the prioritisation of objectives central to strategy, while the operational dimension is the attempt to achieve strategic outcomes by means of campaigning. This centrally entails questions of resource allocation and use in a sequencing of time and space. Tactics are the resulting battlefield actions. In all of these dimensions, geography plays a role, as context and more.

The pervasive impact of geography on war can be seen clearly at the tactical level, and it is there that we begin. The tactical level both profoundly affects operations (and thereby strategies), and also engages the overwhelming majority, both of participants in conflict and readers about war. This is notably so when the latter are concerned with 'the face of battle', an approach, focused on the experience of fighting, that has been especially influential since the 1970s.[1]

Conflict takes part in particular locations which are mentally mapped by the participants; and it is the character of these locations as thus understood that attract attention. Most clearly this is so with discussion of battles and sieges. The battle-descriptions always capture the movement of troops across terrain and/or through cover: they 'toiled up the hill', 'charged down the slope', 'surged across the river', or 'fought back from the wood'; and so on. Ships move amidst squalls and the spray of waves. Pilots see their opponents if in charge of fighters, and the ground if of bombers, through 'a gap in the clouds'. Alongside such language, the detail of the physical geography also plays a role in the consideration of the specifications and impact of the particular weapons employed, both at these sites, and more generally.

Moreover, this is not the limit of geography's impact. It is notably at individual sites that conflict is memorialised with monuments, and therefore, alongside the descriptions offered, their physical nature take on especial interest, as does the exact location of the monument or monuments. Contention over the memorialisation of war makes this more of a potential and potent issue.[2]

The influence of geography on battle can be far more significant than appears at first glance to the modern observer, or earlier counterparts, not least because aspects of it are not apparent to the eye. In part, this is because much of the relevant geography is a matter of the factors that led two armies to fight at a specific spot; while, separately, much is sub-surface, affecting, for example, past drainage patterns. In the First World War (1914–18), deep and surface geology and terrain were important when trench systems were dug, influencing their strength and vulnerability and affecting their placement. Both deep and surface geology were at issue.[3] Furthermore, rock mechanics and soil mechanics were each developed as disciplines during the Second World War (1939–45), in which more geologists served than in the previous conflict,[4] while more had done so in that conflict than in previous wars.

Terrain features, such as hills, valleys and slope profiles, survive most clearly from past physical geography, but combatants also recall other aspects of geography, both physical and human, ranging from surface features, most significantly vegetation and drainage, to weather, particularly temperature, rainfall and wind, with both intensity and direction for the latter two. Such factors help provide a geographical context for tactics, although armed forces are not passive recipients of the influence of physical geography.

The most obvious geographical feature was the advantages of slope, which offered visibility, height and dynamism. Visibility, as with Iron Age hill forts in Europe, or those of the Qulla (Colla) of western Bolivia (CE 1100–1450) and, also far more generally, provided situational awareness of one's own side and one's opponents; but tactics were, and are, not simply a matter of functionality in those terms, and readily measurable accordingly. Instead, visibility, and with both troops and fortifications, was also a question of display and a means thereby to encourage supporters, influence the undecided, and intimidate the enemy, whether or not conflict was intended at that moment and/or on that particular site. Indeed, display and intimidation, and the related use of terrain, were a major feature in the struggle over morale that is integral to conflict; including with reference to the negotiations and/or deterrence, explicit or implicit, that are often part of wars or confrontation.

Height and slope also provided defensive advantage against cavalry, being particularly valuable against steppe nomadic cavalry, as in India,[5] but also for infantry resisting cavalry in Europe, as for the British at Waterloo (1815). In very different contexts, the surveillance, intimidatory and strike opportunities of height were all shown by the German defenders of Monte Cassino in Italy against Allied attack in 1943–4,[6] and by drones in 2020 when successfully used by Azerbaijan against Russian tanks deployed by Armenia and by Ukraine against Russian invaders in 2022.

Height was very important to fighting, and notably, although not only, at the tactical level, and, as a result, drew together natural features and those added to the landscape by settlement, by fortification, permanent or temporary, by the use of animal mounts, or at sea by the importance of the relative height of vessels, such as the effective Venetian galleases against the Ottomans at Lepanto in 1571. In using missiles, whether stones, javelins, slingshot, arrows, or shot from firearms and artillery, height gave greater range, aided aim, made it easier to fire on the rear ranks of opponents, and reduced air resistance. As far as stabbing and slashing weapons were concerned, height potentially provided much greater downward impact, which was a factor in the use of both infantry and cavalry. Moreover, dynamism was given by the real and apparent advantages of advancing downhill with a greater speed and force obtainable for the effort expended, as with the Allies totally defeating the Turks outside Vienna in 1683.

As a consequence, major efforts were made to gain and use particular hills in battles, as at Vitoria in 1813, a British victory in the Peninsular War. In 1863, on the second day of the battle of Gettysburg in the American Civil War, the movement of Confederate troops to the flank, which was readily observed, was successfully countered by the Union, benefiting from its interior position, switching troops to Little Round Top in order both to block them and to use the height of that position.[7]

Conversely, those firing or advancing uphill, or defending against those attacking with the advantage of slope, were at a disadvantage in each of these respects. This factor helped explain William the Conqueror's use at the battle of Hastings in 1066 of the Saxon advance forward of their shieldwall from the commanding hilltop. However, as a reminder of the uncertainty about events discussed in the last chapter, there is debate about how far the Norman retreat that enticed the Saxons forward was planned and how far expediency. Firepower, as with the Norman archers at Hastings, was one way to confront this problem of height. The vulnerability of hilltop positions was also shown with their blockade as with Alesia in 52 BCE during Julius Caesar's conquest of Gaul or in 1573 with Protestant-controlled Sancerre during the French Wars of Religion.

In 1762, during the Seven Years War (1756–63), Frederick II, 'the Great', of Prussia increasingly used artillery-based tactics against the Austrians, not simply due to the enhanced capability of his artillery and the decline in his reserves, but also because the defensive Austrian use of hill positions in the north Bohemian and Moravian hills had revealed the defects of the Prussian tactics, and in particular of the attack in the oblique order, a method, in which force was concentrated on one flank, that was appropriate on the flat. Instead, at Burkersdorf and Freiberg in 1762, the Prussians used dispersed columns successfully in attack. In turn, the Austrians were more successful in 1778–9 in the War of the Bavarian Succession in relying on strong defensive positions in the hills to hold off Frederick who could not benefit from mounting flank attacks on their positions.

The advantage of terrain could be tempered when moving from the defensive to the offensive, a frequent test of fighting and command skills. At Towton in 1461, during the War of the Roses, the Yorkists benefited from a dip in front of their position, but when they came to attack the Lancastrians, they then had to charge not only downhill but then uphill.

However much already affected by field fortifications, the overall situation only really changed when the range and volume of firepower increased to the point that those who were visible were highly vulnerable. This was very much a consequence of the greater use of artillery in the Napoleonic period, and caused heavy casualties for the Prussians when attacked by Napoleon at Ligny in 1815. To avoid the risk, the British, notably under the Duke of Wellington, including at Waterloo, increasingly deployed their forces on the reverse side (back) of slopes and/ or lying down in order to minimise the impact of preliminary French bombardment.

As so often, however, tactical understanding was not necessarily preserved. Thus, the lesson about reverse slopes had to be relearned in the early stages of the First World War, as at Ypres in 1914. There the British 7th Division took many casualties from German fire by holding a forward slope, other British formations having already learned the perils of doing so in fighting on the River Aisne.

As a battlefield instance of the ambush, terrain could also be used to screen moves, as at Towton in 1461 with the late arrival of John, 3rd Duke of Norfolk's men who were hidden by a ridge until they attacked the Lancastrian left-flank, a crucial development that contributed to Yorkist victory. At Rossbach in 1757, during the Seven Years' War, the Prussians under Frederick the Great used the ridge of the Janus Hill accordingly in preparing his successful attack on the French. Mountain passes were classic sites for ambush, as with the Bulgarian destruction of the Byzantine army in 986 at the battle of the Gates of Trajan, and, in 1136, with the comparable success over the Byzantines by the Seljuk Turks at the battle of Myriokephalon.

The mapping of topography was to be more common and more precise by the late nineteenth century, by which time the surveying and mapping of height had improved, not least with the use of contours, but there were useful devices prior to that. One such was the use of numbers to indicate the relative height of ground. Known as relative command, this technique was taught by François Jarry, a French refugee who became topographical instructor at the newly-established British Royal Military College in 1799, and influenced the teaching of reconnaissance to the Royal Engineers. This helped Wellington as he planned in 1815 how best to respond to a French invasion of Belgium. Relative command was used on what is termed the Waterloo map which Wellington reputedly marked up the day before the battle and gave to the Quartermaster-General with instructions to deploy the troops accordingly. In turn, early on the morning of Waterloo, Napoleon briefed his commanders with maps spread over the table before him. The British were not alone in advancing the mapping of height. Major-General Karl von Müffling, who was Chief of the Prussian General Staff in 1821–9, developed a system of hachures marking the gradients of hills on maps which became known as the Müffling method. An understanding of the landscape was becoming central to the technical side of command.

Slopes are rarely uniform, and the detailed folds of topography greatly affected advances and, to a lesser extent, defences. In particular, the formation of advancing units could be disrupted, broken up, or funnelled, thus providing opportunities for the defenders, and notably so if the attackers for their fighting effectiveness, required cohesion, as with pike-squares into the seventeenth century, or, indeed, any other formation that was close-packed and regular. Advancing lines of infantry, stopping and using volley fire faced this difficulty, but columns could also be forced to advance on too narrow a frontage.[7]

A separate issue was that of the drainage, and the very varied water-retention characteristics of particular soils, rocks and settings. These issues could readily extend to a waterlogged character for the terrain, which was significant for infantry, cavalry and artillery. Soft ground was particularly difficult for the last two, as for the French at Waterloo, helping indeed to delay the start of operations that day. At Konotop in Ukraine in 1659, Cossacks dammed the river Sosnivka, flooding the valley, and lured the heavy Russian cavalry into the boggy ground where it was slaughtered by the Crimean Tatars, a light cavalry force, in alliance with the Cossacks. Subsequent changes to the drainage have frequently altered the historical landscape, and the latter needs to be reconstructed in order to understand battles, and thus clarify command decisions.[8] Water features themselves offered many tactical advantages to the defence. They could define the battlefield, notably thus protecting flanks, as the Cock Beck did at Towton. Moreover, that potential was enhanced by the use of water in fortification defences, as with the locks on rivers to flood the surroundings, for example in the French fortifications at Strasbourg, Verdun, Valenciennes and Gravelines.

Water features provided an obstacle for advancing forces and, linked to this, a defensive position, including indeed the basis for an attack at a particular location. Defenders could be deployed to cover a crossing, relying in particular on choke points, in the shape of fords or bridges, as with the Khalka Mongols thwarting an invasion of the Zunghars of Xinjiang in 1731–2, or the Confederates defending what became known as Burnside's Bridges over Antietam Creek against successive Union attacks for over three hours in the battle of Antietam in 1862. During the Cold War, the Americans planned the destruction of bridges as part of the defence against any Soviet attack into West Germany.

Defenders could also rely on the river itself as a means to break up the cohesion, pace and/or dynamic of the attacking force. In 1510, near Merv, the Safavids staged a feint retreat, only to attack the Uzbeks just after they had crossed a river, first breaking the bridge in their rear. At Zenta in 1697, an Austrian army under Prince Eugene heavily defeated a larger Ottoman (Turkish) army that was advancing across the river Tisza: the Austrian attack found the Ottoman force divided by the river. A similar technique was to serve other commanders, including Russians fighting the Ottomans near the Danube.

Being behind a river was usually more advantageous, but there could be an advantage in having a position resting on a river to the rear, as it reduced the opportunities for envelopment, as the Russians showed in the face of Napoleon's attack at the hard-fought battle of Friedland in 1807, and the Soviets over a longer period in thwarting German attacks at Stalingrad in 1942. In the American War of Independence, Daniel Morgan placed the Broad River a few miles to his rear to discourage the militia from panicking and fleeing when he fought the British at Cowpens in 1781, although that was not the reason for his victory. Retreating in these circumstances could be difficult and costly, as for the Lancastrians at Towton in 1461: the river added to the difficulty and cost of the retreat.

A bridgehead position could be difficult, not least with insufficient room for manoeuvre, as Napoleon discovered when advancing across the Danube against the Austrians at Aspern-Essling in 1809, only to be defeated. As such, a bridgehead position was like a beachhead one, vulnerable to counterattack and bombardment, as the Allies found at German hands at Salerno and Anzio in Italy in 1943 and 1944 respectively, and also difficult to exploit.

As a variant to a river, the Mughal centre redeployed behind a ravine at the second battle of Panipat in 1556. In 1616, also in India, a ditch in front of the Mughal army at the battle of the Paitan River broke the cavalry attack by the forces of Malik Ambar of Ahmadnagar. In 1632, at Lützen, Wallenstein deepened a ditch to the front of his position in order to hinder the eventually-victorious Swedish attack. In 1759, in the battle of Chinsurah in Bengal, the British-Indian force of the British East India Company defeated their Dutch opponents who advanced only, unexpectedly, to find a broad ditch protecting the British centre. Blocked by this, they were within range of British fire, and had serious losses before retreating.

River lines and their equivalents could be breached, as at Wenden in 1578 when, in the face of Russian defenders, the Swedes and Poles successfully forded the River Aa, each cavalryman taking a foot-soldier on his horse; or in 1632 when, crossing under powerful artillery cover, including the smoke produced, King Gustavus Adolphus of Sweden forced his way across the River Lech into Bavaria defeating the army of the Catholic League under John, Count of Tilly. Conversely, abandoning the river line in order to attack, as the Hungarian cavalry did with the Borza River, in order to attack the Ottomans (Turks) at the battle of Mohacs in 1526, could be disastrous.

Defensive reliance on a river line could lead to a standard attacking method of 'fixing' the defender at the river by means of attack or threat by part of the army while a detachment was sent to cross upstream and roll up the defender's flank. This tactic was repeatedly used successfully, as by Hannibal and his Carthaginian army crossing the Rhone in 218 BCE against Celtic opposition, William III of Orange at the expense of James II at the Boyne (1690), the battle that determined the fate of Ireland, and by Sir William Howe at that of George Washington at Brandywine Creek (1777), a battle that opened Philadelphia to British occupation. Gustavus Adolphus had intended this ploy at the Lech, while, at Wittstock in 1636, the Swedish army under Johan Banér successfully used a detachment to move behind an Imperial flank. These were instances of the classic need for adaptability in attack and defence. However, at the battle of New Orleans in 1815, the British under Sir Edward Pakenham failed when they sought to use a flanking manoeuvre, because the flanking force across the Mississippi River could not dislodge the defenders there so as to fire at the main American force under Andrew Jackson, a force which was covered by the river on its right, a marsh on the left, and field entrenchments to the fore.

In 1547, at Mühlberg, aside the River Elbe, the defending forces of the Schmalkaldic League of German Protestants had destroyed the bridge across the river, but the Imperialists, under the Emperor Charles V, both built a temporary bridge and found a ford, launching a victorious surprise attack. In 1592, in the French Wars of Religion, the Army of Flanders, the major Spanish strike force, under Alexander, Duke of Parma, thwarted Henry of Navarre, the Protestant leader, outside Rouen by building a bridge of boats over the River Seine. In 1717, the Austrians under Prince Eugene crossed the Danube by pontoon bridges east of Ottoman (Turkish)-held Belgrade, which they then besieged. In 1914, Belgian forces broke the bridge at Visé over the River Meuse, but the

Germans crossed at a ford; while, in 1943, the British responded to the demolition of Sicilian bridges by the retreating Germans, which left very steep riverbanks, by using mules.[9]

However, it was not always possible to find fords or easy to construct effective pontoon bridges, not least in the face of resistance, while, as the Germans and Austrians discovered in Serbia in 1915, storm-spate rivers made these bridges unusable.[10] In 2015, in the re-enactment at Waterloo, a Prussian unit, instructed not to run cannon across a small bridge constructed over a ditch near La Haye Sainte for the Allied re-enactors to cross over, did so, causing the bridge to break, and it took forty-five minutes to repair.

The importance of rivers and bridging points for transport and supplies helps explain the location of fortifications. Thus, because there were no bridges over the Meuse River north of Maastricht, that fortress was of particular interest for operations in the region, as in 1579, 1632, 1673, 1748 and 1794. Nearby Liège and Fort Eben-Emael played comparable roles in 1914 and 1940 respectively.

In the English Civil War (1642–6), part of the British Civil Wars of 1639 to 1651, control over bridges, such as those at Upton-upon-Severn, Pershore and Tadcaster, was very important both in local campaigning and for the movement of field armies, while control over the crossings over the River Trent was important to the course of the war in the East Midlands. In the West Midlands, the bridge over the Avon at Stratford was broken by the Parliamentarians in 1645 in order to cut Royalist communications between their base at Oxford and the west, their remaining area of support.

As a result of these factors, rivers and bridging points explain siege targets, such as Kehl (1733) and Philippsburg (1734) on the Rhine, both French targets during the War of the Polish Succession, Kunjpura on the River Yamuna in India (1760), and Izmail on the Danube which the Russians took in 1770 and 1790. So also with the setting of battles. These included St Gotthard in 1664, when the Ottomans were prevented from advancing across the river Raab by the Austrians; and Kagul in 1770, where the Russians defeated the Ottomans whose rear was to the Danube. As with Kunjpura on the route from the Khyber Pass to Delhi, or Liège, Maastricht and Namur on the River Meuse, such bridging points were often significant for bringing together road and river routes.

Very differently, a lack of drinking water could be a key factor for both troops and animals, and contributed to the serious defeats of the army of the crusading kingdom of Jerusalem at Hattin in 1187 by Saladin, and of the Chinese in 1449 at Tumu by the Mongols. As with the extent to which marshes, forests and mountains could be penetrated, this was an aspect of the local situational awareness that was so important to defining the battlespace. Proper reconnaissance was crucial. Cutting water supplies was an important means in trying to seize fortifications, as unsuccessfully by rebels against Ottoman rule at Aleppo in 1520.

A variant was supplied when using disease in order to contaminate water sources. Thus, in 1646, the Uzbeks fouled the Balkh River in northern Afghanistan, helping to cause an epidemic among the invading Mughal army. In turn, corpses could be fired into besieged positions to cause weakening diseases, as with the surrender of Portuguese-held Fort Jesus in Mombasa to the Omani Arabs in 1698 at the close of a long siege. There could also be the inadvertent impact of disease making positions untenable, as in 1757 when the mass slaughter in Indian cities, such as Agra, led to a cholera outbreak that helped lead the victorious Afghan invaders to return home. Even without such episodes, the health problems posed by the human and animal waste produced by armies challenged water supplies and could make it difficult to keep clean at particular sites where the ground water was readily contaminated. As a result of this problem, fortified positions could not always be retained.[11]

Like water features, dense woodland could serve as a definer of flanks, as for the English in their victory over the larger attacking French force at Crécy in 1346 in the Hundred Years War, and for Babur, the Mughal leader, at the first battle of Panipat near Delhi in 1526. At Panipat, the challenge posed by the far larger Lodi army was magnified by the mobility and speed of its cavalry, so that Babur chose a battlefield to limit and counter the cavalry. At the same time, the physical advantage, of being between two blocks of forest, which channelled the attackers and prevented them outflanking the defenders, was enhanced by human action in the shape of field fortifications in terms in 1526 of deploying a line of wagons linked by ropes of hide and breastworks, and digging a ditch. There are differing accounts of the reasons for Babur's victory, as also for that over the Rajputs at Kanua the following year, but the use of field fortifications in order to create an appropriate battlefield geography played a significant role.

Such fieldworks, seen also with the English use of wooden stakes at Crécy in 1346, indicated the overlap between geography and fortification, which was a key element of human military geography. Although a *wagenburg* failed the untrained German peasants fighting the cavalry and cannon of Landgrave Philip of Hesse at Frankenhausen in 1525, wagonfort-centred deployments, known in Turkish as *tábúr cengí*, were repeatedly successful, as for the Hussites of Bohemia in the early fifteenth century, and for the Ottomans at Chaldiran (1514) and the Safavids (rulers of Persia/Iran) at Jam (1528), at the expense of the Safavids and Uzbeks respectively. The Imperial army used a line of linked wagons against Swedish attack at Wittstock in 1636.

So also, but without wagons, with the successful Spanish use of a trench and earth parapet in the Italian Wars against the French at Cerignola (1503), and against the French and Swiss at Bicocca (1522), and with the field fortifications effectively used by Oda Nobunaga at Nagashino in Japan in 1575. At the same time, contradictory explanations of Nagashino underline the problems in discussing and explaining the significance of geographical features, and, more generally, the practice of military history as both descriptive and explanatory.

More commonly, dense woodland acted as a disruptive obstacle, and thus usually to the benefit of the defence. In 1944, Lieutenant-General Sir Henry Pownall observed of fighting in Burma (Myanmar): 'It is bound to be a slow business, I fear. That jungle is so infernally thick you literally cannot see ten yards into it, and to winkle out concealed Japs, one by one (and they have to be killed to the last man) is the devil of a business.'[12] In France during the Second World War, Resistance fighters used the *maquis*, a very dense shrub with small trees, to hide their supplies, and the Resistance was often referred to as the Maquis.

However, although this led to delay, it was possible to advance through woodland, as the Prussians did in their approach to Waterloo in 1815, albeit benefiting greatly from not having to face any French opposition at this stage. Furthermore, dense woodland could aid penetration techniques and thus attackers by offering surprise and providing cover, as for the Japanese during the Second World War. Much depended on the density of the trees, the nature of the ground cover, the force structure of the two sides, and the experience, skill and confidence of both troops and commanders, and on both sides. In India, in response to gunpowder, forts were increasingly built in the fifteenth century on steep, rocky hills, and in the midst of forests, both of which hindered attack. Conversely, in North America in the seventeenth to nineteenth centuries, the builders of log stockade forts cleared the woodlands for several hundred yards around so as to prevent a surprise attack shielded by the trees and to provide an unobstructed field of fire.

In general, the requirements that commanders and units had of physical features varied with weaponry and mobility (neither constant features), and with the understanding of them. Thus, in tracking Communist insurgents in Malaya in the 1950s, the British recruited Iban trackers from Sarawak as they were able to interpret the slightest irregularity on the ground or in jungle foliage as indicators of recent human presence. Accordingly, the Sarawak Rangers was constituted as a unit. These men were used again in the 'Confrontation' with Indonesia in 1963–4, with this time the tracker skills required on the island of Borneo.

Several factors were frequently involved in the use of terrain. Thus, at Falkirk in Scotland in 1746, the Jacobites succeeded over government forces that were hindered by fighting uphill, by growing darkness, and by the heavy rain wetting their powder. A lack of fighting spirit was also significant,[13] one that presumably owed much to these factors, as did the ineffectiveness of the government artillery. The Jacobite commander, Lord George Murray, commented on 'the infinite advantages' the Jacobites:

> 'had from their position – the nearness of the attack, the descent
> of a hill, the strong wind and rain which was in their back, and
> directly in the enemy's face; and that they had some mossy ground
> upon their right, which prevented the enemy's horse from being able
> to flank them; and that by reason of the badness of the road, and
> steepness of the hill, their cannon were of no use to them; in a word,
> the Highland army had all the advantages that nature or art could
> give them.'[14]

Moreover, engagement with the terrain and cover varied with doctrine and training, as with the Australians fighting the Japanese in New Guinea in 1943:

> 'All companies must retain their mobility and be capable of
> dealing with enemy parties endeavouring to infiltrate between the

companies... Standing, reconnaissance and fighting patrols must be constantly active... At least three days food, water and ammunition must be placed in each perimeter. It is inevitable that, when attacked by large and determined forces, perimeters will be surrounded, but defenders must hold out. In every instance where this was done the enemy were beaten off and the defenders were relieved... On occasions when withdrawals were attempted the casualties suffered were heavy ... the rules of hygiene and sanitation and anti-malarial precautions must be strictly observed at all times, no matter how hard the fighting, or how weary the troops... Patrolling must be aggressive and continuous and is the key to success in the jungle... A high standard of training is necessary.'[15]

Knowledge in advance about relevant physical features differed considerably, while their depiction on maps varied, not least in terms of the expectations of precision. Whereas, for example, there had been considerable stylization in the depiction of physical features in medieval and sixteenth-century European maps, as the map-makers were primarily concerned with recording the existence of these features, rather than their accurate shape and extent on the ground, the trend thereafter was towards precision in the portrayal of the crucial physical outlines, notably coastlines and rivers. This change reflected the nature of the available information, as well as shifts in conceptual standards. At the same time, maps also moved away from using pictorial images (specific presentations) towards symbols that served as a generalised representation that was easy to compare with other maps, as with the depiction of woodland.

There were also obstacles at sea, notably shallows, shoals and coastlines of whatever type, greatly affecting operations and the options for operations, both maritime and amphibious, more especially battles and blockades, but also movements. These features could be used to try to structure an engagement to particular advantage. The Athenians did so at Salamis (480 BCE), using the straits between the Greek mainland and the island of Salamis to restrict the naval force the more numerous Persians could bring to bear against them in a decisive battle that the Athenians were to win. As at Salamis, most naval battles, prior to the use of deep-draught vessels from the sixteenth century, were usually fought close to the shore, which greatly increased the significance of the land-sea interface. The nearby presence of defended anchorages also offered shelter.

Permanent parts of the physical environment at sea, particularly currents, could be affected by additional aspects of it, notably the seasons, and, frequently linked to them, the climate and the weather. The impact of high winds made shoals, shallows, and coastlines, all far more dangerous; and, indeed, every aspect of navigation. Aside from the seaworthiness of individual ships, it was very difficult to hold a fleet in position in difficult, let alone bad, weather.

The marine environment is currently being transformed by global warming, notably with the opening up of the Northwest and Northeast Passages due to Arctic ice melting, but also with more powerful storms at sea. These are major environmental changes akin to desertification, the ploughing up of grasslands, and deforestation on land. All of these have greatly altered the physical environment on land and therefore affected or transformed the possibilities for military operations. At one level, the basic tactical questions of terrain and cover were a consequence of these factors and, therefore, changes. The pace of change has been particularly notable in the last century, but deforestation is a much longer process, as in many parts of the world is desertification.

Weather is a problem on land as well as at sea, and this remains the case, with weather affecting both radio and radar. Earlier, on land, wind was an issue for missile weapons, notably, but not only, arrows, as at the battle of Towton in England in 1461, a major defeat for the Lancastrians in the War of the Roses in part because the greatly-outnumbered Yorkists took advantage of the strong wind to outrange the opposing archers which led the Lancastrians to advance to the attack. Wind also affected firearms, and particularly so in the matchlock era when wind could make it harder to ignite the match.

More generally, in the age of black powder firearms, the wind could mean that smoke would be blown into the faces of one side. Their opponents had a clear field of vision and were free from the choking grittiness of only part-combusted gunpowder. On a heavy day, this could combine especially unpleasantly with humidity, which was made worse by a shortage of drinking water for troops held in position for many hours. Dehydration, and for animals as well as troops, was but part of the oppressive character of battle, and its insistent physicality. Wind was also crucial in the First World War when using poison gas. The Germans, who first employed gas, faced the problem that the prevalent winds were westerlies.

Wind has the advantage that it dispelled fog which was one of the most disorientating contexts for battle, on land, at sea, and in the air. Indeed, that of Belgrade in 1717 saw Prince Eugene's ability to respond in fog to the resulting confusion important in his major victory over the Turks. The contrast between clear and obscured battlefields remained a factor with differing technology, and although the tactical situation could be more radically transformed, as Sir John Dill, commander of the British I Corps in France, noted in 1939, in response to calls for an emphasis on tanks: 'The argument was that it is fire power, not man power that is wanted on the battlefield. That may be true up to a point but at night, in fog and when the enemy uses smoke, one must have men on the ground.'[16] Night-vision equipment has greatly altered the situation in recent decades, although increasing the already heavy equipment-load that had to be supplied, maintained and moved.

Rain could be far more difficult than wind. It affected weaponry, notably by preventing the ignition of firearms. Rain damped gunpowder. At Fornovo in Italy in 1495, the artillery duel at the start of the battle between French and Italian forces was ineffective as rain had dampened the powder. Alongside ammunition shortages, surprise attack, the close engagement, and the obscuring nature of drizzle, mist and the terrain, the impact of overnight rain on the Enfield rifles firing the new Minié conical bullets used by the British helped ensure that the difficult battle of Inkerman with the Russians in 1854 during the Crimean War of 1854–6 saw unusually heavy reliance on the bayonet in bitter hand-to-hand fighting. Even with such percussion cap firearms, which were far more reliable than the former flintlock muskets, wet weather affected performance: with the percussion cap weapons, powder still had to be poured down the barrel, which, if damp, had a bad habit of failing to fire off.

Rain could also make the going underfoot much tougher, adding effort to every step for the troops and making equipment, notably cannon far more difficult and unmanageable to move, which made movement difficult in the battle of Lauffeld in 1747 during the War of the Austrian Succession, and, also in Belgium, delayed the start of the French attacks at Roucoux in 1746 and Waterloo in 1815, lessening the time for attack in the latter case before Prussian intervention on the side of the British. Terrain therefore was a factor in part in terms of the need for firmness in order to support the fire of artillery, as well as the movement both of the guns and of their supplies. Indeed, this problem helped not only to complicate static battles but also, repeatedly, attempts to combine firepower with mobility.

Rain, moreover, seriously affected siege works, as with the unsuccessful Ottoman siege of Varad (Oradea) in Romania in 1598 and the trenches of the First World War (1914–18). Unexpectedly heavy rain, notably in August, proved a major problem for the British in the Passchendaele (Third Ypres) offensive in 1917, with five inches of rain in total and much reduced evaporation. Heavy rain and mud sloughs were a problem again in October, hitting morale and energy and making it difficult to move artillery. The ground was waterlogged.[17] The significance of weather features was increased by the difficulties of protecting against them, and also by the lack, for long, of any reliable means to predict the weather accurately.[18]

Rain also raised water levels in streams and rivers, which could make them difficult or impossible to ford and could also inundate the banks. The British under Charles, 2nd Earl Cornwallis might have caught the American Patriots under Nathanael Greene in the 'Race to the Dan' River in North Carolina in 1781 had he not had to divert around to find fords due to the spring thaw having flooded the rivers: in contrast, Greene had pre-staged boats at the crossings. Thus, the size and shape of the combat zone could alter in an unpredictable fashion, and on a daily basis. A good example is the severe flooding that affected, notably due to the movement of reinforcements and commanders, the battle of Shiloh in the American Civil War, fought in southwestern Tennessee on 6–7 April 1862, which may have been an El Niño year.[19]

So also with the expansion of boggy areas. The muddy terrain was a factor for the cavalry at Fornovo, while, at Pavia, also in Italy, in 1525, marshy and brush-covered terrain delayed the French cavalry making them targets for Spanish fire. Particularly strong in cavalry, the French in the Italian Wars benefited when on good cavalry terrain, as in defeating the Spaniards at Ceresole in Piedmont in 1544. Marshy ground delayed the Swedish advance at Wittstock in 1636. Even when rivers did not flood, melt-water and/or heavy rain might give them more power and thereby create problems, as for the British crossing the Jordan in order to attack the Turks in March 1918, or with the Weser, Aller and Leine in north-west Germany when the British had to cross them in April 1945.[20]

These and other factors might in part only be an extrapolation or aspect at the tactical level of wider operational-level considerations, but that did not lessen their impact, instead being an aspect of it. So also with another key environmental element, disease. This could both kill and weaken combatants and help lead to the abandonment of operations, as with the British siege of Spanish-held Cartagena in Colombia in 1741 during the War of Jenkins' Ear. A key element was yellow fever which affected expeditionary forces, as with the Chinese invaders of Burma (Myanmar) in the late 1760s, rather than long-term garrisons, for survival brought immunity and the disease depended on new hosts.[21] The Chinese failed with heavy losses to disease. Conversely, despite such losses, the British siege of Spanish-held Havana in 1762 was successful. The British were helped by not having to campaign into the interior.

Disease was not so fast-acting as to be a factor in most battles, as they were usually over only a day or two; but some battles lasted longer, and this was even more the case with sieges. The two could overlap, as in both world wars when battles, such as Verdun (1916), Kursk (1943), and, very differently, Iwo Jima (1945), were, to a degree, sieges of partly- or wholly-surrounded defensive positions. So also with the siege of Sevastopol in 1854–5 during the Crimean War. The impact of disease was generally a factor for both sides, as with the British and Turks in the Jordan valley in 1918, but, at the same time, could have very different consequences for them and for their moves.

Moving on, the tactical impact of the built environment was a continual factor, not least in shortening lines of sight, but also a changing one, entailing, for example, the addition of features such as railway cuttings and embankments as well as buildings. These were apt to provide particular opportunities for the defender as they offered what were already defensible sites, ones that gave cover, and/or ones that broke up the cohesion of attacking units. Providing strongpoints and defence in depth, Wellington made excellent use of farm buildings, notably those at Hougoumont and La Haye Sainte, both fixing large numbers, accordingly at Waterloo in 1815, of French troops and delaying the latter, thus limiting the pressure on his centre. The Soviets use of factories at Stalingrad in 1942, especially the Tractor, Red October, and Red Barricades factories, showed how the increasing use of reinforced concrete, for the construction of industrial plants and other installations, changed their defensive value in the man-made geography.

Again, this brought an element of the overlap of siege and battle. However, the use of such positions as part of a wider struggle was key. Thus, at the battle of Blenheim in 1704 in the War of the Spanish Succession, the French, while able to use villages to anchor their defence, notably those of Blenheim and Oberglau, fed their reserves into them, providing the British under John, 1st Duke of Marlborough, with an opportunity to break through the French centre, where there was no such village.

The tactical level could also be affected by pre-existing features that aided movement to, or on, the battlefield, and of troops and/or supplies. This was especially important when roads and, later, railways reached the actual battlefields, and notably so depending on the interaction of these routes with the terrain. Thus, in the American Civil War (1861–5), the nature of the terrain, often heavily wooded and with a low density of roads and tracks, affected tactical coordination or operational execution, as many battles and campaigns demonstrated. In turn, this situation enhanced the very significance of the links that were available, while the position was much easier where such links were more common. This contrast remains the case, and notably so in heavily-forested, marshy and mountainous terrain.

An embankment around a large pond was an important battlefield feature at Plassey in India in 1757, providing the British Robert Clive with a viable defensive feature against the Nawab of Bengal, one he used with great effect. A very different type of human alteration to the environment was provided by the drainage of marshlands and, therefore, by the breaking of dykes in order to create defensive zones, as by the Dutch in Holland in 1574 and 1672 against Spanish and French attackers respectively, and by the Germans near Anzio in Italy in 1944. The Belgian flooding of the Yser area in 1914 against the German advance was based on the example of flooding this area in 1793–4: the sluices were raised in 1914 during high tides, creating a wide flooded area and stabilising the Yser Front which became a part of the Western Front that then changed least during the war.[22] This was operationally and strategically important in helping protect the Channel Ports from German attack.

More generally, the low terrain and the high water-table in the Low Countries (Belgium and Netherlands) affected siege operations, usually forcing attacks onto very narrow frontages, and making the undermining of defences impossible, and easing the waterborne relief of besieged positions. The last was shown at Alkmar in 1573, and Leiden in 1574 when, during the Dutch Revolt, they were unsuccessfully besieged by the Spaniards. Rivers also made it easier to move cannon and their heavy shot, as repeatedly in Belgium.

The diversion of water defences was long a method of siegecraft, being mentioned by Sextus Julius Frontinus (*c.* 30–104 CE) in his *Strategema*. In Japan, the success of Toyotomi Hideyoshi in the 1580s and 1590 in sieges, owed much to the use of entrenchments to divert the water defences offered by lakes and rivers, these entrenchments threatening fortresses either with flooding by rising waters, or with the loss of the protection by water features on which many in part relied. Despite major and costly efforts in 1626–9, the Spaniards failed to construct a canal between the Rhine and Meuse (Maas) rivers that in part was designed to dry up Dutch water defences, causing floods elsewhere, and creating a barrier to impede Dutch advances.[23] Defending the city of Khartoum in Sudan against Mahdist attack, Major-General Charles Gordon dug a line of defences to link the Blue and White Niles which converge there, only for the city to be taken in 1885 when the river levels fell and the Mahdists were able to cross on foot, finding a gap, to outflank the city wall.

Canals, notably the St Quentin one for the defence of the German Hindenburg Line in France in 1918, were also significant tactical factors and, in the case of the Suez Canal in the Yom Kippur War of 1973 between Egypt and Israel, an operational and strategic one. The ability of, first, the Egyptians and, then, the Israelis to cross the canal was crucial in that conflict, each benefiting from surprise. That factor was also crucial to the success of the bold German airborne assault in 1940 on the Eben Emael fortress bordering the Albert Canal, the capture of a key position in the Belgian defences. Built by the Pakistanis as part of the protection against any Indian advance on Lahore, the Ichhogil Canal, which had defensive features on the western (Pakistani) side, was an important feature in the Second Indo-Pakistani War, that of 1965.

Agricultural methods were also significant in affecting the battlespace. For example, in the eighteenth century, the linear tactics of Frederick II, the Great, of Prussia (r. 1740–86), were most suited to the particular worked environment of East-Central Europe, especially the large spaces of the unenclosed agricultural farmland of Bohemia and Silesia. In turn, the limitations of these tactics were to be revealed in the French Revolutionary War from 1792, in the face of French troops fighting in open order and/or assault columns, rather than tightly-packed lines, in the enclosed and wooded country of Belgium and the Rhineland. Enclosed farmland was also an issue in Flanders in 1914 and, in the shape of the dense hedgerows of the *bocage*, Normandy in 1944, the latter providing plentiful cover for the defence, especially anti-tank guns, and thereby hindering offensive tank operations. So also in India with the contrast between the flat plains of the north and the more broken and forested terrain in the Deccan and in Bengal.

Terrain features, both human and physical, could break up battles into separate engagements, which underlined the need for tactical skill and rewarded the ability of commanders to integrate these engagements if at all possible. This was always a factor, but became more so, first with advances in columns rather than lines, and, secondly, as the scale of operations increased, not least with the independently-operating corps of the nineteenth century. Failures of integration, as with the poorly-commanded attacking Union army at the battle of Antietam in 1862 in the American Civil War, were as significant as terrain obstacles, or could accentuate the impact of the latter.

Fortification, both that constructed prior to conflict, and that constructed during it, as an instance of the responsiveness of the built environment to war, reflected the need to understand particular localities. The increased role of artillery demanded the renewed planning of defensive sites, the better to deploy optimum firepower to thwart enemy attack from all sides. Investment in fortifications was knowledge-driven. Cesare Borgia (*c.* 1476–1507), the illegitimate son of Pope Alexander VI and the successful Captain-General of the Papal army in 1499–1502, asked Leonardo da Vinci, among much else a gifted physical geographer adept at surveying, to examine the Papal fortresses. Da Vinci provided accurate maps, for example of the city of Imola in 1502, which were useful tools for planning defences.

The geometric style of fortification encouraged the use of plans and of drawing to scale. Developed from the 1450s, the polygonal bastion was spread across Europe by Italian architects. In a defensive system known as the *trace italienne*, that in some respects was a revival of Classical models, bastions, generally quadrilateral, angled and placed at regular intervals along all walls, were introduced to provide effective flanking fire. Books on fortification, such as Battista della Valle's *Vallo libro continente appertinente a capitanii, ritenere et fortificare una città con bastioni*, which went through eleven editions from 1524 to 1558, were, with their focus on spatial considerations, a form of theoretical geography. Galileo's first publication, *Le Operazioni del Compasso Geometrico e Militare* (1606), focused on military engineering and emphasised the importance of applying mathematical rules.

Alongside the desire for geometrically perfect shapes, a desire that matched the Chinese commitment to *feng shui* (see Chapter 3), fortification techniques had to be adapted to the terrain, which made the ability to understand the latter crucial. Mud and bamboo were used in the absence of stones in India, south-eastern Asia, and south China, and *trace italienne* systems were not required there. Built in the mid-eighteenth century, the mud walls of Bharatpur Fort in eastern Rajastan remained impervious to British 18-pounder artillery and storming attacks in 1805 during the Second Anglo-Maratha War, leading to heavy British losses: over 3,000 men. Fifty feet high and eighty feet wide mud walls, surrounded by triple wet and dry ditches, each of which was about forty-five feet wide, constituted a formidable defensive structure. The moat could be filled from a nearby lake. However, in the aftermath, Ranjit Singh, the Raja of Bharatpur, made terms with the British. In 1825–6, a second siege led to the capture of the fortress, in part thanks to capturing the lake so that the moat could not be filled. The people of south-east and south Asia also used bamboo stakes driven into the ground and covered with loose layers of earth and vegetation as premodern minefields.

A concern with shape and its possibilities was important not just for fortifications, but also to the deployment of units in particular formations. Organisation in terms of formations was a means to hold the chaos of battle at bay, as well as to maximise tactical advantage, and the use of weapons. This order enabled more effective fire and more sophisticated tactics in moving or withholding units on the battlefield, including the crucial use of resources. So also with line-ahead tactics at sea, which provided a degree of cohesion and reflected a move away from battle as a series of struggles between individual ships and, instead, toward a degree of control and co-operation.

Functionality was related at least in part to ideas about the inherent value and virtue of particular forms, such as columns, lines and squares, as in lengthy and often heated discussion of the topic in eighteenth-century France, discussion which included consideration of the methods and formations of Classical warfare including the Macedonian phalanx.[24] This question was generally also very much one tempered by the experience of conflict with opponents. Thus, in the 1780s, following a Russian pattern successfully used at the battle of Kozludzha in 1774, the Austrians developed tactical formations to counter Turkish cavalry superiority, especially infantry squares arranged in mutually supporting checkerboard pattern, helping them to defeat the Turks in 1789, whereas the Turks had heavily defeated the Austrians in 1739 in the previous war. Similarly, the growing use of light infantry by European powers in the late eighteenth century reflected experience of their value, not least in North America.

Environmental factors, both physical and human, were all more significant geographically because they did not exist in a uniform fashion. Instead, such features varied greatly, both within and between regions. This helped ensure that the impact of geography was a matter of the local, as much as the regional or global factors that tend to attract attention, with the local focusing requirements for information and reconnaissance. The principal geographical variations at the tactical level in part reflected those of these wider regional patterns. There were particular interactions of importance, as with the significance as sites for combat of oases and, more especially, fresh water sources both in dry areas and on coastlines.

An understanding of such variations is often strongest at the level of particular communities, thus providing a variant at the tactical level of what is termed strategic culture. For example, Kurds have proved extremely good on their own turf and, as mountain fighters, know every valley, cave and peak. Caves, more generally, are of particular significance in providing hidden fortresses, and offer an instance of the variety found both in fortification and with reference to 'small war' techniques. They can pose a challenge, as with the natural caves at Tora Bora in

Afghanistan, which provided an al-Qaeda refuge in 2001, although one that was taken. In the shape of guerrilla warfare, 'small war' can provide a geography of conflict different from the one of apparent control over territory, a situation that is far from new.

Some areas and terrains proved particularly appropriate for guerrilla warfare. Marshy regions proved difficult for regular forces, whether the Mughals in the valley of the Brahmaputra in the seventeenth century or the Germans in the Pripet Marshes in 1941–4, although the development of the hovercraft altered the situation from the 1960s. Woodland was more lastingly significant. Thus, the wooded and boggy terrain of Ulster was propitious for sudden attacks on English armies, as at Clontibret (1595) and Yellow Ford (1598), with a strategic defensive by the Irish successfully combined with a tactical offensive, a situation more generally the case with guerrilla warfare. Thus, so also with uplands and successive Corsican rebellions in the eighteenth century against first Genoese and then, from 1768, French rule. The value of North American woodland for ambushes was frequently shown, and most dramatically so with the successful ambush by French and Native American forces of a British force under General Edward Braddock advancing on Fort Duquesne (now Pittsburgh) in 1755.

In turn, as Braddock demonstrated, outside forces lacked such knowledge, and thus were obliged to turn to a geography of control in which they either co-opted it through local allies or sought to overcome it through fortifications and other means of power. The balance, of deterrence and reprisal, that was frequently thus embraced, had a tactical level in terms of the location of fortifications, for example the barbed wire and blockhouses used by the Spaniards against rebels in Cuba in the 1890s and by the British against the Boers (Afrikaners) in the latter stage of the Boer War (1899–1902), in each case successfully so. However, this balance also had a less certain operational dynamic arising from military and political assumptions about how best to conduct war,[25] while the effectiveness of deterrence and reprisal owed much to the response of opponents.

As far as fighting is concerned, there have been relevant changes through time in tactical geography. This is notably so as a consequence of the introduction of different weaponry and the related changes in formations. Both weaponry and formations have consequences for the scale and character of the battle-space, and the resulting context for the tactical dimensions of conflict. Thus, during the nineteenth century, the need to understand the battle-space changed greatly with the increasing range and lethality of firearms, both handheld and artillery. A host of developments were significant, including percussion caps, bullets (as opposed to shot), bolt actions, rifling, breech-loading, steel artillery, machine guns, and automatic re-siting mechanisms. In turn, each of these developments entailed continuing processes of improvement, frequently involving trial and error.

The net effect was a greater range of weaponry that required maps covering a larger area, and an enhanced lethality of weaponry. This led, in general, to less dense troop formations, the so-called 'empty battlefield' and, therefore, again, the coverage of a larger area. In turn, when the autumn manoeuvres of the Saxon army (part of that of Germany) were reviewed in 1909, the thickness of the firing lines was severely criticised, because it exposed the troops to this lethality.[26] Moreover, rifled artillery permitted greater range, which enabled the artillery to move back out of the now longer range of accurate infantry fire without losing impact: the British failure to do so in 1899 led to serious losses at Boer hands in southern Africa, as did their reliance, early in the Boer War (1899–1902), on massed infantry formations. As with many wars, there was a learning curve to respond to the particular military environment established by opponents' fighting practices.

The improvement of artillery barrels enhanced their range, accuracy and, crucially, lifespan, for durability is a key element of weapons effectiveness that is very important to maintaining capability. Thus, heavy and accurate artillery fire from the hills around Sedan was crucial in the defeat of the French attempt to break out on 1 September 1870, and led to the surrender by Napoleon III to the Germans there the next day. Meanwhile, the physical character of the battlefield was affected not only by the greater difficulty of closing to bayonet point, but also by the replacement of black-powder firearms in the 1880s by those using smokeless powder which helped, as for the Boers fighting the British in southern Africa in the Boer War, to keep the positions from which fire was coming secret, and was an element that was very difficult even to suggest on maps.

Firearms capability was the crucial driver of change in the nineteenth century. The relationship with topography was now over a larger area, and this relationship encouraged an overlap, in conflict and planning, between tactical and operational levels and criteria. At the same time, there was a looking back in terms of presenting the physical frame of reference for earlier battles, both narrowly and more broadly. Thus, the *School Atlas of English History* edited by S.R. Gardiner (1892) included battle plans of Hastings, Bannockburn, Crécy, Poitiers, Agincourt, Edgehill, Marston Moor, Naseby, Dunbar, Steinkirk, Neerwinden, Blenheim, Ramillies, Quebec, Quiberon Bay, the Nile, Copenhagen, Trafalgar, and Waterloo, as well as maps to illustrate campaigns and wars. This tendency was also later to be seen in staff rides, the inspection of battlefields as a form of military education.

Despite the greater range of weaponry, an important element, and at all levels, remained that of the ability, in both battle and campaign, to create and use an 'open' zone in space and time, with both room for manoeuvre, usually outflanking opponents, and a tempo permitting the retention of the initiative. The failure to do so, as in many of the battles of the American Civil War, was important to producing what, as a result of firepower, was either an impasse, or a cause of heavy casualties, or both. Mechanisation in the twentieth century made the search for an 'open zone' more possible, and notably so during and after the Second World War.

The tactical level of conflict during the world wars and the Cold War is addressed in part in Chapters 11, 12 and 13. In geographical terms, there was a considerable degree of continuity, with the issues of height and cover remaining of great significance. At the same time, air and submarine warfare introduced new geographical spheres, while communication and surveillance capabilities were transformed by radio and radar. Thus, sonar became a key element in submarine warfare. The majority of combatants involved in war, however, continued to fight on land, where mechanisation and, with it, mobile firepower proved a key change in the twentieth century, and, indeed, meant that factors such as height, cover, and 'going' (the firmness of the terrain) acquired new considerations and meanings.

Thus, in the First World War, observation aircraft effectively provided intelligence of enemy movements and positions, and directed artillery fire against enemy gun positions hiding behind ridges and unobservable from the ground. By 1944, in the Normandy campaign, German forces could not safely move during the day due to Allied air superiority. At sea, the height of aircraft provided advantages against both submarines and surface shipping, including surveillance and attack.[27]

At the same time as change, notably motorisation, most infantry and artillery continued to operate in an established fashion, the German army, despite its vaunted mechanisation, making extensive use of horses in the Second World War, although this was for logistics and not combat. More generally, artillery plotted lines of fire in the accustomed manner. However, elements of continuity did not necessarily equate with a lack of effectiveness. The British artillery, in particular by 1918 and 1944–5, was able to deliver concentrated fire across a broad frontage, both in a pre-planned fashion and against targets of opportunity on a variety of axes. In service from 1940, the 25-pounder gun on its firing platform proved very mobile, flexible, versatile and durable. The gun could be used for both direct fire and high-angle-fire.

At present, the tactical nature of conflict is changing. Improved communications, especially now with drones, on which see Chapter 14, are highly relevant. In a rapid development, drones are increasingly a source of firepower as well as reconnaissance, a transition that was earlier rapidly made with aircraft. However, the most instructive feature is that basic infantry training continues to adopt similar doctrine and practice to that of decades ago. This continuity is worthy of consideration in what follows.

The geographies of war are important to the tactical tenets frequently discussed, notably manoeuvre, mass, objective, firepower, tempo, deception, surprise, economy of force, shock and moral cohesion, providing leverage in combat,[28] as well as the very settings for operating and fighting. These factors were made more significant by the role of combined-arms combat. Thus, in the Second World War, the defensive effectiveness of anti-tank weaponry ensured that mixed or combined-arms formations were more effective than those that focused solely on tanks. In February 1945, Field Marshal Montgomery, then commander of the British 21st Army Group, argued that close co-operation with infantry was needed in order to overcome German anti-tank guns: 'I cannot emphasise too strongly that victory in battle depends not on armoured action alone, but on the intimate co-operation of all arms; the tank by itself can achieve little',[29] a theme he had earlier adopted in North Africa in 1942–3. Indeed, artillery was important to the set-piece fighting that involved support-in-depth.

The formula of a carefully-prepared firepower heavy offensive, was deviated from by Montgomery with the bold, if not foolish, airborne Arnhem operation in September 1944, and with disastrous consequences;[30] although the verdict would have been different had the operation succeeded. This is often the case with war and at the tactical, operational and strategic levels. Other instances include the Gallipoli operation in 1915, and the Anglo-German naval battle at Jutland in 1916.

These instances and factors were, and are, subject to interpretation, both in terms of command decisions and with reference to cultural norms, the latter of which can be harder to disentangle.[31] There is the significance for these norms, both of particular sites, as in specific mountains, but also of general situations. For example, the view of standing behind, or before, rivers varied. As far as Classical commentators (from different cultures) are concerned, Vegetius, the Roman author of the fourth-century CE *Epitoma rei militaris*, a summary of the art of war that remained influential in Europe into the fifteenth century, advised against fighting with a river to the rear, which sounds sensible. In contrast, Sunzi, the Chinese author of the fifth century BCE *The Art of War*, recommended doing so in order to motivate the troops to fight harder. Thus, even some basic-looking intersections of geography and war are subject to cultural perspective.[32] So also with the use of horses, or the need to consider what to do with civilians. These cultural elements affect the very basic elements of tactical issue and response, and, again, reflect the complex interactions of physical and human geography.

Chapter 3

Operations

'He [Napoleon] established a temporary command post in the stables of the White Horse Inn. He studied two maps spread on a high bench in a corner.'

'In the middle … was placed a large table, on which was spread the best map that could be obtained of the seat of the war…. This was placed conformably with the points of the compass … pins with various coloured heads were thrust into it to point out the situation of the different corps d'armée of the French or those of the enemy. This was the business of the director of the bureau topographique … who possessed a perfect knowledge of the different positions … Napoleon … attached more importance to this [map] than any want of his life. During the night … was surrounded by thirty candles … When the Emperor mounted his horse … the grande equerry carried [a copy] … attached to his breast button … to have in readiness whenever [Napoleon] … exclaimed "la carte! [the map]"' Ernst, Baron Odeleben, reporting on French headquarters in Germany, 1813.[1]

At the operational level of war, again, the emphasis is on the human as well as the physical environment, although the latter tends to attract the greatest attention. The direction and timing of campaigning can clearly be linked to topography and climate respectively. Whereas the tactical issue discussed in the last chapter essentially related to where army and navy units would be located, the operational one was in part a matter of how, and why, they both got there, and then moved on.

Each of the factors mentioned in the previous chapter had an operational dimension; but the contextual contrast with the tactical one was so great that most can do with re-examination. Thus, the topography and cover that helped explain where, and how, a specific clash was conducted do not necessarily explain how that particular area came to be in dispute. The next chapter, on strategy, focuses on the intentionality at stake in the specific geography contested by the two sides, but this chapter considers campaigning at the operational level. The latter was not free-floating, as the particular goals that were pursued were understood in terms of a specific timescale. Nevertheless, operational matters in terms, for example, of the availability of food for humans and animals, and of ease of communication, were highly significant in explaining why hostilities were pursued in certain areas.

Again, the division will be, first, physical and, then, human. The former saw climate, rather than weather, as the factor, and mountain ranges in place of individual slopes. At the same time, the impact of climate at a particular moment was in terms of weather; and so on. Referring to the constraints of the climate, Field Marshal Garnet Wolseley (1833–1913), the multi-purpose and successful British commander of the age of empire, who was to be satirised in Gilbert and Sullivan's song 'I Am the very Model of a Modern Major General' from *The Pirates of Penzance* (1879), wrote in 1873: 'I always seem to be condemned to command in expeditions which must be accomplished before a certain season of the year begins.' Indeed, his Red River expedition in Canada in 1870, 'a minor masterpiece of logistics and sheer physical effort',[2] had to succeed in advancing from Lake Superior to Winnipeg before the lakes froze; and that against the Asante in West Africa in 1873 before disease struck, which had been the fate of the 1864 British expedition. In each case, Wolseley did succeed.[3]

The key element in climate was that of opening up, or closing down, conflict in particular regions. Most academic writers on war in recent decades have lived in temperate zones, as did the Classical writers who are frequently cited. As a result, the key climatic control for them was generally that of the movement from winter cold to spring warmth, with campaigning usually beginning in late spring, both because river levels by then had fallen after the spring snowmelt- and icemelt-fed spate, and due to the start of grass growing to provide forage for the cavalry and draught animals. Warmth, notably the end of frosts, also eased sleeping overnight in the fields for troops and animals, while summer brought longer days (and shorter nights) for campaigning and conflict. This routine still pertained in 1941 when the Germans invaded the Soviet

Union in late June. Earlier in that year, the rivers were very high and much of the ground saturated, a situation exacerbated by higher than normal rainfall. The seasons also greatly affected naval operations, with longer days during the summer and, usually, calmer weather.

In turn, the onset of winter created a whole set of problems, both practical (for combat and logistics), and related to morale. This situation acted to discourage winter campaigning, as with Attila and the Huns leaving Italy in late 452, or the Ottoman abandonment in 1514 of the city of Tabriz, which they had captured from the Safavids of Persia earlier in the year: instead of campaigning further to the east next year, as Sultan Selim I had intended, he had to retreat. Winter campaigning repeatedly posed problems. In January 1863, Ambrose Burnside tried to move round the left of the Confederates under Robert E. Lee in Fredericksburg, Virginia, only for the Union army's 'Mud March' to be brought to a halt by heavy rain swelling the Rappahannock River. However, as with so many single interpretations of success or failure, other factors played a role, in this case not least dissension among the senior Union officers.

The British wanted to take Québec in 1759, and to retake the Falkland Islands in 1982, in each case before the winter weather broke in (in the latter case in the Southern Hemisphere); and the onset of winter was also seen as a factor in discouraging British provocation of the United States in late 1862, in particular because the freezing of the St Lawrence would hinder the reinforcement of Canada in the event of American attack, which would be overland.[4] Alongside concern about Western responses and also the Chinese navy, the winter weather helped ensure that the Japanese army's plans for a major landing in Chihli province during the 1894–5 war with China were not pursued. 'General Winter' hit the German attack on Moscow in late 1941 hard, greatly affecting both troops and equipment; although strong Soviet resistance was a far more significant factor in leading to total German failure.[5] The Germans, however, were apt to underrate Soviet fighting quality.

In turn, the situation was very different in climates not defined by the dichotomy of winter cold and summer heat, as well as all stages in between. Indeed, in tropical and semi-tropical regions, the summer was often too hot for campaigning, which therefore generally began later in the year. This was seen in India, the American South and the Caribbean. Furthermore, in the Portuguese-Spanish war of 1640–68, the nature of the campaigning zone encouraged a resort to cavalry, not least because of the difficulty of mounting operations with large infantry forces in what, due in part to the climate, were short campaigning seasons, in which such forces moved slowly.[6]

The monsoon was a major factor in south and south-east Asia and in coastal east Africa: heavy tropical showers during the rainy season made military operations on land impossible. Dry streams became big rivers, and the latter changed their courses causing floods. In turn, the monsoons and the floods resulted in lush, dense vegetation which enabled the elephant-centric armies of south-east and south Asian states to campaign. In addition, the deposit of silt along the river valleys made the soil fertile and bumper crops became available. This made possible supporting a large population and the agricultural resources that were utilised or consumed in constant internecine warfare. Other areas that enjoyed such river-borne silt were also significant providers for campaigning, notably the lower Nile valley in Egypt and the Tigris and Euphrates valleys in Iraq.

In 1760, campaigning between the Marathas and the Afghans stopped near Delhi in the monsoon season, which provided an opportunity for inconclusive negotiations. In 1762, British operations against Spanish-held Manila were successfully pushed on because of the breaking of the monsoon. In 1791, with the monsoon about to break, the British withdrew from their position outside Seringapatam, the Mysore capital in southern India, although this withdrawal also reflected logistical issues and the absence of reinforcements. In 1799, Seringapatam fell to British attack before the monsoon broke. As a result, the level of the River Cauvery, part of the defences, was low.

Conversely, in 1820, in an area without the extremity of the monsoon, José Rinón, the new royalist commander in the Papantla region near Veracruz, Mexico, abandoned the practice of a rainy season break in campaigning and thus both denied the rebels an opportunity to recover and his own troops freedom from the disease of that season. The two sides accepted a settlement that December.[7]

Because humidity could be a major factor in summer heat, wind conditions could ease the situation. However, at sea, there was the related complications of typhoon and hurricane seasons. Nevertheless, the monsoon winds, the understanding of them, and the use of the lateen sail, made possible long-distance oceanic voyages across the western Indian Ocean between the western coastline of the subcontinent and the coastal areas of East Africa. This was an instance of how, on land and sea, the seasonal contrast in movement was greater than it was to be from the mid-nineteenth century, when steam-power came into play, as was the contrast between operating in good and poor weather. Yet the use of neither steamships nor railways could end these contrasts.

The climate's impact on campaigning interacted with its affect on the harvest, and that of the harvest on the campaigning. In large part, this was a matter of food availability (for humans and animals), and the resulting assumed equations about when (and where) to campaign, with what numbers, and for how long.[8] There was also the need for labour (human and animal) for the harvest, and the resulting implications for campaigning, and notably so prior to agricultural mechanisation. Across much of the world, mechanisation only really began in the twentieth century, dramatically cutting the requirement for manpower. Again, this factor varied across the world, and as part of the interaction of physical and human geography. Thus, alongside the constraints of the former, there were the types of crops chosen for cultivation and the means employed, especially irrigation.

At the same time, constraints can be overplayed, not least because their consequences could be minimised. Repeatedly, armies (although less so navies) ignored maxims about limitations, and successfully so: as with Henry of Navarre (Henry IV of France) who regularly campaigned during the French Wars of Religion in winter, for example in 1589–90 and 1591–2; or again in early 1742, when the Austrians successfully overran Bavaria. Similarly, Ireland in the early 1600s saw winter campaigning by the English and their Irish opponents, producing, moreover, a verdict in the shape of British victory at the battle of Kinsale in 1601. Northern Italy witnessed a remarkable level of activity in the winters of 1703–4, 1733–4, and 1745–6, including sieges, stormings, and the relief of besieged cities. In the American War of Independence, Cornwallis advanced into north Carolina in January 1781. The harshness of winter brought no end to the fighting in the Russo-Turkish War of 1877–8, with the Russians having starved the fortress of Plevna, Bulgaria into eventual surrender in December 1877, encircling another Turkish army at the Shipka Pass the following month, and then pressing on to take the cities of Plovdiv and Adrianople, and to threaten Constantinople with attack.

Moreover, as another more general instance of lessening limitations, it was possible, where food was not plentiful, for there to be an emphasis on the speedy verdict of battles, rather than sieges, and also on smaller forces. These responses helped ensure that it was still possible to conceive of plans and to implement them.

While climate was a prime geographical context at the operational level, terrain was another. It was more significant at this level than at that of tactics, for, whereas relatively small numbers could deploy and fight in adverse terrain, for example deserts, permafrost and high mountains, the situation was very different for large numbers and for operations intended to produce significant results. From this perspective, although the situation changed by the season, much of the world's land surface, and part of its oceans, were totally unsuitable for operations, and more was partly so. These constraints, however, were to be eroded over the last century, partly by air-support, particularly in the provision of supplies, by submarines being able to operate under the ice, and by well-supplied high-tech land forces successfully attacking in desert conditions, notably in the Gulf Wars of 1991 and 2003, but already in North Africa in 1940–3 during the Second World War, and in the Arab-Israeli wars, especially in 1956, 1967 and 1973.

These capabilities were new, yet there had previously been significant advances across deserts, for example those of Alexander the Great through the Gedrosian Desert of Baluchistan (in Pakistan) in 326 BCE in his move west from the Indus River, and of the Moroccans across the Sahara to the Niger Valley in 1590–1 to victory at Tondibi over the Songhai forces; although, in crossing, each army suffered very heavy losses and took a lot of time. Aside from this, there had been fighting in deserts, with some groups especially well-attuned to operating there, notably in Arabia against successive imperial powers, for example Egyptian forces in the early nineteenth century. Sandstorms, furthermore, could benefit combatants, as with the Manchu success in the crucial battle of Shanhaiguan in 1644, with their cavalry turning Li Zicheng's flank in a sandstorm. Nevertheless, the constraints posed by desert warfare had still pertained for most militaries. In the twentieth century, these constraints received a new twist given the serious difficulties of motor-borne mobility particularly in desert terrain: fuel and engine maintenance, fuel and water availability, and 'going'. As a result, the Six Days War of 1967, and the Gulf Wars of 1991 and 2003, were dramatic displays of new capabilities, with, in each case, unlike with the North African campaigning in 1940–3, the very rapid delivery of total success, at least in so far as short-term military verdicts were concerned.

Mountains in the event have proved an even more durable obstacle than deserts. They shaped operations by constraining advances, which could tend to mean obliging advancing forces to move through via valleys or round the mountains. This could have deleterious tactical and operational consequences. Their role as a barrier was more significant for cavalry and artillery than for infantry, so that the force structure (composition) of armies operating in this environment was greatly affected as a consequence, as with the current Chinese-Indian confrontation in the Himalayas.

The impact of mountains was influenced by other geographical factors, notably season and relative location. Winter snow could leave passes closed, thus enhancing the barrier posed by the mountains, one prolonged during spring melt. Conversely, if mountains, such as the Alps, Apennines or Taurus, were close to water, it could be possible to avoid them by bypassing them at sea.

Even if not so, mountain ranges were not necessarily a bar to campaigning, as shown by the invading Carthaginians under Hannibal who crossed the Alps in 218 BCE from France into Italy, and by Mughal rulers who campaigned into northern Afghanistan, as in 1546, 1549 and 1646, as well as into Kashmir through the Pir Panjal Pass, and into Baltistan and Ladakh in 1637–9. In addition, Ahmad Shah of Afghanistan successfully sent armies into northern Afghanistan in 1751 and 1768. In 1819, Simon Bolívar invaded New Granada (Colombia) from Venezuela via the allegedly impassable Pisba Pass in the Andes, with heavy losses on the crossing, but gaining the element of surprise.

Prior to the major changes brought by air transport, including the supply of Nationalist China from Indian airbases over the Himalayas or 'Hump' in the Second World War, accessibility was not the sole factor. In addition, mountainous regions were unwelcome for campaigning due to harsher weather, the difficulties of obtaining supplies, stonier or rocky soils, the opportunities offered by defenders and the effect of altitude on humans and animals. The last has had a major impact during recent conflicts in the Himalayas involving China, India and Pakistan.

Lower terrain was also significant. In the map 'The Role of the Environment' in J.S. Lay's *Pictorial Atlas of English History* (1919), terrain, in a map of southern Scotland and the Borders, above 1,000 feet was marked and readers were urged to 'notice that the battle fields are close together in the plain between the highlands and the sea'. At the same time, local topography was also crucial and that was not shown on the map, as with the site of the 600-foot high Halidon Hill, a battle near Berwick in 1333. In that battle, Edward III of England used the hill, his archers firing on the advancing Scots with devastating effect. Another map was highlighted 'note the level country on the Belgian frontier where the Germans invaded France in the Great War' in 1914. The role of local topography in northern England was also seen with the Roman Emperor Hadrian building a section of his wall on top of the natural physical barrier of Whin Sill, thus reinforcing the effectiveness of the terrain while gaining additional height for the wall.[9]

The operational importance of passes, and therefore the tactical place of locations within them, reflected the role of mountain ranges. Famous passes included Thermopylae in Greece, where a small number of Greeks, most prominently Spartans, delayed the attacking Persians in 480 BCE, fighting to the death, and Hulao in China, where a road wound through high loess escarpments and the Tang were blocked in 621 CE until the defenders came out to fight.[10] At a different level, passes were analogous to the gates that were so significant in attacks on fortified positions. The Iron Gates was the term for a gorge on the River Danube.

Yet there were no inevitable consequences of physical features. Whereas, in 1739, Nadir Shah of Persia was to push on from Afghanistan to invade northern India, capturing Delhi after a major victory over the Mughals at Karnal, there was no such advance in 1622 and 1648, after Abbas I and Abbas II of Persia respectively captured Kandahar in Afghanistan from Mughal forces. Terrain was not the prime constraint: instead, the strength of the Mughal opposition was a major element, as was the development of the Safavid (Persian) state into a sedentary and less expansionist polity.[11] In the latter, less expansionist, context, the use of force could be a product of the failure of established means of controlling frontiers by clientage or garrisons, as when the commander of the garrison of Kandahar, fearing execution by his sovereign, surrendered it to the Mughals in 1638.

Mountain ranges could serve as a defensive means which was operationally significant. However, depending on context and circumstances, both consistently key in the geography of warfare, the ranges could be decisive, or could simply increase the varied costs of operations. These costs include casualties, delay, logistical requirements, and force deployment. This element was very much demonstrated in Italy in 1943–5 and Korea in 1950–3. In each case, east-west mountain ranges increased the potential for the defence, and minimised that for motorised equipment. In neither case were advances prevented, but pushing up their cost, as well as holding decisiveness at bay, served to alter strategic practicalities, and for both sides. Invading Sicily in 1943, the Allies 'found themselves canalized by geography', with the terrain, mountaintop towns, and small roads, all a problem for their mechanized forces, and, in the face of effective German opposition, this became still more problematic in mainland Italy where there were many steeply indented valleys.[12] Indeed, this situation helped lead the Allies in 1944 to divert forces from Italy to Operation Dragoon, an invasion of southern France. Yet, again, though, as an instance of the need to move away from determinism, the political dimension of Allied debates over strategy were more significant.[13]

In part, the situation with mountain ranges was a projection onto the operational level of the impact of geography at the tactical level, but with the time constraint to the fore. Hannibal crossing the Alps in 218 BCE was a key instance of operational deception producing strategic surprise when the Carthaginian army suddenly appeared in force on the north Italian plain.

Separately, at both the tactical and the operational levels, terrain frequently limited the capability of combined arms forces, as well as ensuring that attacks, which usually in such terrain were the responsibility of the infantry, were executed sequentially rather than simultaneously. An element of this was seen with the battle of Keren in Ethiopia in 1941, as the British defeated Italian defenders in the hills of Eritrea. Further south, the mountains of the Tigray region of Ethiopia, for example the Tembien mountains, posed a challenge to the Ethiopian army as it sought to subjugate opposition in 2020–2.

In turn, terrain gives a series of advantages to the defence. With reference to Julius Caesar's successful campaigns against Pompey's sons in Spain in 45 BCE, a Roman writer noted:

'the hilly type of country by no means unsuitable for the fortification of camps. In fact, practically the whole region of Further Spain, fertile as it is and correspondingly well watered, makes a siege a fruitless and difficult task.... A large proportion of the towns are established in naturally elevated positons, with the result that the approach to them, involving as it does a simultaneous climb, proves a difficult task.'[14]

It is probable that an understanding of the impact of mountains began from the outset of conflict at any scale, in other words well before mapping. Subsequently, the mapping of terrain was easier for the operational level, requiring less precision and detailed work than at the tactical. Vegetius stated that a general must have:

'itineraries of all those regions in which the war is being fought very fully set out, so that he might become fully acquainted with the distances between places in terms not only of mileage but also the quality of the roads, and may have at his disposal reliable accounts of the short cuts, alternative routes, mountains and rivers: indeed the more able generals are said to have not only annotated but pictorial itineraries of the provinces in which they are operating, so that they could decide which way to take not merely by mental calculation but by visual inspection too.'[15]

Rather than geography in the shape of terrain becoming less significant, it was more so as the requirements of armies increased. Thus, movement became a requirement for cannon which, unlike siege engines, could not be made at the spot from locally-obtained timber. Indeed, geographical information, especially maps, was particularly important for the employment of cannon. This was not so much at the tactical level, because of the problems into the late nineteenth century of recording and mapping heights and, in the beginning, of a limited range for cannon. Moreover, line-of-sight fire was coordinated by eye. Instead, maps were important at the operational level posed by the need to retain mobility, because they provided indications of where artillery could be transported. Maps could be inadequate in their depiction of roads, but there was an awareness of the need to use maps for information to aid troop transport, and it was increasingly called and catered for. For example, in England, Sir Thomas Elyot praised the utility of maps in *The Book Named the Governor* (1531), a manual on statecraft.

At the tactical, operational, and strategic levels, terrain was made a more significant factor by the interaction with fortifications, a factor that looked back to human society at its most basic, a situation indeed when these levels were collapsed together into one. Fortifications moved from being a matter of natural features that provided shelter and/or enhanced strength, notably caves, ridges, thickets of vegetation, and marshlands, which variously provided shelter against the weather, animals and other humans. Instead, fortifications became man-enhanced, as in stone walls across the front of caves, and then manufactured. The nature of the environment was an important variable in this process: arid environments were more exposed, and thereby dangerous, than jungles where trees provided camouflage, cover and protection; and both humans and animals are more exposed in flatlands. The physical environment also varied greatly in the availability of materials for fortification.

A measure of safety was provided by hilltop settlements, which could be fortified and also provide sight-lines for intelligence and communication, as with Iron Age (and earlier) settlements in Europe, those of the Qulla (Colla) civilisation (CE 1100–1450) near Lake Titicaca in South America, and many other pre-modern civilisations. The physical environment, moreover, helped to direct, indeed determine, trade routes, and therefore to condition settlement, fortification, and military purpose. Thus, the Bronze Age fortress of Mycenae between c.1550 and 1100 BCE, dominated the main road between Argos and Corinth, the two great ports of the Peloponnese in Greece. Indeed, the ability to provide protection for, and thus to encourage, direct, and tax, passing trade at choke points, whether natural or artificial, often funded the construction of fortresses.

A particular instance of terrain-climate combination was that of marshy areas and their constant or seasonal propensity to fever, as in the Danube, Jordan and Brahmaputra valleys. Marshy areas did not necessarily have the detailed consideration for combat arising from height and slope (although they often did), but were also significant at the operational level, in that armies sought not to operate in them. More generally, disease was an issue at the tactical, operational and strategic levels. Particular environments, notably in the tropics, were deadly. General Thomas Blamey, the Commander-in-Chief of the Allied Land Forces in the South West Pacific Area, wrote in 1942 from New Guinea where Australian and American forces were deployed against the

Japanese invaders: 'The wastage in tropical warfare in undeveloped areas is immense. For example, at least one third of our force at Milne Bay is already infected with malaria.'[16] There were related (but also separate) issues as a result of the very massing of troops and animals, and the problems of sanitation.

At sea, the operational-level considerations were again the tactical ones writ large. Most notably, the direction and force of winds and currents affected the possibilities for operations, and particularly so before the Age of Steam. It was necessary to understand and work with these possibilities. Thus, the pattern of Mediterranean currents is at once simple, yet also complex. The former is explained by the major current moving in a counter-clockwise direction eastwards along the coast of North Africa, then from south to north past Israel and Lebanon, before moving back westwards along the northern shore of the Mediterranean to the Strait of Gibraltar. Yet complex, because of differences in surface, intermediate and deep water masses and because the Mediterranean is in part a product of subsidiary seas – from east to west, the Aegean, Adriatic and Tyrrhenian – and there is significant disruption to currents and weather produced by islands, notably Cyprus, Sicily, Crete, Sardinia and Corsica.[17]

Alongside currents comes the pattern of the winds, which change very greatly by season and in response to weather systems. Thus, summer winds in the eastern Mediterranean tend to come from the north-west. Winds, such as the Mistral, a strong southerly that blows onto the coast of Provence, wrecking ships, made being able to take shelter in harbours very important. The operational impact of the weather was greater in the technology of the past. Galleys had a low freeboard and therefore were vulnerable to high waters in poor weather which was one of the reasons why they, as opposed to high freeboard-ships, were unsuited to Atlantic waters. In turn, sailing ships with higher freeboards found it difficult to move against the wind, and wind directions therefore greatly affected campaigning. The Japanese referred to the 'divine winds' of the typhoons that wrecked Mongol invasions in 1274 and 1281, and Charles V's attack on Algiers in 1541 was similarly ruined. In turn, 'Protestant winds' prevented invasions of England, notably by Spain in 1588 and 1719, by France in 1744, and by France and Spain in 1779, and by France of Ireland in 1796. Conversely, after initial failures, winds aided William I of Normandy and William III of Orange to invade England in 1066 and 1688 respectively.

Technology, in turn, altered the operational situation, Henry, 3rd Viscount Palmerston, responding to pressure to focus on the navy by telling Parliament in 1860 'that steam had bridged the [English] Channel', a remark directed at the superseding of the previous dominance of winds and one successfully designed to encourage an expensive process of coastal fortification aimed to provide protection against French attack. The risk of such attack was enhanced by the major improvement to the harbour at Cherbourg.[18]

So also with airpower. While it is heavily dependent on both climate and weather, airpower, nevertheless, has become less so as a consequence of technologies including radar, infrared and GPS, as well as improvements at airfields and on aircraft carriers.

Human geography greatly affected the patterns of naval possibility because routes were supplemented by harbours and the related facilities. These were of particular significance for logistical reasons; and geography affected conflict for such reasons more at the operational level than at the tactical. As a consequence of the significance of geography for logistics, it was necessary to acquire information on sources, routes and facilities for the provision and movement of resources. The particular requirements for them were in part a matter of force structure, in terms of both the size and composition of the military, for example the number of horses, and that again underlined the need for information, and for both sides. So also with the possibilities of expedients as a solution for problems, which was a key feature of military activity, and remains so: the distinctive can-do approach is necessarily a matter of the solution-driven response to particular tasks and circumstances.

Changing the geography by means of improving communications was a classic instance of the solution. In pursuit of his eventual conquest of Dacia (Romania), the Roman Emperor Trajan had a 3,724-foot (1,135 metres)-long bridge built across the Danube in 103–5, the first bridge built over the lower Danube and a major engineering achievement. In turn, the bridge was destroyed by Hadrian, probably in order to thwart any 'barbarian' invasion of the Roman Empire from the north. In Japan, Oda Nobunaga, who rose to power in the 1560s, facilitated the mobility of his forces by building pontoon bridges across rivers and improving the road system. So also with British forces in North Africa in 1942, creating vehicle-bearing routes across the Saharan sand. Such methods not only helped troop movements, but also changed the logistical situation.

Yet it was necessary to take advantage of new routes within the context of wider possibilities. Thus, in 1783, Russian troops entered Georgia, following up by improving the road linking Russia and eastern Georgia through the Dariel Pass, one of the only crossings of the Caucasus mountains. However, commitments elsewhere against the Turks led to the withdrawal of Russian troops in 1787, and the road, which became the Georgian Military Road, did not come into its own for over a decade. This route was important to Russian power-projection in the region.

The interaction of physical geography and roads was also seen in the public discussion of operational-level warfare, as in the presentation in Ramsay Muir's *New School Atlas of Modern History* (1911) of the Peninsular War of 1808–14 and more particularly the Lines of Torres Vedras constructed by the British in 1809–10 to protect Lisbon:

> 'Note how the campaigns were determined by the direction of the river valleys and mountain ranges, and by the greater military roads, which are shown; also how the physical barriers in which the country abounds not only prevented effective co-operation between the various French armies and thus added to their difficulties, but accentuated the strong provincial sentiment of the various provinces of Spain. Note the magnificent strategic position of the Torres Vedras lines, a vast natural fortress, commanding the best possible base for an Atlantic naval power, and also controlling the best roads into the heart of the peninsula, from which it was possible to threaten equally all the scattered French armies.'[19]

As a separate point, physical and human geography, notably terrain and agricultural production, could combine to ensure that campaigning concentrated in particular areas, especially flat agrarian zones, such as Lombardy in northern Italy, not least in successive conflicts from the 1510s to 1740s, and in the 1790s. At the same time, supporting or clashing with that point, the need for transport infrastructure could be lessened by deciding to live off the land, rather than rely on supply routes or, indeed, the fortified positions that anchored them. Alternatively, the size of forces deployed could be reduced, as in Germany in the latter stages of the Thirty Years War (1618–48).[20] Nevertheless, even in economically benign areas for operations, the situation could be dramatically changed by the impact of bad weather on the harvest as well as by the cumulative pressures brought by campaigning.[21]

Human and physical geography could combine differently when routes helped open up economically and strategically significant areas to occupation. In his 'General Situation' memorandum of 21 January 1945, Field Marshal Bernard Montgomery wrote: 'The main objective of the Allies on the western front is the Ruhr; if we can cut it off from the rest of Germany the enemy capacity to continue the struggle must gradually peter out.'[22] The Ruhr was Germany's leading industrial zone, and, indeed, it was totally cut off in subsequent operations. In turn, during the Cold War, the Fulda Gap, sixty miles northeast of Frankfurt-on-Main, was seen as an obvious way for Soviet tanks to break through NATO defences and advance from East Germany to Frankfurt and the Rhine Valley, thus outflanking NATO defences to north and south as well as denying the Americans the large airfields in the Frankfurt area. Atomic Demolition Mines, and missiles capable of carrying nuclear warheads, were used by the Americans as part of the protective system for the Gap.[23] The Gap was an instance of the changing significance of particular areas and routes, as, although an invasion passage on occasion, it had been of no real consequence during the successive Austro-Prussian wars between 1740 and 1866, nor subsequently, until used by the Americans to advance eastwards in 1945.

Conversely, there were operational-level physical obstacles, as in 1945, when the Western Allies had to confront the key physical obstacle of a Rhine crossing in order to be able to cut off the Ruhr, again an issue that had not been significant militarily for a considerable period. That was the consequence of strategic need and circumstance, particularly the previous world war not continuing into the 1919 campaigning season. Yet the inhibiting operational potential of physical features was also affected by technology. Thus the Rhine was less of an obstacle to the Allies in 1945 than it would have been had their forces advanced there in the event of the First World War continuing into 1919; not least by 1945 with less of a reliance on existing bridges. Instead, for the Allies in 1945, there was a repeat of the possibility of invading France in 1944 without having to focus from the outset on seizing ports, such as Cherbourg and Le Havre, in order to tackle logistical issues. It was possible, with the Rhine, to mount a large airborne assault, with over 16,000 paratroopers successfully dropped in Operation Varsity on 24 March 1945.

Furthermore, bridge-building techniques were also far more advanced as a consequence of the development of combat-engineering, which led to expedients such as the Bailey Bridge, a pre-fabricated portable bridge that was easy to assemble and produced in Britain from 1941, being first used, in North Africa, in 1942. The Americans adopted that technique in 1942, and these bridges served to replace those destroyed by the Germans, notably in Italy. Bridge capabilities were made more significant by the heaviness of the tanks deployed, a situation that is still very pertinent today as in discussion of the NATO reinforcement of the Baltic Republics against possible Russian attack.

Physical obstacles and their passage, in turn, took on meaning given the time sequences of the units on the respective sides. Thus, in 1805, the Austrians were outmanoeuvred and enveloped by the rapid advance of the French from the middle Rhine to the front of the Austrians, to the Danube in their rear. In 1973, the Israelis counterattack against the Egyptians proved able not only to advance to the Suez Canal, but also to launch a surprise assault across it, using, first, troops crossing on rubber dinghies and, then, tanks ferried on motorised rafts.

At a broader scale, envelopment attacks benefited when opponents fought forward in defence of their frontiers, as the French in 1870, Poles in 1939, and Greeks in 1941, did when successfully attacked by the Germans. Such invasions proved far less successful when the opponents did not fight forward, relying, instead, on a defence in the interior, as with the Russians in 1812 when attacked by the French under Napoleon. The latter was an aspect of the extent to which distance repeatedly was a strategic reserve that had to be challenged and overcome by attackers, an ultimate form of geography in warfare, as with the Habsburg forces invading France in 1636 and the British and/or Austrian and Prussian forces doing likewise including in 1708, 1743 and 1792. Fortifications took on a delaying value in this context, as with invasions of France, for example in 1524, 1544, 1708, 1744, 1747 and 1793, none of which really achieved their strategic purpose.

In late 1846, when war was declared, American forces under Zachary Taylor, operating from Texas across the Rio Grande into northern

Mexico, captured the provincial capitals of Monterrey and Saltillo. The last, however, is about 550 miles from Mexico City. These distances were part of Mexico's natural defences and underlined the marginal character of operations in Mexico's northern provinces as far as Mexico's centre of power was concerned. In contrast, in 1847, the bold stroke of a strike at the Mexican centre was launched by an American amphibious landing near Vera Cruz, from which a successful advance was made on Mexico City. This was a matter of sound strategic choice, but also a political matter: troops were transferred from the army under Zachary Taylor, a rival of President James Polk. Conversely, advancing to a centre of power, as the British and French each did to Madrid during both the War of the Spanish Succession and the Napoleonic Wars, and the French to Moscow in 1812, did not dictate victory.

Separately, human adaptation to the physical environment could lead to a distinctive fighting style that posed difficulties for others. For example, in the forested valley of the River Brahmaputra in what is now north-east India, the Ahom proved a serious challenge to the Mughals from 1612. Although outnumbered, Ahom fighting techniques were well adapted to the terrain. They relied on infantry armed with muskets or bows and arrows, used flexible tactics, including surprise night attacks, and rapidly created fortified positions based on bamboo stockades which made attacking them a costly and difficult task. The riverine and jungle terrain were very different from the plains and low hills of Rajasthan where the Mughals had campaigned from the 1520s. There was a parallel with Britain's Indian Army, long familiar with the dry, high North-West Frontier of India, most recently in the Waziristan campaigns of 1939–9, but sent to fight the Japanese in the dense tropical forests of Malaya and Burma in 1941–2. There, it was heavily defeated, and then forced to adapt.[24] The Mughals had indeed done so in the Brahamputra valley, not least with the use of elephants, boats, and infantry.

Technology was not solely a matter of change over the last 120 years and the new operational concepts linked to it, as earlier developments were also of great significance. Key instances included stirrups, as the combination of mobility and firepower was thereby affected. Nevertheless, the major elements of environmental impact, both physical and human, did not alter fundamentally during the pre-industrial period. Probably the most important were those of global climatic changes, notably the

'Little Ice Age' centring on the seventeenth century, with the impact that it had on growing seasons and thus on the productivity of the crucial agrarian economy.[25] Colder temperatures also increased vulnerability to disease; and for animals as well as humans.

To include climate change in this section underlines the extent to which there are precedents for the unpredictabilities of the present. Climate change also pushes to the fore long-standing issues in tension and conflict over control over fresh water, as well as grazing land. Idris Aloma, ruler of Bornu (1569–c. 1600), an Islamic state based in the region of Lake Chad, made careful warlike use of economic measures, attacking crops or keeping nomads from their grazing areas in order to make them submit. So also with the goals and means in conflict in the *sahel* in the early 2010s, notably in Darfur in west Sudan, but, by the late 2010s and early 2020s, more generally, and particularly so across the great expanses of Mali, but also more widely. Yet again, however, the physical geography takes effect in large part due to changes in its human counterpart, notably the dispersal from Libya, following the overthrow of the Gaddafi regime in 2011, of troops and weapons.

A less relevant operational level for the present might be that of spiritual geography, one also found at the tactical and strategic levels, and one overlapping with such powerful and lasting symbolic and anthropological dimensions of warfare as display and the calling forth of success. However, functional explanations are necessarily incomplete when assessing spiritual geography. In Oriental cultures, the understanding and use of space had a spiritual character in the shape of geomancy or *feng shui*, and the specific positioning of fortifications, as with other buildings, was important to their effectiveness.[26] Thus, fortifications could take the place of missing hills to produce a geomantic pattern that was effective in defence. The enhancement of the environment for defence, and to harm opponents, was regarded as a key component for both *feng shui* and martial arts. Mountains and water were essential elements to ensure the proper martial positioning and circulation of energy to help achieve success. Thus, in Japan, it was thought necessary to appreciate local geomantic configurations, while in China, iconographic warfare played a role in the location of walls. An element of continuity in the location of border walls has been seen as reflecting both a practical understanding of the topography and its possibilities, and, on the other hand, beliefs about the structure of the universe and concerning a border between China and the 'barbarians.'[27]

In addition, storms, notably, but not only, at sea, could be blamed on hostile spiritual forces. This was a process validated by the discussion of war in texts such as the *Iliad* and the Old Testament of the Bible. Indeed, the histories of war very much provide a way to approach the geographies of war, and vice versa.

Religion, which overlaps with both these histories and these geographies, is generally an underrated dimension of war, and particularly so of modern warfare, but, for long, the idea of humans as occupying a world defined, as well as created, by spiritual forces was matched by a sense that the essential parameters had a real physical existence. If this was true of Heaven and Hell, that reflected the belief, as in St Augustine's *City of God* (426), that the agents of good and evil had bases, a real presence, and a determination and ability to intervene. Their continual metaphysical rivalry was the key conflict, but one shaped by, as well as shaping, the struggles between humans. In this view, evil was in part believed to be expressed in other religions, as with the Muslim notion of *Jihad*. Heathens were defined as hostile. The language was that of war, and the campaigning was linked to those of military forces, including religious ones such as the Christian Crusading Orders, or, in part, of religious bodies with a militaristic ethos and/or organisation, such as the Jesuits.

Conflict linked to religious observance ensured that human geography played a major role in religious struggles in the shape of the existing distribution of rival faiths. Given the role of religious tensions within individual faiths, as well as of political struggles between co-religionists, this factor did not preclude others; but it was significant, and has remained so to the present, as with civil wars over the last thirty years in the former Yugoslavia, the former Sudan, and Iraq. Religious sites have also been frequently attacked, including in Afghanistan, Bosnia, Egypt, Iraq and Pakistan; and the resulting geography of their protection includes an emphasis on gates, walls and guards. More generally, the possibility of proselytism and/or 'ethnic cleansing,' as in Bosnia and Kosovo in the 1990s, and both Arakan in Myanmar and the Kurdish areas of Syria in 2019–2020, emphasises the extent to which human boundaries were malleable. This is a situation that still remains the case, although there is far less international tolerance for territorial frontier changes today than in the past.

Another possible aspect of symbolic geography was the extent to which the long-standing practice of fighting at particular places was culturally-driven. An alternative explanation is of topographically-driven choices as in where a battle could be held. There is certainly evidence to suggest a correspondence, as in Ancient Greece and Anglo-Saxon England, between places appropriate for assemblies, legal, political, and/or religious, and for peace-making ceremonies, and places appropriate for conflict. As aspects of 'markings on the land',[28] these places were often associated with forests, heaths and river crossings, as well as with specific waypoints, such as barrows or other monuments. These places had pragmatic benefits, including logistical ones, as in access to routes of communication, visibility and space for large numbers of people to gather. They could also have sacral significance and explicit associations with kingship, as in places where gods or other figures had shown themselves, or barrows associated with a legendary ancestor. As these places were memorialised, and the battles that took place there were recorded, they could convey territorial control and collective identity.[29] So also with conflict elsewhere, for example in Oceania, as in Hawaii.

As a different issue, while the political boundaries of territories changed often in the past, there were still physical obstacles with which the states had to cope. Thus, Moroccan forces were sent across the Sahara in 1590–1, conquering Songhai in the Niger Valley; but, once established, the trans-Saharan Moroccan empire could not be expanded, or, in the end, eventually sustained. Yet much about the impact of geography on expansionism and war concerns the nature and consequences of influence and possibility, rather than of certainty and determinism in outcome and means.

To note that boundaries can be changeable and/or porous does not deny the role of this influence, for fixity is not a necessary proof of influence. However, this very absence of fixity also underlines the extent to which it is inappropriate to use the conceptualisation and vocabulary of determinism. Such a conceptualisation, indeed, is a problem with some of the modern literature on geopolitics and related popular pieces on so-called 'the return of geography'.[30] In practice, geography never went away, but nor did it dictate outcomes.

And so, moreover, with the operational and tactical conceptualisation of techniques, for example the exploitation of interior lines, a classic Napoleonic technique. That technique, and others, relied on skill rather than having success inherent to the method itself. Napoleon took a central position in order to divide more numerous opposing forces, and then to defeat them separately. In turn, a strategy of envelopment was used against weaker forces: they were pinned down by an attack mounted by a section of the French army, while most of the army enveloped them, attacking them in flank or, in preference, cutting their lines of supply and retreat, the *manoeuvre sur les derrières*.

A very different organisational spatiality was involved in the structure of the military, for example the Napoleonic development of the system of corps (combined arms groupings of divisions), and the consequent relationships between units, including as they advanced on campaign. Corps could operate independently, which increased the frontage of any advance, as in Napoleon's successful 1805 campaign in Germany with the *Grande Armée*, but such an independence and frontage made co-operation between them more necessary. Indeed, under the friction of actual contact with circumstances, the Germans, despite at that stage not facing insuperable opposition, failed to maintain co-operation between their units when advancing into France in 1914, providing an opportunity for the successful Anglo-French counterattack in the battle of the Marne.[31]

Indeed, because war is a process in which there is always more than one stakeholder and participant, success in part depended on the response of opponents and its rapidity. Thus, in 1805, it was the slowness of the Austrian response that was important to Napoleon's success. Similarly, in 1866, 1870, and 1940, the responses of opponents were necessary to Prussian and German success. This is an aspect of the absence of determinism.

In addition, tactical capability and operational-level effectiveness (up to a point) were not necessarily decisive at the strategic level, as the Germans were to discover when attacking the Soviet Union in 1941. Again, aside from the response of opponents, the goal was important; and notably whether the occupation of territory, or the destruction of opposing forces, was crucial. This was a frequent issue in war, as for the Germans in 1941. In this case, as in many others, the geography was generally seen as subservient to the strategy; although the viability of the strategy, in turn, was affected by both physical and human geography. So for example in 1747, when the viability of the French attempt to break through the Piedmontese defence of the Alpine passes into Italy became an unsuccessful attempt to break through the defended Assietta Pass, where redoubts and a palisade provided an opportunity for deadly defensive fire.

Repeatedly, the impact of geography was in part a matter of assessment and, therefore, perception. For example, the Allies, in considering where to invade German-occupied France in 1944 during the Second World War, could see the Calais region as closer, because there was a shorter sea crossing from England and a shorter route to Germany, but Normandy was closer to key invasion ports on the south coast of England, notably Portsmouth and Southampton. In the event, underlining unpredictability, the need subsequently to cross the River Seine, rather than landing east of it, was apparently one of the principal hazards of the Normandy option, but, in the event, did not prove too difficult. The Normandy option might seem to have made a German counter-attack more difficult than one in the Calais region. However, in practice, the Allies failed to isolate the Normandy battle zone and the Germans were able to move up forces so that, once off the beaches, the Allies had to fight harder in Normandy than they had anticipated; although, conversely, their defeat of the Germans there meant that less of an effort than planned for was required in order to cross the River Seine. In a reminder of the folly of some types of geographical determinism, this was one of the many physical obstacles that did not prove the anticipated barrier.

More generally, as in other periods, but more so given the greater number of formats in which conflict could be waged, a variety of factors was always at play in helping shape the relationship of war and geography in the twentieth century. Thus, the civil conflicts in China in the 1920s, the warlord era, indicated the multifaceted nature of contextual environmental influences. The significance of rail links and of control over cities helped ensure that there was a stress on rapid advances on key positions, rather than on continuous fronts; but there was more at stake including the essentially unstable background of coalitions between warlords. This was a geography of war that was very different to that of conflict between states, as the latter had inherent fronts in the shape of frontiers, and these served as the starting place for attempts at territorial aggrandisement and/or preservation.

Historically, this was especially so of frontiers linked to walls, whether they were primarily for defence, or as a base for further offensives, or for trade and migration control, and/or a mixture of all three, but in which ratios? Alongside providing a physical barrier, wall systems could also offer observation and early-warning structures. The geography of frontiers was related to that of walls and, in particular, the question of whether the frontier should be seen as a line or a zone. There was no inevitable geographical basis for either a line or a zone, in war or peace, although specific features, notably rivers, readily lent themselves to an emphasis on a line.

Whatever the set of assumptions, they were in a dynamic relationship with the respective strength and intentions of the two sides. Thus, from the seventh century, the essential Byzantine strategy involved letting Arab armies across the border, having the entire population and their crucial livestock retreat into fortified settlements in order to deny easy plunder to the raiders, and, instead, shadowing the larger Arab armies with field forces. As a result, the fortified points served as refuges while also providing crucial logistical support for a mobile defence force. The extent to which the logistical strain of distance was a continual challenge, and often for both sides, was particularly significant at the operational level of warfare.

The operational level of the geography of war will recur in later chapters. At this point, however, it is necessary, yet again, to note that there was no invariable process that can be regarded as deterministic. Instead, the environment acted, and was acted upon, in a 'possibilist' fashion. Success in war is about decision-makers having a holistic view of the theatre of war, and no single decision, act or factor is likely to lead to success. Fighting and succeeding in war is a complex business.

Chapter 4

Strategy

'The paramount importance of geography ... has been brought home to Englishmen by the late war in South Africa [Boer War, 1899–1902], which has forced them to realise how impossible it is to understand events in their connection without a knowledge of such things as the relative position of towns and villages; the relative course of rivers; the nature of the frontier; remoteness from or indentation by the sea; etc. All these circumstances must be taken into account in drawing up the strategy of a campaign, strategy being in a great measure the art of adapting military movements to the geographical conditions of a given country.... The present atlas endeavours to initiate the student into the knowledge of the strategy of events, and to accustom him to look at history from that most fertile of points of view, the geographical correlation of events.' Emil Reich, *New Student's Atlas of English History* (1903).[1]

The role of geography in military strategy, a practice that long preceded the vocabulary,[2] focuses primarily on its impact on the strategic elements of war: the formulation, prioritisation and implementation of military goals and tasks. For all powers, geography plays a role in this sphere, both in general terms and with reference to what is termed the strategic culture of specific states. The latter, inherently a geographical approach to strategy, relates to long-term concerns at that level; and many of these concerns were expressed, at the time or subsequently, with reference to particular geographical goals. These included the goal of obtaining allegedly natural frontiers for France,[3] a theme in *Atlas historique* (1900) by Vast and Malleterre, both of whom taught in the Military Academy; and, alternatively, the drive for warm-water ports for Russia; or of spreading from 'ocean to ocean', the Atlantic to the Pacific, for the United States. The overlap in strategic formulation and prioritisation with geopolitics, the subject of the next chapter, is readily apparent, but, for the moment, the focus is on implementation as that overlaps with the last chapter. Indeed, there is no fixed bounding of strategy, and the understanding of it varies within, and between, national military cultures.

Geography is present and (differently) presented in strategy not only in terms of spatial considerations, including those reflecting the underlying geology,[4] but also with reference to a space-time continuum, in that these considerations had to be addressed and mastered in the period of opportunity. The size of the war-space (as opposed to both the tactical battle-space, and the operational-campaign space) is a key element in strategy. Thus, in the Thirty Years War (1618–48),[5] there were the issues arising from the size of the disputed areas where campaigning focused, essentially modern Germany, and the security, as a result of their distance from them, of the key political centres of Vienna, Paris, The Hague, Stockholm and Madrid, each of which was largely safe from attack; although less so in the first two cases, both of which were threatened. Similarly, the royalists could not seriously challenge the Parliamentary heartland – London and the south-east, in the English Civil War after 1642; nor the Manchu that of China prior to 1644; nor the Rebellion of the Three Feudatories Manchu control of northern China in 1673–7.

There was, as a related aspect of the war-space, the force-space ratios of the combatants. Thus, the force-space ratios of conflict in Latin America during the Wars of Independence from Spain and Portugal of 1809–25 were very different to those in Western and Central Europe during the French Revolutionary and Napoleonic Wars (1792–1815). This difference had major implications, not least the greater logistical problems faced by campaigning in Latin America. In both regions, however, the interaction of different areas was such that success in one did not pre-empt countervailing action originating from another, which delayed an overall verdict. Indeed, for France to do well in one region often entailed moving troops from elsewhere, and weakening its position there, which was seen repeatedly in the Peninsular War of 1808–13 in Spain and Portugal, and also with regard to moving French troops to or from Spain as consequence of commitments elsewhere in Europe. Ultimately, such interactions contributed to Napoleon's complete failure in Europe, although, in variance with that approach, his repeated defeats in his main field of operations, in 1812, 1813, 1814 and 1815, were necessary to this outcome.

Distance continued to be an issue in subsequent conflicts. Once independence had been won in Latin America, there was then the tension, notably in Mexico, between central government and, on the other hand, *caudillos* (strong men) based on the military commandancies (regions) created in 1823,[6] and in Argentina in the parallel struggles between *unitarios* and federalists. In the American Civil War (1861–5), although Washington, the capital city and a Union base of operations, was very vulnerable to Confederate attack, and therefore strongly protected, more distant Boston, Chicago and New York were not so protected as they did not need to be. In the First World War, Paris proved more exposed to German attack than the centres of Russian power, although it was to be Russia that surrendered. If the margin of safety was very narrow when the Germans advanced on Moscow in 1941, the Soviet regime had already established an alternative centre at Kuybyshev (now Samara), on the Volga River. Indeed, in October, much of the government was moved there, returning to Moscow only in the summer of 1943. Yet again, however, geography was not the determinator: the French could have moved their centre of government in 1940 to Algiers or, even, London, but chose rather to surrender and to retain a limited territorial presence in France based in Vichy.

Force-space ratios in part arose from the extent to which goals were defined, both from the outset and with regard to the events and issues that arose during the war. Thus, in 1866, during the Austro-Prussian War, the Prussians advanced towards Vienna after their victory at Königgratz (Sadowa) in Bohemia, reaching the outskirts of Bratislava, where they were held off in the battle of Blumenau. However, the Prussians wanted a speedy end to the conflict, not least in order to prevent France from considering armed mediation and pursuing a demand for territorial gains. As a result of this limitation of the Prussian goal, there was no final battle, no siege of Vienna to prefigure the lengthy one of Paris in 1870–1, and no territorial gains for Prussia from Austria, as opposed to the important ones from Austria's defeated allies in Germany. Thus, in the case of 1866, as more generally, the assessment of the geographies of conflict has to consider one of the most important and underrated building blocks in military history. These were (and remain) campaigns, as well as wars, that did not take place, but that were still considered and, therefore, were aspects of the planning and assessment of capability of the period.

Again, as in the last two chapters, physical and human geographies played a role, but, at the strategic level, the emphasis was generally on considerations at a greater scale, and usually including entire states. The most significant aspect of the physical environment is propinquity (closeness) and its reverse, distance; and, at the human level, the distribution of population, as people provide the key target for control, and the means of this control, but also of resistance. Again, there have been important changes in scale with technology and development, notably transport innovations and population growth, but the essential points remain valid. The understanding of them is also a factor at once constant and changing. Thus, people providing targets for control helps ensure the significance of cities to both strategy and operations. They are where the human environment most affects the physical one of fighting. Buildings provide a readily contestable terrain, as at Stalingrad in 1942, Warsaw in 1944, Berlin and Manila in 1945, Hue in 1968, and Mosul in 2016–17. Moreover, control over the populace was a clear desired outcome, as opposed to simply the outcomes of territory overrun, and opposing combatants killed. Thus, in 2020, in its conflict with the rebellious province of Tigray, Ethiopia primarily sought to gain control of the regional capital, Mekelle.

The contrast between outcome and output, a central tension in war (and military commentary), helps drive different strategic methods. So also does that between timetables for victory, as in the Vietnam War, with the American drive for short-war counterpointed with their opponents' readiness to fight for longer. This readiness was vindicated by eventual victory in conquering South Vietnam in 1975 after American departure in 1973. In turn, and with the difference not solely linked to technology, that situation helped in that conflict to ensure a geographical stress on particular areas: the American emphasis more maritime and their opponents' more inland. This contrast, which in part looked to lines of communication, helped structure the geography of the battle for dominance.

For the Americans, there was also the standard geography of strategy, in the shape of the contrasting emphasis placed on particular commitments, as in Europe versus Vietnam in the 1960s, as there had been, for instance, war against Germany versus war against Japan in 1941–2; and, for Japan, war against the Soviet Union or America in 1941.

And so for other powers, for example for Russia, the Baltic or southwards, from the fifteenth to the eighteenth centuries; and for Germany, in the early twentieth century, the relationship between expansionism to the west and the east. The distribution of troops, such as Roman legions, Russian forces in the eighteenth century, or American garrisons between 1815 and the Civil War, was a product of such issues, and has been readily represented spatially,[7] as also can be that of warships. At the same time, the ready conclusions in terms of deliberate planning drawn from such distributions can be questioned,[8] while it is necessary to appreciate that unit location is not necessarily a measure of equivalence in size or in fighting quality.

Varying strategic commitment to particular sites and/or types of territory was a facet of insurrectionary/counter-insurgency warfare, notably in the Cold War, but, again, was found more widely in conflict. In particular, control over settings of legitimacy, especially capital cities, took on special significance in civil wars, as in the English and American Civil Wars, the French Wars of Religion, the *Frondes* (French civil wars of 1648–53), and Chinese civil wars; but far less so in struggles between neighbouring states in which no permanent absorption of a territory was intended. Civil wars were also different in that they forced all areas of a state at least potentially into the equation, with local issues subordinated to larger ones, but, in turn, the political geography of the former affected the latter.

The incremental style of strategy designed to acquire border provinces and focused on sieges of relevant positions, as under Louis XIV of France (r. 1643–1715), not least with his presence for example at Mons in 1691, and the related show-of-force/'pacification' processes of imperial powers such as China, were both therefore based on a specific type of war and a particular view of territory. This specificity and particularity had implications in terms of the force structure and doctrine of the militaries of these and other powers. Indeed, the focus on gaining political advantage and territory in short conflicts, one often referred to as *ancien régime* or cabinet warfare, can be seen into the modern age, as in the Franco-Prussian War of 1870–1, German plans in 1914 and 1938–41, and, very differently, Indian and Israeli strategies in post-independence conflicts.

So also with continuities in the strategies of defence; although they cannot always be so readily separated from attack as might appear.

Separately, the need for a fixed defence system, generally in the form of fortifications and even walls, is not somehow constant in requirement, location, type or cost. Thus, what primarily emerges as tactical and operational terms, as in why do these defences take this form, and at this place, can best be explained in terms of strategic choice. Neither the Romans nor, very differently, President Donald Trump (r. 2017–21), required walls, but they built or proposed them for particular strategic reasons. In the Roman case, in part this was due to the fixing of a border to defend after a period of expansion had closed, thereby for consolidation, although other factors also played a role. In the case of Trump towards Mexico, the strategy was that of domestic politics, with the ostensible 'military' component directed against criminals and illegal immigrants.

Walls, more generally, were a product of a wish and/or need to shelve, as well as consolidate, ideas and practices of expansion, but, more especially, in a context of immediate concern and requirement. The resulting geography of military preparedness is becoming clearer through archaeology, and notably so for areas for which written sources are limited. However, partly due to the latter, it can be difficult to assess the purpose and value of particular fortifications. Much of the world has not been adequately studied from this perspective, and archaeological work anyway is greatly affected by the extent, nature, and accessibility of the remains that are available. Material that throws possible light on strategic geography continues to be unearthed even for major states such as the Ottoman (Turkish) empire.[9] So also for the 195 kilometre-long 'Great Wall of Gorgan,' or 'Red Snake,' from east of the Caspian Sea that was constructed and maintained by the Sasanian rulers of Persia from the fifth to seventh centuries in order apparently to stop invasions from the north by the White Huns. As part of a wider geography of defence, this work was apparently matched by the Wall of Derbent to the west of the Caspian Sea.[10]

China had a long history of wall-building, repairing and garrisoning, with the location of walls an aspect of failure and success, as, with the former, in those of the fourth to sixth centuries CE being further south than earlier ones. In turn, the Tang dynasty (618–907), in its more successful early stage, pursued expansion, with fortresses and military colonies from Xinjiang to Sichuan. A different geography was at stake under the Northern Song (960–1127), with linear defences, including a network of hydraulic defences such as deep irrigation channels and marshes to protect the vulnerable province of Hebei. The Northern Song also developed new fertile land, which helped to sustain the new garrisons, and new towns, which was a classic instance of a strategic direction in which the local was subordinate to the imperial state. In contrast, the location of many of the castles in medieval Europe was due to the local considerations of local landlords seeking to control and protect their domains, and related to the particular nature of their holding and the threats to it. In response to renewed Mongol success in the mid-fifteenth century, there was a new Chinese emphasis on a defensive strategy based on walls. Especially in the 1470s, the Great Wall of the first Qin Emperor was reconstructed, and there were also new fortifications.[11]

The nature of the geographical information involved in the location of past fortifications is generally unclear, as direct evidence is usually lacking. Nevertheless, this location would have required a spatial sense, one derived in part from a general geographical sense of the nature of the relevant territory and routes. This was especially so as fortresses were intended to form defensive systems, as with Henry I of Germany constructing about fifty fortifications between 929 and 936 to protect the eastern border of Saxony,[12] or in Spanish-ruled Lombardy in the seventeenth century where the forts of Novara, Alessandria, Tortona and Valenza were regarded as links in a chain aimed at the defence of the state from attack from the west. This was the direction of Savoy-Piedmont and, more seriously, France. The latter had to attack across the Alps, but that was not an insuperable barrier outside the depths of the winter.

Human geography was very much part of the process and led to a variety of processes. These included the use of scorched earth policies by defenders, as with Crimean Tatars opposing Russian expansion in the seventeenth and eighteenth centuries, notably in the late 1680s and late 1730s. The establishing of settlements in the form of colonies, for example by the Romans and the Chinese was also significant, and widely seen. Faced by attacks by the Jurchens of Manchuria, Korea in the fifteenth century established a chain of defensive positions to consolidate the frontier, using settlement as part of the process. Rather differently, the wall systems used by Russia's rulers in the seventeenth and eighteenth century to protect from attack by Tatars to the south helped to consolidate power, but also to mark successive stages of expansion and would-be expansion. These systems required significant effort, and thus were the product of an autocratic society able to deploy labour.[13] In response to the large-scale millenarian White Lotus rebellion in the late 1790s, the Chinese government introduced military-agricultural colonists as part of their major, and successful, counter-insurgency campaign. At the same time, the location of wall systems, in China as elsewhere, was part of the process of affecting identities by seeking to make frontiersmen fix their identity.[14] So also with the Pakistani fortification of its frontier with Afghanistan in the early 2020s.

Walls play no role at sea, and the image of ships as wooden walls was fanciful due to their dependence on the weather; but maritime strategy was very much linked to bases and routes. The operational factors discussed in the last chapter were significant to this, but the need to supply warships, even fleets, was closely related to where it was felt to be appropriate to maintain a presence. That was in part apparently 'fixed' by geography as a constant, but, in practice, the latter was also a construct, with specific naval tasks, and therefore geographical requirements, adopted accordingly. And so also with the nature of 'fixing' by geography. Thus, the relocation of the principal English (later British) bases reflected a task-based approach: from facing the Dutch (Chatham), to the French (Portsmouth, Plymouth), to the Germans (Scapa Flow, Rosyth), and then back to an Atlantic orientation linked to a Soviet threat to the North Atlantic (Portsmouth, Plymouth, Faslane). From the sixteenth century, Spain moved from an emphasis on the Mediterranean to one on the Atlantic. The British geography of bases will be affected by Scottish independence if/when it occurs, as both tasks and options will change.

More generally, technological developments were part of the equation in the geographical influence on naval power, not least in affecting the responses to the parameters of the maritime physical environment. Changes in the power source for warships were significant, with coaling stations around the world crucial in the Age of Steam. Earlier changes in methods for establishing the location of a ship were also vital. They, for example, provided British ships with new opportunities for navigation in the Indian Ocean in the seventeenth century.[15] Changes in communication systems, notably with radio, were also fundamental.

The technological dimension of the human environment also provided opportunities and constraints that could change. This was noted by Sir

Frederick Barton Maurice, a former Major General, in his inaugural lecture as the Professor of Military Studies at King's College, London in 1927, when he emphasised the logistical impact of 'the development of railways, roads, and mechanised transport of all kinds.'[16] The opportunities thus offered for force-projection could, however, be lessened by opposing action, notably bombing, especially in the shape of aerial interdiction, or could be limited by asymmetrical warfare in the shape of insurgencies.

In turn, air power had its own requirements,[17] with a strategic capacity offered by a logistical infrastructure. Thus, in Britain, in preparation for war with Germany, under a plan of 1936, fuel storage tanks were constructed, and then a secret underground pipeline to link Bristol's Avonmouth Docks and Liverpool's Stanlow Refinery was operational by 1942. It was expanded to link to major RAF airfields in eastern England.

Although operating in accordance with geographical parameters, most obviously range and climate, air power to a degree neutralised the benefits of geography that defending forces had formerly enjoyed. It provided three-dimensional access to the battlefield and to the theatre of operations, and on both land and at sea. A river, mountain range, or body of water, no longer served as an obstacle to thwart an attack, while height permits better visibility. Defenders had to turn to cover and adopt camouflage, as occurred in the Middle East and Central America in the 1920s in response to British and American air power respectively.[18] In the Second World War, the British and American bombers, from 1939 and 1942 respectively, could fly over the frontlines and attack targets at a considerable distance as airpower theorists had earlier predicted. Moreover, airpower allowed the attack on tactical, operational and strategic targets simultaneously.

Technology is not the only driver of strategic change. There is also strategy in an assessment of what are supposedly past lessons[19] and in a broader geographical setting of priorities within states, or really their ruling groups. In part, these priorities are task-based, as in Japan in the 2010s and 2020s with the move from an orientation directed against Russia to one against China. They are also reflected in, and affected by, expenditure and the related parameters of the military.

Related to this have come priorities between the branches of the military, as the geographies of strategy are in part a matter of competing military interests. Thus, for Japan, the naval focus today is on China, and the army one on Russia. In a very different geopolitical context, there was also a marked contrast in Japan in the early twentieth century, with the army most concerned about China and Russia, and the navy with Britain and the United States. This tension was particularly acute in differences over Japanese policymaking in 1939–41, and, indeed, led to a dysfunctional element in Japanese warmaking during the Second World War.[20]

There is repeatedly a competitive-context and response-character to decisions about strategy, force-structure, and procurement. Thus, in South Korea in 2020, the decision to build a first aircraft carrier, due to be launched in the late 2020s, reflected concern about the prospect of a surprise attack on its air bases by North Korea, and was linked to the wider international context that is so crucial to strategy, namely being a product of the failure of American-North Korean negotiations. That failure led to South Korean interest in being able to retain aircraft able to attack North Korea from a carrier located in the Sea of Japan or the Yellow Sea, thereby, on the Cold War pattern, providing a strike capability even if faced by a devastating North Korean first strike. That capability is seen as a deterrent.

This point underlines the extent to which geography is both a structural element in war, as in one with irreducible facts of location and the physical environment, and also a contested one. The latter is the case both in that the military consequences of these 'facts' will be disputed, and because the very elements that help mould the understanding of these facts, and, indeed, the search for them, are far from fixed and, in addition, are debatable and often debated. This includes the always problematic issue of learning from previous conflicts, and the critique that this entails then plays a role in preparing for others.

At the same time, there were not only political tensions within states and their militaries, but also international differences between cultures and ideologies that affected their attitude to conflict. Thus, in south-east Asia in the sixteenth century, most cities were not walled, and, in so far as the attitudes can be recovered, the notion of fighting for a city was not well established culturally across the entire region. Instead, the local culture of war was generally that of the abandonment of cities in the face of stronger attackers, who then pillaged before leaving. As in sub-Saharan Africa where labour was won with slaves and profit gained from their sale, captives, not territory, were the general objective of operations. In contrast, the standard geography of Western strategy in south-east Asia reflected a different culture. This geography was one of an interest in annexation and the consolidation of control by fortifications, especially of the coastal ports that provided the crucial bases, the latter still seen with the Americans in the Vietnam War. One strategic geography was not more correct, essential, nor progressive, than the other.

The focus in this context on fortifications was not restricted to Westerners. It was seen even more clearly with China, which, separately but on a linked point, on land did not have the semi-autonomous forces seen more clearly with Western expansion. Instead, the Chinese relied on garrisons, walls and soldier colonies. The Ottomans were more similar to the Western powers, not least in having both semi-autonomous forces and, differently, formal garrisons able to express and consolidate control, indeed many of the latter. Thanks to both, there was an ability to define and protect frontier zones, both internal and external. Thus, fortifications were built along the roads from Damascus to Cairo and Mecca, and on Africa's Red Sea coast from Suakin to Massawa.

The choice of sites for fortification reflected a grasp of the relationships between tactical, operational and strategic factors. Thus, positions on, or near, the mouths of rivers, for example Ochakov on the Dnieper and Azov on the Don, were important sites for fortification by the Ottomans, providing points for transhipment between river and sea vessels, and also controls over access to the river systems, and thus the relationship between Ukraine and the Black Sea.[21] Having been fought over before, these two positions were finally seized by the Russians in 1736 and 1788 respectively. So also with Strasbourg, captured by the French in 1681, 1918, and 1944, and recaptured by the Germans in 1870 and 1940, not that the politics were seen in that light by the French. Strasbourg controlled passage along the River Rhine and, what was less common, a crossing point over the river, serving for France as a protector for Alsace and a means to move forward into southern Germany, and a symbol of relative strength.

Fortification in a different fashion was provided by air bases, which served both defensive and offensive purpose, although with longer runways required of the latter due to the emphasis on bombers. Strategy was bound up in their location, as with America ensuring bases on Saipan and Tinian in the Mariana Islands in 1944 from which Japan could be bombed. As with so much with the strategic dimension in the Second World War, this looked forward to the geography of the Cold War, albeit in a different geopolitical and, eventually, technological context.

Geography frequently arose as an operational friction with strategic effect, as with the British failure at Saratoga in North America in 1777 and at Wadgaon in west India in 1779. These two defeats indicated similarities in the 'frictions' affecting well-trained forces from the world's most wide-ranging military power. Such a force could only achieve so much, especially if on difficult terrain, in the face of considerably more numerous opponents and with limited 'situational awareness' due to poor reconnaissance. In India, the situation was more difficult because the British could not match their opponent's light cavalry, which was not an issue in North America.

In turn, there could be a 'structural', as in long-term and, thereby, strategic response. One such, reliance on *sepoys* (Indian soldiers), was encouraged by the impact of disease. This, for example, hit British operations near Pondicherry in the summer of 1760: 'the then approaching season made it absolutely necessary, as the Europeans in general suffer greatly by the excessive heat of the weather ... but notwithstanding all possible precautions the army has sustained great loss by sickness.'[22] Yet, there was also the dispatch to India from the 1750s of regular units from the British army.

At the same time, it is important not to see India, or North America, or Europe, or the West Indies, as undifferentiated geographical units. Strategy, in part, entailed an interaction between specific environmental contexts and the effectiveness of particular systems, whether, for example, of weapons or of logistics, and this could involve confronting different environments, as when Central Asian forces moved into southern China in the thirteenth century and into India repeatedly.[23] In India, British-trained infantry proved more effective in operations on the Carnatic coast, near their base at Madras, and in the marshy Lower Ganges valley, close to their base at Calcutta, than they were to be in conflict against the Marathas and Mysore in regions that favoured light cavalry. The latter was serious as it was necessary to operate beyond the security of coastal bases in order to raise and secure revenues and supplies, and so as to be able to attract, support and retain Indian allies such as Travancore.

Moreover, India was differently exposed to British penetration and to French intervention, which was easier for example in southern India than in Punjab. At the same time, the possibility of French intervention appeared an issue for the British across India, challenging the sense of power on which they were reliant. Thus, in 1770, Lewis Grant, wrote from Patna, the capital of Bihar: 'It seems to gain credit daily with the people of this country that the French will make an attempt to get some footing in Asia … threaten us with a powerful fleet from Mauritius loaded with European troops.'[24]

There was also great variety in geographical contexts elsewhere. For example, in the West Indies, the scale of the French colony of Saint-Domingue (now Haiti) made it a very different target to the more limited spaces of Martinique and Guadeloupe, and one that was far more difficult to control, as the French found in 1802. In Europe, the logistical challenge of supporting an expeditionary force in Portugal, where the agricultural base was poorly-developed, was far greater than in Germany where supplies were more readily available; as the British were to discover in 1762.

The physical environment was not the sole issue. Thus, in India, the Madras and, to a greater extent, Bombay presidencies of the East Indian Company lacked the resources of the Bengal presidency, and neither made great headway against local rivals. Nevertheless, wealthy Bengal enabled the Company to act as an effective territorial power, not only in the Ganges Valley, but also elsewhere in India. This was far from easy, however, with both allies and opponents creating problems in India, as elsewhere. These problems, in turn, created geographies of opportunity and crisis, and those geographies were part of the mental strategic perspective of leaders. Thus, the system was one of multiple links and patterns of causation.

In responding, leaders sought to understand the geographical relationship between territories. That understanding, on which see also Chapter 7, was a key element of strategy, albeit serving contrasting purposes, for example possible linkages between these territories, and, as a result, the risks entailed in intervention. Differently, a geography was part of the process of understanding, presenting and defining priorities, threats and responses,[25] as with the delimitation and implementation in the late nineteenth and early twentieth centuries of the view that Afghanistan was a buffer state against Russian expansion, and, therefore, of particular value to British India.[26] Politics helped define (and eventually, for a while, defuse) the response of the powers involved. At the same time, location was a key issue for the rival strategies of British India, Russia, Persia and Afghanistan, with the last pursuing independence in terms of the interplay of the great powers and the ability to take advantage of it.

In contrast, when the target was set by the clash of armies itself, then the location in question in this case was not say a specific physical factor, such as, in Afghanistan, the Amu Darya River or the Khyber Pass, but, instead, the destruction of the opposing army. However, gaining control over particular sites was seen as likely to further this process.

In 1815, the primacy of such destruction was seen with the Waterloo campaign, the geography of which was instructive, and can be readily understood as the goals of each side are well-covered in the sources. To defend Belgium without knowing the likely axis of French advance, the British, Dutch and Prussians had to deploy their forces over a large area in order to cover the possible routes of attack. In practice, the French advance would depend on a paved road, notably in order to transport the artillery, but, compared to most of Europe, there were a large number of roads that could be used. Moreover, the Allies had a number of places of interest to defend, including the Belgian North Sea ports, notably Ostend, the naval base at Antwerp, the court of the exiled Louis XVIII at Ghent, the Belgian capital at Brussels, and the strategic positions on the River Meuse: Namur, Liège and Maastricht, which would open the way for the French into both Germany and the eastern Netherlands.

In practice, from the perspective of both sides, all of these positions were instrumental. As Napoleon's principal objective was the rapid defeat of the opposing armies, so that he could then turn against the Austrians and Russians, in contrast, the preservation of these armies was the key objective for the Allies. Indeed, the places above were secondary goals for both sides, instead establishing the geography of the conflict and its initial character as the interplay of places and armies, with both sides manoeuvring in order to pursue primary and secondary goals. Thus, in an instance of the prioritisation that was so important in operational and strategic geography, Napoleon's opportunity rested on the degree to which the Allied protection of secondary goals, in particular of lines of communication, provided Napoleon with an opportunity to secure his primary goal of defeating their forces. In his mind, there was none of the confusion between securing key positions and inflicting defeats that were to be seen with many offensives, for example with Hitler and his unsuccessful invasion of the Soviet Union in 1941, or, to a degree, with the Allied advance in France and the Low Countries in 1944.

For the Allies in 1815, in turn, in an operational mode, it was crucial to get within the French decision loop (the OODA loop in modern parlance), as a rapid response to French moves would enable them to concentrate their forces and to engage the French from a position of numerical superiority. This response would also let the Allies protect the places that were deemed essential. However, any Allied concentration that was not near the frontier, if followed by a battle that left Napoleon able to advance, would pose a challenge, as one or other of the Allies' armies would probably find it difficult to retreat along secure lines of communication.

The choice of a place of concentration dramatised the military geography at issue. Initially, the Prussians proposed that the Anglo-Dutch and Prussian armies retreat to Tirlemont, about twenty-five miles east of Brussels, a position that would take the Prussians nearer to their lines of communication to the east. Wellington, however, thought this proposal militarily and politically unwise, the two combining in the anxiety that the French would be able to take Brussels and, as a result, that the loyalty of the Belgian forces (part of the Dutch army only since 1814) would be affected. Such a concentration would also risk the French conquest of western Belgium and cut Wellington off from the port of Ostend and the sea route to Britain. Alternatively, had the Prussians concentrated there, and the British to the south of Brussels, then Napoleon would really have been able to defeat the two armies separately. As a result, Wellington pressed for a deployment by both armies south of Brussels. The Prussian commander, pending the arrival of Field Marshal Gebhard von Blücher, was Lieutenant General Count August von Gneisenau, who had served in Canada on behalf of George III in the Ansbach forces in 1782–3. Keen to co-operate with Wellington, he agreed, a decision that was to be of great importance for the campaign.[27]

Because they both, in the event, deployed south of Brussels, the Allied armies, however, were close to the French frontier and, therefore, vulnerable to attack as was to be shown on 16 June 1815, the day after

Napoleon invaded, in the battles of Ligny and Quatre Bras. More specifically, as the events of that day were to indicate, these armies risked contact engagements, that they did not want, in order to disengage prior to concentration. The concentration, both of the individual armies and of the two together, moreover, would require marching across the axis of French advance.

Complicating the situation for both Allied armies, and providing additional opportunities for Napoleon, the Prussian I Corps blocked the French advance north on Brussels via Charleroi, the crossing point he chose over the River Meuse. Yet, instead of Prussian forces to the north of this corps' area of deployment, there was Wellington's reserve round Brussels, ensuring a south-west to north-east division between the Allied armies. This division meant that the I Corps was not protecting Prussian positions to the north and also suggested that the axis of Prussian concentration, and, if necessary, withdrawal would be east/north-east along the Prussian lines of communication and towards where the other Prussian units were located, thus opening up a gap with the British forces.

The Allied armies in Belgium were Napoleon's strategic target, as their defeat would provide both the appearance and the reality of success. Operationally, he aimed to use a central position in order to defeat his enemies in detail. To do so, he planned a secret concentration south of the junction between Wellington's and Blücher's armies, followed by a rapid advance designed to defeat them separately before advancing on Brussels. He had his chance when the armies were separately engaged, first at Ligny (Prussians) and Quatre Bras (British) on 16 June, and then in the initial stages at Waterloo on 18 June. However, Wellington beat him off on the 18th, winning the defensive part of the battle, and the Prussians were able to arrive in time to draw off French forces for that and then to help win the offensive part.

The Waterloo campaign was more generally typical of a situation in which choices of tactical, operational and, most significantly, strategic geography, were all set by a tasking that, in turn, was established by a politics that drew on assumptions about geography. Yet these assumptions took weight in terms of political views and wishes, and this remains the case. Successful decision-making is a complex process, in part affected by the nature of the geographical information available.[28] Both politics and geography (physical and human) play their part in all three of the tactical, operational and strategic elements of decision-making.

Chapter 5

Geopolitics

In 1904, Halford Mackinder, Britain's leading geopolitician, advancing his notion of a Eurasian heartland that was both impregnable to attack by sea but also a threat to the whole of Eurasia, claimed that, in the heart of Eurasia, there was a 'geographical pivot of history'. Railways, presented as key demonstrations and enablers of power, Mackinder argued, had made the heartland power, now Russia, more potent, reversing the earlier emphasis on the value of maritime power projection, which Britain had dominated. Pressing for a united British empire able to resist the heartland power, Mackinder wrote 'it is desirable to shift our geographical viewpoint from Europe, so that we may consider the Old World in its entirety' and that 'in the world at large she [Russia] occupies the central strategical position held by Germany in Europe.'[1]

In practice, the First World War was to show that the powers, including Germany which repeatedly defeated her, had greatly exaggerated Russia's military potential. Nevertheless, Mackinder testified to the continued usage of the geographical image of a tension between the power or powers in central or core Eurasia and those at its periphery, the former being frequently presented as nomadic raiders from the steppe and the latter as settled societies under pressure. Indeed, Mackinder envisaged a reversion, with rail, to the core power held by nomadic raiders, a reversion after what he termed, with reference to Christopher Columbus, the 'Columbian era' of maritime hegemony.

Considering essentially the Trans-Siberian Railway, begun in 1891 and finished in 1916, although only, as with many long-distance railways of the period, single-track,[2] Mackinder argued that the primacy of maritime links had been replaced by those of rail. In his eyes, this transformed the military possibilities, both for the dominance of central Eurasia, which he proposed as the supposed pivot of world history, and then of military expansion from it. He very much linked strategic possibilities of space and distance to changing technologies and their military application.

This dichotomy between core and periphery was an important tool for understanding circumstances, and remains a potent historical theme, not least as offering an all-embracing account. It is classically geographical, in that a spatial relationship is at the centre, and that element provides an analysis that can be variously described as structural and systemic. At the same time, this approach faces the challenge that it can be both overly reductionist in its methodology and simplistic in its analysis. So, indeed, with many geopolitical theses. When explicitly expressed, the theory may seem flawed; but, nevertheless, the theory is frequently implicitly present in much of the discussion of war. Indeed, with a particular focus on the 'Barbarian invasions' at the time of the fall of the Western Roman Empire in the fifth century, the concept of the nomadic attacker from the steppe has long been, and remains, a central one in much of the discussion of war in Eurasia until the early-modern period, with the Manchu overthrow of Ming China in the 1640s usually seen as the last major successful episode.

Edward Gibbon developed the theme in his epic *The History of the Decline and Fall of the Roman Empire* (1776–88), and it was given a cartographic depiction, as in the 1924 edition of W. and A.K. Johnston's *Historical Atlas of British and World History*, which provided a map 'Europe showing the General Direction of the Barbarian Inroads on the Fall of the Roman Empire', that presented physical features: desert, highlands over 3,000 feet and 'grassland and steppe, mainly Black Earth region, the route of Nomad Invasions from Asia'. The description of the Black Earth region was, and remains, valuable, because such a reading of evidence was usually left to inference. This theme was also taken in the map 'The Realms of Civilisation *c.*200 AD and the Natural Conditions Affecting their Relations' in the 1928 edition of the Philips' *New School Atlas of Universal History*.

At the same time, the situation, and notably that of nomadic invasions, was historicised by being discussed in terms of cavalry, which was, and remains, generally seen as inherently anachronistic. This assessment is somewhat surprising, as cavalry continued to be important in much of the world until the nineteenth century, being in no way incompatible with firepower, and also providing a mobility that infantry lacked until mechanisation. There were also instances of the successful use of cavalry in the early twentieth century.[3]

Moreover, far from being inherently anachronistic, the steppe societies were long successful, both politically and militarily. Indeed, in 1961, Basil Liddell Hart, the most influential British military commentator of the time, explained that his bookplate included not only the 'Globe – to represent a global view and subject', but also Mongol horsemen: 'because my theory of future mechanised warfare was evolved originally from my study of the campaigns of Genghis Khan's all-mobile army of Mongols'.[4] References to the Mongols, and Genghis Khan ruled from 1206 to 1227, also proved a continuing way to think of geopolitical tensions within Eurasia, but not necessarily helpfully so. Thus, in 1946, Field Marshal Sir Claude Auchinleck, Commander-in-Chief India, the last British holder of the post, had to explain to Lieutenant Sir Francis Tuker, Head of Eastern Command in India, also the last holder of the post, that the latter's proposal for a British protectorate over what he termed Mongol territory from Nepal to Bhutan was unrealistic. Tuker had wanted to prevent any threat to India from the north.[5] At that stage, the challenge appeared to come from Kuomintang (Nationalist) China, but it was soon to come from Communist China. Tuker went on to publish *The Pattern of War* (1948), in which he proposed the existence of persistent patterns.

As with much discussion of geographical influences and the spatial dimension of operations, Mongol warmaking improves by being understood, as opposed to being regarded as a type of natural phenomenon. The Mongol tsunami method of conquest was especially effective: they invaded and devastated a large region, but then withdrew and held only a small section of territory. By doing so, the Mongols thus created a buffer zone that made it impossible to attack them and also weakened the enemy's resources. Also, by only occupying small chunks of territory, they did not tie down troops in garrison duty. Instead, a relatively small force could control the region while the civil administration moved in and integrated territories into the empire, the border troops then moving forward anew to add new territory.

Eventually, the Mongols made a transition to city-taking conflict, but different geographical factors thereby came into play, and at the tactical, operational and strategic levels. To move from raiding and victory in battle to seizing territory required an ability to capture fortified positions and, largely by using Chinese expertise, as part of the incremental pattern of the conquest of China, proficiency in siege warfare developed.[6] Thus, the

Mongol military system should be understood as an effective changing phenomenon and, eventually, as a hybrid one. This was also to be true later of the Manchu system, which, similarly, responded to the conquest of China. More generally, as a result of such hybrid behaviour, strategic cultures and military styles were, and are, often less consistent than is generally implied, and this both reflects and creates differing responses to the geography, both physical and human.

The physical environment can repeatedly be seen at play in the role of light cavalry, both with the Mongols and with Timur the Lame (1336–1406) who, based in Central Asia, campaigned with great success from the Aegean to north India. Indeed, the use of horses on the steppe grasslands brought mobility, and the relatively low population density in those areas provided an opportunity for creating a rulership from which power could be projected to those areas where resources were denser. Steppe forces were difficult to fight as they could always ride away, which made difficult control over the steppe against them. Neither holding territory nor defeating armies in the field were necessarily viable in conflict with steppe forces, which encouraged subsidies to them as a means to address the problem. In turn, the absence of determinism was shown by the varied success of steppe forces, and by their dependence, as earlier, with the Huns in the fifth century and the Magyars in the tenth, on a continuation of able leadership. Mongol decline in the fourteenth century, due in large part to divisions, was matched later by Timur's failure to plan for the future; and these elements did not reflect geographical factors, other than in the sense of the problems of having to govern such a large area.

There was also a contrast between, on the one hand, advances from the Eurasian core toward the periphery that arose from the separate attack on those who were advancing on the periphery by more powerful core rivals on the steppe; and, alternatively, those, as with the Mongols or the Afghans in India from 1748, that were not thus motivated. In the former case, key instances were provided by the Huns invading the lands of the Goths in the late fourth century, leading the latter to move into the Roman Empire, defeating and killing the Emperor Valens at Adrianople in 378; by the Turkmen who successfully pressed in the eleventh and twelfth centuries on Byzantium and the Crusader states;[7] and later by the Mughals in the early sixteenth century, as they were pushed out of Fergana and Samarqand by the Uzbeks. This led the Mughals to concentrate, instead, on the prospectus offered by the wealthy agricultural zone of the Punjab and then, more generally, in north India.

There was no common narrative nor inevitability of peripheral or settled pressure on the core, as opposed to elsewhere on the periphery. Thus, whereas Aurangzeb, as a Mughal prince had campaigned (ultimately unsuccessfully) into Afghanistan in the 1640s, he focused, as a ruler, further south; and no other, or later, Indian ruler, until the British in the 1840s, changed this focus. Nor did the Persians repeat the campaigning to the north-east against the Uzbeks they had followed in the sixteenth and early seventeenth centuries, with Abbas conquering Herat in 1598, until Nadir Shah did so (successfully) in 1740, and his short-term effort was not repeated.

However, there are always problems in using countries as the inherent building blocks of the system and practice of conflict. Nadir, a Turkic tribesman who became a successful general from 1729, indeed ruled Persia from 1736 until his assassination in 1747, but he had a more far-flung ambition than his recent Safavid predecessors, one that was similar to that of Timur. As such, there was a parallel with China, where, from the late seventeenth century, Manchu interests, ambitions and commitments were more far-flung than those of the previous Ming dynasty. A certain style of combat went with these politics, a style which emphasised boldness, battles rather than sieges, and continual conflict in order to hold the group together with activity, prestige and loot.[8]

Moreover, to take further the problem with using countries or states or, indeed, empires as the inherent building block of strategic geography, they were diverse within themselves, both as physical and as human environments, and also with reference to their borders. 'India', for example, or 'China', was very diverse (as well as different) in practice under the three criteria of physical and human environments and borders; and this situation very much affected their tasking and military activity.

As a separate, but, as usual, related issue, another problem with using states, or, in this case, military systems, as units, is that there is a degree of syncretism in most such systems, and notably so across apparent divides, for example those of infantry- or cavalry-based systems. Such divides certainly existed, but there was also adaptation, not least in terms of borrowing techniques and weaponry, and hiring units. Thus, for example, the infantry-based imperial systems, such as Rome,

Byzantium, and Britain, borrowed from their cavalry-based opponents, such as the Goths, Huns and Marathas respectively, with the mobility they offered. The units among their opponents that were willing to serve this end were both militarily significant as force-multipliers, and also politically important because their support was a product of negotiation and therefore conditional. This relationship varied greatly, and in both military and political terms. As far as the latter was concerned, there could be a clear spatial dimension in terms of a relationship with client states, for example that of the Ottoman Empire with the khanate of the Crimean Tatars from the fifteenth to the eighteenth centuries.

The steppe dynamic, a product of the interaction of the physical with the human environment, was not the only long-standing geographical one in Eurasia, the area that deserves most attention as it contained the overwhelming majority of the world's population. Indeed, on the eve of Western expansion in the late fifteenth century, the distribution of world population was about half the world's population in East and South Asia combined, another maybe 13 per cent in south-east and south-west Asia together, about 14 per cent each in Europe and the Americas, about 10 per cent in Africa, and less than 0.01 per cent in Australasia and Oceania. The percentage in Europe and the Americas was to rise subsequently, but that in Asia has risen in recent decades, and, in turn, Africa is due to become proportionately more significant.

Another dynamic in Eurasia was provided by religion, and, in particular, the division between Christendom and Islam. This division was superimposed upon the older divide between 'West' and 'East', in the sense of a civilisation based on the Mediterranean and one located to the east. That division complicated the core-periphery structuring of Eurasia already referred to, but Islam for long was thought of in Christendom in terms of nomadic cavalry forces, first Arab and then Turkic.

The division between Christendom and Islam also opened up major questions about the extent to which war fed new combatants into a geopolitical rivalry between 'West' and 'East', how far it transformed this rift, and how far the discourse of 'West' versus 'East' was a rationalisation of an inherently independent process with a different causation. Certainly, the West's 'East' was far from constant, with Islam's syncretic character helping ensure that it was greatly influenced by Turkic peoples and leaders, and notably so with the Seljuk and Ottoman Turks. At any rate, from the

Christian perspective, religious rivalry created a particular geography, one that was highlighted by a sense of loss stemming from the Islamic capture of holy sites in the early seventh century. This geography had a particular strategic significance during the Crusades, but not only then.

Yet, until the beginning of the sixteenth century, the actual fault-lines between Islam and the Christian West were much more geographically limited than they were to become as a consequence of the European arrival in the Indian Ocean. We might still seem to be in this latter period of contact between Islam and the West across a major range of the Islamic presence, but, in practice, the geography has changed greatly with an Islamic diaspora in many Western cities. That has also led in a few cases to a separate type of conflict, in the shape, variously, of terrorism, as in New York and London, and of particular areas of lawlessness, for example some of the *bidonvilles* around Paris.

That interaction was different to the period of European conquest and rule of overseas Islamic societies from 1830 (French conquest of Algiers) to 1962 (French departure from Algeria), but that period also had implications in terms of conflict. Aside from the obvious ones of conquest and counter-insurgency, there was the sense that fighting in one particular area could bridge to another. Thus, in 1922, General Lord Rawlinson, the British Commander-in-Chief in India (see also Chapter 7), argued that war with Turkey, if it broke out over the enforcement of the 1920 peace agreement, as appeared a risk during the Chanak Crisis, would lead to more wide-ranging trouble for the British empire: 'To undertake offensive action against the Turk is merely to consolidate a Pan-Islamic Movement.'[9] In the event, there was no conflict.

Other religions, fault-lines repeatedly saw violence, not least against religious sites, as when the Romans destroyed the Jewish Temple in Jerusalem in 70. The (Muslim) Afghans devastated Sikh sites in Lahore (now in Pakistan) in 1762, only for the Sikhs to destroy mosques there in 1764.

Structuring a geography of potential conflict in terms of religious difference, as with Samuel Huntington's notion in the 1990s of a 'clash of civilisations',[10] underplays the extent to which there was also persistent conflict within civilizational blocs, including religions and, conversely, often significant co-operation across them, the latter frequently being very important to military co-operation. The germane point is that of the role of human agency and variation in geography, as opposed to structural determinism and simplification. Failing to rise to the challenge of probing that point conceptually, methodologically and empirically, can involve wrenching situations out of context.

So for example with the role of agency, as opposed to determinism, in Chinese maritime policy. Whereas the Mongols, once in control of China, had pursued (unsuccessfully) maritime expansion against Japan and Java in the thirteenth century, and the Ming had launched maritime expeditions into the Indian Ocean in the early fifteenth century, Manchu goals by sea were largely restricted to nearby Formosa (Taiwan), occupied in 1683, and to maritime security.[11] There was no attempt to invade Japan as a counter to earlier Japanese expansionism into Korea in the 1590s, nor any significant wish to expand or extend the brief (and successful) frontier war with Russia in the Amur Valley in 1683–9. The Russians were not to be driven beyond Lake Baikal.

As Mackinder noted, technology could have a role in the geopolitical equation; but this was a matter of possibility and not of inevitability. For example, in the Crimean War of 1854–6, the Allies, principally Britain and France, successfully deployed forces into Russia and kept them there until they had achieved their task of preventing the Russians from exploiting their destruction of the Turkish Black Sea fleet in 1853. Success had eluded Napóleon when he invaded Russia in 1812, but the contrast was in part a matter of tasks as much as technology, as the Allies did not use their forces to strike at the Russian capital, St Petersburg, but, instead, at a peripheral target, Sevastopol, the Russian Black Sea naval base in Crimea, which was captured in 1855 after a difficult siege. This emphasis on a particular task was more important than the change in the distance-movement of force ratios caused by the Allies using steamships as Napoleon, through technology as well as target, had not been able to do. Once ashore in Crimea, the Allies preserved this advantage by making a port, Sevastopol, their target, and there was no deep deployment into the interior comparable to the attacks on Russia in 1812 and 1941–2, by the French and Germans respectively. Earlier in the Crimean War, there had been consideration of operating against the Russians in the Balkans, but Sir James Graham, the First Lord of the Admiralty, warned about the need to relate geography to force-structure: 'If you leave [the port of] Varna and enter the [Danubian] Plain your weakness in cavalry will be a serious disadvantage.' He also noted that it would be difficult to feed the army there in Bulgaria.[12]

The Crimean War saw a British reconceptualisation of the whole of Eurasia as a sphere of geopolitical competition with Russia. Justified anxiety about Russian plans resulted in a wish to win over and bolster Turkey, China, Afghanistan, and the Central Asian khanates, to consider stirring up opposition to the Russians in the Caucasus, and to interest in a new geopolitics in East Asia, Rear Admiral Sir James Stirling, the thoughtful Commander-in-Chief in China and the East Indies, arguing that 'As the Schemes of Russia in Eastern Tartary, and the command she will thus acquire over Northern China are thus developed, the vast importance of a close connection with Japan becomes more obvious.'[13] In 1885, when a Russian invasion of Afghanistan, and maybe British India, for which Afghanistan was a would-be buffer zone, appeared possible in the Penjdeh Crisis, the British placed the Royal Navy on full alert, and their plans included the occupation of islands off Korea and attacks on the Russian ports of Kronstadt (Baltic), Batumi (Black Sea), and Vladivostok (Sea of Japan).[14]

The wider European world as a whole was, at least to a degree, being structured by a geopolitics focused on military rivalry between Britain and Russia, a situation that helped cause the Crimean War[15] and that affected the world thereafter, providing both the background to Mackinder's 1904 lecture referred to at the outset of this chapter, and a model for the later Cold War. Yet such a geopolitics did not dictate the role of other powers. Indeed, while Japanese Asianists saw Russia as a competing power in China, with Japan closely linked to Shanghai, Korea and Manchuria, they were not dependent on an Anglo-Japanese alignment, as lines of causation, or, indeed, only influence, were often not fixed, but geographical factors were important. These included the mismatch between Japan's population increase and resource poverty. This situation helped encourage its expansionism, culminating in 1931–41 with the launching of successive wars accordingly. Resources were a key element of the geopolitics of warfare, and remain so.

Reporting from Moscow in March 1946, as the Cold War developed, the British diplomat Frank Roberts, who had been posted there in January 1945, saw longterm geopolitical factors, rather than simply Communist ideology, which had only prevailed from late 1917, as crucial in Soviet attitudes:

'There is one fundamental factor affecting Soviet policy dating back to the small beginnings of the Muscovite state. This is the constant striving for security of a state with no natural frontiers and surrounded by enemies. In this all-important respect the rulers and people of Russia are united by a common fear, deeply rooted in Russian policy, which explains much of the high-handed behaviour of the Kremlin and many of the suspicions genuinely held there concerning the outside world.'[16]

Roberts shared with others, including the American Deputy Chief of Mission, George Kennan, an analysis that played a role in the development of the thesis of containment,[17] although what that was to mean in practice was less clear. Indeed, as with strategic geography, so also with geopolitics. Again, there was a sense of inherent certainty, but also a response that was open to different circumstances and interpretations.

This was very much the case with the central geopolitical organisational device, that of the tension between a Eurasian Continental world and a maritime-based one. This tension was a key concept superseding that of a division of the world into continents, itself an abstract conceptualisation.[18] Indeed, the division was particularly unhelpful when considering the warfare of the Achaemenid Persian, Macedonian, Roman and Ottoman empires, each of which spanned Asia, Africa and Europe.

The concept of geopolitics preceded the term, which was devised at the end of the nineteenth century, and used thereafter, in order to provide apparent scientific credibility for ideas of developing the synergy of territory and power. In turn, the employment of geopolitical concepts was important in the 1900s and 1910s, as commentators sought to shape the opportunities and threats they discerned in any international arena, and to use geography as a key element of this shaping.[19]

The audience response in 1904 to Mackinder's lecture added the very new complication of air power. Furthermore, Japanese victory soon after in the Russo-Japanese War of 1904–5 scarcely suggested that the supposed Eurasian pivot power was necessarily successful, and railways themselves had their limitations and vulnerabilities, both of which were serious. As a writer on geopolitics, Mackinder proved somewhat flawed, and, although a MP, his political career was limited. Nevertheless, as Director of the London School of Economics, he provided the home in 1907–14 for a course for the training of officers for the higher appointments in the army's administrative staff.[20]

In turn, geopolitics was pushed to the fore during and after the First World War, and in the following world war, as commentators sought to explain what they presented as both threat, need, and opportunity. In part, this was a variant on the geography of strategy, with geopolitics different as it sought more explicitly to engage, persuade and instruct the public. The scenario varied by government, with the right-wing geopoliticians of Weimar and then, even more, Nazi Germany, very different in intention and methods to those presenting President Franklin Delano Roosevelt's views during the Second World War. Notable in his case was the immediate strategic relevance to the United States of what had hitherto appeared distant lands, which was a reversal of the usual American concept of hemispheric defence. The role of oceanic frontiers was subliminally part of the American emphasis on protecting (and presiding over) the Western Hemisphere, as with the mid- and late-1930s development of the B-17 Flying Fortress bomber for 'hemispheric defence' and, differently, with the Havana Conference of 1940.

Geopolitics is best at this task of explanation because the map is made fluid and didactic by devices such as arrows and bold titles and typeface, with the latter often also employed for the relevant text. These practices are another instance of the role of human geography as aiding the understanding and use of physical geography, indeed, in part as an aspect of human adaptation to the latter.

That point may appear far distant from war, but is relevant because the geopolitical exposition of spatial links as existing, necessary and indeed under threat, is both highly significant for strategic assessment and important for public support. Neither element is free-floating. Instead, at every level of war, it is assessment, and the relevant tools – practical, conceptual, and psychological, that are of consequence.

In turn, the need for care in assessment, and notably with reference to the information used, was made clear on 11 June 1877, as British anxieties about Russian expansion in Europe and Asia reached new heights, threatening a war that was in the event narrowly averted. The more cautious Robert Cecil, 3rd Marquess of Salisbury, the Secretary of State for India, and later Prime Minister, declared in Parliament:

'I cannot help thinking that in discussions of this kind, a great deal of misapprehension arises from the popular use of maps on a small scale. As with such maps you are able to put a thumb on India and a finger on Russia, some persons at once think that the political situation is alarming, and that India must be looked to. If the noble Lord would use a larger map – say one on the scale of the Ordnance Map of England – he would find that the distance between Russia and India is not to be measured by the finger and thumb, but by a rule. There are between them deserts and mountainous chains measured by thousands of miles, and these are serious obstacles to any advance by Russia, however well planned such an advance mighty be.'[21]

Despite improved mapping of the region, no such map in practice was then available. The American 'Domino Theory' of the 1950s and 1960s in south-east Asia, enunciated by President Dwight Eisenhower in a press conference on 7 April 1954, was an instance of the same process of readily-imagined and easily-graspable threat based on a transferable challenge; as was the anxiety in 1979 that the movement of Soviet forces into Afghanistan represented a threat to the Persian Gulf. That was the case as far as the Afghan airbase at Kandahar was concerned; but Afghanistan itself is distant from the Persian Gulf.

Scale was, and is, not the sole issue in assessing geopolitical challenges and the need to respond to them. Perspective was also important. Thus, the geographer Charles Fawcett, in his *Political Geography of the British Empire* (1933), produced maps centred on London, Canberra and Durban in order to convey the differing geostrategic vantages within the British Empire, the range of which made a good spatial understanding necessary. The maps illustrated the sheer power of distance in shaping strategic perspective. Fawcett used the technique of drawing an orthographic (one seen as if from outer space) globe, centred on say Canberra, and then 'peeling' the dark side of the planet around the edges from the back.

More generally, the use, for political and other purposes, of the centring of maps as a distinctive cartographic device was frequently seen, and it had growing military applicability in that period in terms of assessing bombing, both for offensive and defensive purposes. Thus, both political and technological changes could make the methods used by mapmakers inherently dynamic.

The greater potential of power made possible by steam had already encouraged the idea of long-range power-projection, with the geopolitical concepts that arose from this interacting with the particular characteristics of naval command practices and culture, notably the effective independence of overseas squadrons and ships. Naval steam power, combined with far more global trade and the extension of the Western empires, helped lead to a greater emphasis on the potential of naval strength, not least in doctrine, as in Admiral Théophile Aube's *La Guerre Maritime et les Ports Françaises* (1882). Aube was a key supporter of the *Jeune École* group in French naval thought, which sought to develop asymmetrical methods for use against the stronger British navy, notably the use of fast, relatively lightly-armoured, ships to attack British trade.[22]

From a different perspective, in his *Rulers of the Indian Ocean* (1927), George Ballard, a retired British admiral, argued that the rise in American and Japanese naval power had transformed the geopolitical situation as it was no longer sufficient for Britain to prevail over European rivals in order to win global naval dominance, adding:

'As regards its present form or fabric the Empire may be roughly divided into an occidental half – including the British Isles – and an oriental; which are held together commercially and strategically by the Imperial lines of communication across the Indian Ocean … If those connections are cut, the two halves of the Empire will fall apart as surely as night follows day.'

The opening of the American-built, administered and controlled Panama Canal in 1914, a canal around which, in a classic instance of geopolitics, a new state, Panama, was created, had transformed the strategic place of the Caribbean in naval plans, and greatly increased the flexibility of the American navy by making it easier to move warships between the Atlantic and the Pacific, and thus to confront challenges in either.[23] Like the Suez Canal, opened in 1869, this was an instance of man-made geopolitical transformation.

In turn, the capacity for mobility and tactical advantage offered by air power ensured that, from the early 1920s, it was increasingly seen as a major strategic asset and one that offered a new approach to geopolitics, a view that encouraged government support for the development of air services to link imperial possessions, notably in Britain, but also in particular in France and Italy. The Second World War was to bring these ideas to fruition in new views of a world at war.[24] The resulting geopolitics was very much presented with the maps of the innovative American cartographer Richard Edes Harrison, for example, 'One World, One War?' Echoing the traditional British concern with India, and drawing on Mackinder's work, Harrison in this piece referred to India as where the Allies would: 'have to fight one of the great decisive battles of history: The Battle for Asia,' adding:

> 'If Japan and Germany are allowed to join hands in India, the Axis will have the advantages of "the inner line" - on a world scale. Uninterrupted Axis control of Eurasia's huge land masses, from Le Havre to Shanghai, would transform the New World into an island and the two surrounding oceans into highways of invasion.'[25]

The discussion hitherto leads also toward what is known as 'critical geopolitics', a term employed to describe a branch of literature concerned to demonstrate the degree to which geography is a branch of power and a reflection of power relationships, an argument that has been particularly deployed since the late twentieth century in order to critique the United States, Western power, and international capitalism.[26] The use of geography and, more particularly, geographers to assist in planning for war, as discussed in Chapter 7, is an aspect of the critique. However, in part, the literature is based on a matter of the obvious, in that no subject is value-free; but there can also be a simplification and reductionism in 'critical geopolitics'.

Separate to this debate, geopolitics is presented at the most fundamental level in the perception of a different civilisational basis in contrasting modes of organisation for conflict. Societies with a smaller population, and a lower population density, generally lacked a defined state system, and certainly did not have the taxation base of settled agrarian societies with the permanent specialised military units they could support. The 'little war', of raids, skirmishes, and limited-scale clashes, of the societies with a smaller population, was also related to the specific circumstances of particular geographical contexts and constraints, and at sea as well as on land; but generally so in a different fashion to the militaries of the large, settled, agrarian societies. The latter had organisation, notably in logistics, to help overcome the constraints, but, in turn, provision of these supplies posed a new set of geographical issues.[27]

In addition comes the specifics of particular areas, and their relationship to opportunities for and in war. In part, this was a matter of long-term differences between continents, with disease and animal life both being of significance in this. As a result, the interaction with physical geography was not just a matter of humans. Thus, the horse was not native to the Americas, nor to Australasia and Oceania; and was not found across much of Africa south of the savannah belt nor in south-east Asia or Ceylon [Sri Lanka], in part due to disease. However, despite the impression sometimes arising from discussion of Eurasia, and notably the steppe, far-flung land empires were not created by cavalry alone. Thus, the successive empires of the Andean chain in South America, including the Chimú (c.700–1475) and, far more, its conqueror, the Inca (1438–1532), showed what could be achieved by infantry armies. Caveats can be added in terms of the need for appropriate physical and human environments for such an achievement, not least the lack of rival cavalry. The Incas also benefited from the extent to which the farming villagers in the tropical forests to the east of the Andes did not pose a military challenge, no more than the nomadic hunter-gatherers to the south-east. Equally, the Incas did not try to extend their power far into these areas, especially the former, and this limitation represented a sensible response to their environment; while these forest people did not seek to conquer the upland. In an instance of the wider pattern of environmental adaptation, the forest people, based on their hunting, used archers, while the Incas, coming from treeless uplands, did not. This contrast gave the former a marked advantage in conflict.

Yet again, determinism is of scant value. The actual spread of an animal was less important in military terms than its usage (or non-usage), a process that entailed a variety of practices, both animal and human. As far as horses were concerned, they were domesticated, first as a source of food, and only later as a means of transport, initially for drawing chariots and, subsequently, for riding.[28] For the latter, horses had to be of the right type, to be available in sufficient numbers, and for there to be a process of training, care and equipment.

Thus, the human geography of access to horses, an important aspect of geopolitics, was a significant variant on that of the distribution of horses. In the seventh century BCE, Assyria was able to create the first empire to span from the Persian Gulf to the Nile in part due to its ability to obtain plentiful horses, on which both its cavalry and its important chariot corps relied. Details, when available, throw light on what could have happened in the other, more numerous, episodes for which they are not available. The Nogais, who lived on the steppe north of the Caucasus, moved their main supply of horses from Constantinople to Moscow in the late 1520s, helping to cement political links, receiving firearms in return, cooperating with Russian forces, and helping, by their horses, the Russians to operate outside the forest belt to which they had largely been confined. This helped tilt the balance for Russia against the Crimean Tatars. Ming China had horses, but there was a shortage of cavalry horses and they were unable to obtain them in sufficient numbers from the steppe, whereas the Manchu, who were a power there, had access and therefore a greater facility to act on the steppe. So also with the Afghans in eighteenth-century northern India: their access to horses in Central Asia was an important aspect of their military presence there.[29]

In Africa, there were both cavalry and non-cavalry forces, and the interrelationship between physical environment and human adaptability was part of the equation. Cavalry was particularly important in the *sahel*, the extensive savannah belt to the south of the Sahara Desert, which was suitable cavalry terrain. However, in turn, this reliance on cavalry increased the dependence of operations on the availability of water and fodder, especially grass, and thereby vulnerability to the climate and weather. The changing animal environment was part of the equation, as with the interconnected spread from North Africa to inland West Africa, from at least the fourteenth century, of larger breeds of horses, new equestrian techniques, and new tactics of cavalry warfare.

In turn, this development created neither a constant military environment nor one without challenges. In the case of the Songhai state of the Niger Valley in the fifteenth and sixteenth century, there were the challenges posed by different environments: of controlling the Sahara desert to the north, fighting for example the Tuaregs in 1505–6, and operating into forest terrain to the south. Linked to the latter, but extending into the *sahel*, were the problems posed by disease, notably the tsetse fly, to the use of horses.[30] Thus, when in the First World War, horses were used in heavily-infected areas in East Africa, the 'equine wastage rate' was 100 per cent. The Mongol invasions of Vietnam from China between 1258 and 1288 suffered from disease, as well as the lack of forage,[31] and this situation contributed to a break on Mongol expansion, although it is also necessary to give weight to the effective Dai Viet resistance. This situation looked toward the lasting limitation of Chinese southward ambition and expansion, one seen as recently as the late twentieth century.

The geography of animal distribution changed greatly with both diffusion and domestication, and notably in the case of the horse, with, respectively, horsed, semi-horsed (horses relatively expensive), and horseless worlds. It is also necessary to give due weight to particular types of horse, especially the distinction between those able, or not, to carry heavy cavalry.

The physical environment was always a factor in such questions, but should be generally seen as permissive rather than deterministic. Thus, in the medieval period, the French emphasis on heavy cavalry was not matched in Spain where, instead, there was a far greater stress on light cavalry which proved more effective against the Moors, less expensive, and better attuned to the arid environment; although heavy shock cavalry still had a value in battle in Spain. There was a related contrast during the Crusades which, albeit at the risk of considerable simplification, saw a clash between light Turkic horse-archers whose highly-mobile techniques had evolved on the terrain of the steppe, and the Franks, who relied on small groups of heavy cavalry supported and screened by infantry and archers. This style had evolved in the relatively closed countryside of much of France, Germany and Italy. There agriculture, which was dominated by grain production, itself expensive in time, effort and area of cultivation, reinforced hierarchic social impulses in order to prevent a focus on clouds of light horse. In contrast, in the Near East, mobile tactics tended to be favoured by the open, dry countryside; and, related to that, it remains the classic land of tank warfare.

Although the horse was the principal war-animal in Eurasia, there were areas where it was less effective. In the sixteenth century, mounted archers led to a decline in the importance of elephants in north India, as with the Mughal defeats of the Bengalis at Rukaros in 1575 and of the

Rajputs at Haldighati in 1576; although Mughal rulers, notably Akbar (r. 1556–1605) and Jahangir (r. 1605–27), continued to have numerous elephants. In forested regions, elephants remained more significant than horses, as in Ceylon (Sri Lanka), Kerala in southern India, Burma, Thailand and Vietnam, all of which were unsuitable for archers on horseback. Elephants did not play a comparable role in Africa, primarily because the African elephants proved much more difficult to train.

A key instance of diffusion was the spread of the horse in the Americas by European settlers, and then beyond the ambit of their power. In about 1730, the Comanche became the first North American tribe to equip an entire people with horses, an achievement that was significant in their rise to dominance over a large area of the Great Plains and of what became the American South-West and northern Mexico.[32] The arrival of the horse brought a far greater mobility, allowing the Native Americans to follow herds of bison or deer for hundreds of miles, and the resulting improvements in diet led to a larger and healthier population. Requiring much organisation and planning, these animal drives served as preparation for human conflict. At the same time, tribal warfare was very much affected by animal movements and by competition for hunting grounds, which was not a new but a long-standing cause of conflict. Indeed, alongside physical and human geography came animal geography.

The problems of assessing geographical influence can be gauged by the case of sub-Saharan Africa where, as in other instances, it is too easy to read from environment, in the shape of terrain, disease, vegetation and climate, to the size of states, and therefore the forces they could deploy and the purposes to which they were to be deployed. In practice, conflict was not simply dependent on the environment, not least because skill was important to success. There can be, in some accounts of geopolitics, a pragmatic, almost mechanistic, search for situational advantage. This is offered in parallel to a misleading semi-Darwinian account of international relations and warfare, one, however, that downplays the extent to which assessments of success vary by and within cultures.

In practice, it was in accordance with cultural supposition about the goals and methods of warfare, that particular goals, methods, territories and societies take on significance for politico-cultural reasons. Such reasons have frequently affected the choice of where, how, and to what end, to campaign. Honour, reputation and glory were all aspects of the context of decision-making, and each potentially a source of strength.[33] The choice of where to campaign then had knock-on effects for other powers, as with the Ottomans from the sixteenth to the eighteenth centuries turning against the Safavids of Persia or, alternatively, the Habsburgs of Austria; and with the Siamese in the eighteenth century fighting Burma to the west, or expanding east and south into modern-day IndoChina and Malaysia.

There were also the extent to which more particular political conjunctures reflected these choices of where to campaign. Thus, the rapid extension of Ottoman power in North Africa in 1517–29, an extension, more swift there than that of the Arabs in the seventh century, that took power as far as the border of Morocco, threatened maritime links between Spain and Italy and, more particularly, Barcelona and Genoa, Naples and Palermo, and with them, the basic axes of Habsburg power. Whereas the Ottomans were able to ground their North African position on strong economic underpinnings, especially the agriculture and commerce of Egypt, the opposing Spanish and (for the Moroccans) Portuguese coastal positions in North Africa entailed continual infusions of funds; which was another aspect of geopolitical competition. Investment was a consequence of military commitment; and vice versa.

Distance played a role in assessing geopolitical concerns, strategic places, and operational options, but it was not the sole factor. For example, the major effort devoted in 1570–1 by the Ottomans to the successful conquest of nearby Venetian-ruled Cyprus, which they were able to cut off from support, contrasted with their failure to provide significant support to the unsuccessful *Morisco* rising of 1568–71 in southern Spain. After the costly Ottoman defeat in attacking Malta in 1565, the western Mediterranean seemed too remote and difficult to allow a large commitment and, prior to attacking Cyprus, Ottoman forces were busy in Yemen (successfully) and southern Russia, unsuccessfully advancing on Astrakhan. Yet, as so often, too much should not be made of physical distance alone. Aside from both Yemen and southern Russia, each of which was distant, the Ottomans had sent fleets to Indian and Persian Gulf waters and, by 1577, were finally to overrun the Fezzan region in inland Libya.

Distance was most important when it was also an expression of mental horizons. In the Mediterranean, these had expanded for the Ottomans in the early decades of the sixteenth century, but closed from the 1570s as concerns about Persia came anew to the fore. The extent to which military factors, in this case in part a matter of Spanish resistance to Ottoman expansion, as with the Spanish relief of Malta in 1565, helped shape these mental horizons varied, and, to a degree, was a matter of an understanding of limits. As for all states, such an understanding was not value-free but, instead, mediated through personal and factional rivalries, as well as with reference both to anxieties about opponents and to the pressures of the constituencies of interests that made up a state and also its alliance system. Drive, both general and specific, was a key element in geopolitics, as, despite a misguided sense in some treatments, as if empires were the equivalent of amoeba, there was no determination to expand continually in all directions, or even in any.

Aside from constraints in the shape of contrary pressures from other states, both imperial and smaller, there were also the extent to which rule, let alone expansion, depended on co-operation,[34] and, linked to this, the roles and views of autonomous interests within empires, such as the Crimean Tatars and the Sharifs of Mecca within the Ottoman Empire. As a consequence of this and other factors, distant and loose hegemony might be all that was required or possible in some directions, with activity in those cases therefore largely to do with responding to threats and problems.[35]

Insurrections in areas distant from the centre of power were part of this pattern, affecting the potential for presence, let alone expansion, in particular directions. In some empires or states, insurrections were a frequent element in the regional equations of power, notably the tension between an unwillingness to respect the wishes of central government and its local agents, and their rival desire to demonstrate control in frontier regions, including over these agents.[36] This situation could be further complicated by the 'inner frontiers' within empires and states, with regions of lesser control, generally those of harsher terrain, less prosperous agriculture, and a different ethnicity and/or religion, challenging any tendency to think in terms of geopolitical uniformity.

Such 'inner frontiers' were prominent in the Mughal empire in India, but were also seen elsewhere,[37] as in China with regions where there were non-Han people, these regions, often physically difficult, frequently seeing rebellions. In 1794–1804, although poverty rather than ethnicity was the cause,[38] the mountainous region between Sichuan, Hubei and Shaanxi was the basis of the large-scale White Lotus rebellion. These and other crises, in China and elsewhere, were, in turn, made more complex by the role of the locally-prominent. They were either in favour of the central government or opposed to it, or both, the last a situation reflective in part of the tensions within many governments. Such tensions themselves affected and reflected the nature and seriousness of civil warfare.

In turn, the territorial limits of power had meanings in part in terms of the strength and ambitions of other states. Thus, France could only wield hegemony in Western and Central Europe, if, as with Charlemagne in the early ninth century, Louis XIV in the early 1680s, and Napoleon up to 1812, other European powers were weak and divided. Once those factors ceased, as from 1688 for Louis XIV and from 1813 for Napoleon, then France's position deteriorated significantly, a process very much seen with German unification in 1866 and with German rearmament and expansionism in 1933–9. Already in 1807, when the somewhat excitable Commodore Sir Home Popham of the British navy worried that Napoleon, a geopolitical bogeyman, and notably so after his 1798 invasion of Egypt, would 'threaten India through Persia' or invade Ireland from Lisbon,[39] that was scarcely viable given British naval strength.

As an aspect of the plasticity of geography, limits were not uniform in character or context. Thus, very differently to Napoleon, Russia was on the 'edge' of Europe, but that does not explain why it was more effective in spreading its power in Siberia in the seventeenth century than the European powers were in North America in the same period. In part this was due to the latter facing stronger local resistance from a more densely-populated Native population benefiting from the extent to which much of North America was more temperate than Siberia. In part also, the contrast arose from competition between the European powers and their willingness accordingly to ally with the Native Americans and provide them with firearms, a factor with the Dutch, English and French from the early seventeenth century. This was not an issue for Russia: neither China nor Japan wished, nor were in a position, to take a comparable role in Siberia.

Geopolitics is taking on renewed significance today, and also, to a degree, being reconceptualised, not least given the rising prominence of issues over food, oil and water 'security'. Thus, the utilisation of rivers, notably for hydroelectric power and irrigation, has become a serious cause of tension in international relations, particularly in the Nile, Mekong, Tigris and Euphrates valleys. It is also an aspect of the struggle for dominance of the Himalayas.

A contrasting type of geopolitics is organised around people and not control over territory. Such a focus has a variety of aspects. For example, rather than seeing soldiers as the product of rulership, and with the geopolitics thereby set by territorial control over the areas where they are recruited, there has been the significance across time of military labour markets, with troops recruited from outside the territory of rulers, most frequently in return for payment but sometimes also for land. With their own geographies, notably of recruitment area and subsequent routes, such markets were particularly important in India and Europe,[40] although also playing a role elsewhere. This frequently underrated element of geopolitics remains significant today, and notably so in Africa and in the Middle East, as was seen by the use in Syria and Caucasus of what were referred to as 'mercenaries'. In practice, the large number of young men who are unemployed or underemployed in many areas, for example the *sahel*, provides a source of manpower, as does the easy availability and use of handheld weaponry. The situation is similar to the availability of large numbers of young men for fighting at the behest of drug cartels in Latin America and other areas.

Another aspect of control over people is that provided by the opportunities for profit and other benefits through enslavement. That was a frequent cause and method of warfare for much of history, but also one particularly appropriate where there were large numbers whom could be enslaved.[41] Thus, human geography was of direct significance to the economics of warfare. In part this could be from the sale of slaves, as on behalf of conquering Roman armies, but their use as labour, including as sex slaves, was also significant, as with Ghaznavid raiding into India from medieval Afghanistan or Comanche raiding in North America.

Slave labour could include slave soldiers, a key instance of 'war feeding war'. The use of captives as soldiers in this fashion is more classically associated with early-modern Islamic forces, notably the Ottoman *janissaries*, and their equivalents; but was much more widespread in pre-modern times, for example being seen in pre-modern African warfare. Such a use continued into the last century and to the present. Thus, Kuomintang soldiers captured by the Communists in the Chinese Civil

War of 1946–9 were used in the Korean War of 1950–3, and with scant concern for casualties. More recently, there has been the seizure of children and others as slave soldiers in West and Central Africa, Iraq, Yemen, Mozambique, and other conflicts; and of enslavement-like conscription by the government in Eritrea.

As in the pursuit of slaves, the role of operations in affecting strategy was in part driven by the opportunities of profit, which, in what are in effect costings, always sit alongside the likely frictions of failure. The opportunities of profit often related to the acquisition of territory itself,[42] or to what could be gained from it in the short term, but another crucial form of profit was that of political success, both domestic and international. Indeed, the role of gaining territory as a means of demonstrating success was a key and persistent instance of the geography of strategy, and one that cannot be readily quantified. So also with seapower, with, again, the cultural dimension of its display being of significance.[43]

Lastly, there is the geopolitics of the entire world, with struggles presented as of universal validity. This might very much appear to be a modern tendency, in terms of the global ideologies and struggles of the last century, and the related rhetoric and methodologies of transnationalism.[44] That is a pertinent approach, but, at the same time, there is also a link back to the earlier would-be worldwide applicability of religious movements. They seek to defy any physical limits, and serve as another reminder of continuities, or at least echoes.

Chapter 6

The Impact of Technology and the Question of Periodisation

Cyber-weaponry is the latest and most complete version of an attack in which troops do not have to cross the geography in the form of an advance across the physical terrain. It is a dramatic demonstration of the degree to which the context of geography can be challenged, indeed transformed, by technological change. This transformation occurs in a number of ways, and has notably done so in the last quarter-millennium, the period of modern industrialisation. Thus, communications have been revolutionised, with minor incremental devices, notably the semaphore developed during the French Revolutionary and Napoleonic Wars (1792–1815), replaced by others with a totally different range, speed and reliability, for example telegrams, telephone, and radio. All of that is highly significant for war, and, as a direct consequence, governments and militaries have frequently been the key players in the relevant investment and application, and especially so over the last 150 years.[1] Indeed, the complexity of war has ensured that preparedness for it is a significant aspect in strategic geography.

Other limiting aspects of physical geography for war have been challenged by developments in food preservation and water purification, each of which became more significant from the nineteenth century. As a consequence, the death gradients of operating in particular disease-environments changed greatly, which helped make it possible to mount sustained operations in such areas, as with America in both the Pacific and Vietnam Wars. Again, the key work was frequently undertaken by the military, as death from disease was often greater than from combat, as for the British in the Boer War (1899–1902), and notably so in the tropics. Thus, in part in response to casualties in its successful 1898 war with Spain, notably in Cuba, the American military put a major effort into understanding the nature and diffusion of tropical diseases such as yellow fever and malaria, and this aided its operating in the tropics, including the construction of the Panama Canal, finished in 1914. As a result, a key strategic tool that made it easy for American warships to move between the Atlantic and the Pacific, the Canal was also an instance of the overcoming of physical geography thanks to the understanding of the constraints of a different aspect of it. In the twentieth century, food and water provision became even more important to the geographies of conflict, as warfare came to involve a presence in 'unnatural' environments, particularly those of submarine operations (where humans were kept for far longer than in aircraft), while, separately, unprecedented numbers fought in the world wars.

Weaponry and the related platforms could help overcome aspects of both physical and human geography, although their impact could be lessened by anti-weaponry, such as anti-tank and anti-aircraft guns, and anti-measures. The most significant weaponry at the operational and strategic level was that providing firepower, mobility and, crucially, range, as the latter could help collapse the Home Front into the front line. However, although ships provided power-projection against opposing states, such weaponry was not really present until strategic bombing was an option. Attempted in the First World War without success, such bombing came to fruition in the Second World War, and then helped define the geopolitics of the Cold War.

Prior to that, as far as land conflict was concerned, the range of weaponry was only such that the front line could be affected, although that did not mean that civilians did not suffer. For most of history, the range and rate of effective fire did not change greatly. It was the product of the combination of missile weapons with both the experience and strength of the soldier, and the nature of the physical environment. Thus, jungle cover nullified range and accuracy. Instead of change in the weapons themselves, it was the diffusion of weapons to people that had not hitherto had them, as with gunpowder weaponry in North America in the seventeenth century, that was the principal development. At the same time, the impact of that particular change was lessened by the extent to which missile weapons, notably bows and arrows, were already present.

Firearms became more effective from the early nineteenth century, which was a period of significant technological change. The mass-produced metal percussion cap was developed in the 1820s, and replaced the flintlock mechanism, producing a reliable, all-weather, ignition system which, by lessening the impact of weather and cutting the risk of misfires, reduced the impact of geography. Percussion muskets were followed by percussion rifles, the rifles producing a more reliable trajectory for the bullets than muskets had done.

There were also changes in artillery and in the prime response, fortification. In the first half of the nineteenth century, as the volume, range and lethality of firepower increased, defence-in-depth in response was provided by developing a ring of detached forts, as round Antwerp and Paris, which meant that less attention needed to be devoted to the main defensive position. This different geography of defence forced a more distant and longer line of investment on the besiegers, and thus posed greater demands on their manpower.[2]

Meanwhile, again affecting the spatiality of conflict, the Prussians developed the 'needle' rifle, named after its needle-shaped firing pin, which penetrated the base of the chamber in order to detonate the propellant. This breech-loading, bolt-action, Prussian rifle had an unprecedentedly high rate of fire, and proved effective in the 1860s, with an accuracy rate of 65 per cent at 700 feet. This provided a form of 'geography' at the tactical level, but that also owed much to the speed of fire – four to seven times a minute – as the combination produced the coverage, and thus helped shape the battlefield. In turn, the nature of deployment and tactics was part of the equation, with the Prussians training all their soldiers to be skirmishers, able to fire their rifles accurately. In 1864, the Danes suffered in fighting the Prussians from shorter-range, muzzle-loading, rifles as well as the lack of rifled cannon. In 1866, in turn, the French adopted the *chassepot* rifle, with its more gas-tight breech and greater range than the Prussian 'needle gun,' and inflicted heavy casualties accordingly in the Franco-Prussian War (1870–1), for example at the battle of Gravelotte-Saint Privat in 1870. The Germans, crucially Prussians, however, in contrast, not only had good breach-loading, steel-tubed artillery, but also used it in a way that defied the traditional geography of the battle: departing from the Napoleonic (I) tradition of gun lines laying down frontal fire, the Germans operated in artillery masses: mobile batteries formed by enterprising officers, which converged on key points, annihilated them with crossfire, and then moved on.

Nevertheless, while important, the geography of weapons capability, that at the tactical level, proved less significant than that of troop movements, that at the operational and, to a degree, strategic levels. This was demonstrated for example by the success of the rapid and large-scale French deployment into Italy in 1859.[3] In turn, against Austria in 1866 and France in 1870, the Prussians had more effective mobilisation and deployment than their opponents, and used this to operational and strategic effect. There was also, at the tactical level, the ability of more flexible Prussian units to adopt new positions more rapidly than their opponents, permitting attacks on opposing flanks, while using small-unit formations that were less exposed to opposing artillery.

The Prussian operational means in 1866 employed the space-mass-time relationship, that of the planned deployment and use of a mass of troops to a particular area and on a specific timetable, more successfully than the Austrians. The latter responded irresolutely to the possibility of using interior lines to defeat the separate Prussian armies in detail. Prior to the battle of Sadowa (Königgrätz), the Austrians were outmanoeuvred by the three Prussian armies which were implementing Moltke's operational method of using exterior lines. Whereas Napoleon I had employed separately operating corps within his army that concentrated prior to the battle, the Prussians in 1866 aimed for a concentration of armies in the battle itself in order to outmanoeuvre the Austrians.[4] Yet, with greater scale, the space that had to be used, and therefore planned, was far greater than hitherto, and that posed significant problems of coordination.

At the same time, although wars delivered results, plans rarely came to fruition, and this was true of the Franco-Prussian War not only for the heavily-defeated French, but also for the Germans. Victory near the frontiers in 1870 did not lead to the end of French resistance that had been anticipated and that was logistically and financially most feasible.[5] More specifically, the success of the garrison in Belfort in southern Alsace in holding off a German siege denied the Germans the opportunity to advance at the southern end of the Vosges Mountains and to annex Belfort in the peace treaty, which meant that, in any future war, they would not be able to advance through the Belfort Gap into southern Lorraine and Franche-Comté. Yet, having lost most of Alsace and part of Lorraine in the war, France now had less space in which to manoeuvre in any future war. Partly as a result, major military bases, such as Belfort and Verdun, were surrounded after the war with fortified positions which posed the Germans, when they attacked Verdun in 1916, with the problems of a strong defence-in-depth; there was no comparable attack on Belfort in the First World War. Ironically, it proved easier to redeploy French forces to protect Paris in 1914, as, due to the territorial losses in 1871, the French right-wing was further back in Lorraine, and therefore closer to the capital.

In addition, French defences in the Alps, defences that took advantage of the terrain and were sited accordingly, were designed to prevent Germany's ally Italy from mounting an attack, and indeed served to deter the Italians from planning one. In the event of Italy attacking, these forts were intended to lessen the need for French manpower and thus to further the strategic goal of concentrating the army on the German threat.

Meanwhile, the increased threat of long-range firepower ensured the obsolescence of existing fortifications, which encouraged the dismantling of city walls. The geography of fortifications continued to be challenged by advances in explosives and artillery in the late nineteenth century, especially the development of rifled steel breech-loaders, delayed-action fuses, and improved pneumatic recoil mechanisms. These had implications in the tactical battlespace, including in the appearance and shape of fortifications, as with armour-plated turrets, disappearing cupolas, and the use of concrete roofs. Extensive fortress complexes offering defence-in-depth were seen in a number of countries, including around Antwerp and Liège in Belgium. Liège was both a major crossing-point over the River Meuse, and an important rail junction.

At the same time, in the run-up to the First World War, the psychological geography of a conviction of the value of the offensive was part of the assessment of the situation. The focus on the offensive then was related to a conviction of its value in terms of both goals and means, and to the related linkage of strategy with doctrine. Thus, General Joseph Joffre, the inexperienced French Chief of the General Staff in 1911–16, anxious, in the event of war with Germany, to coordinate operations with Russia, planned to mount an early offensive against German forces in Alsace-Lorraine, before launching what was intended as a decisive blow against the German centre in eastern Belgium. An emphasis on the offensive, which played a key role in the rewriting of the French regulations in 1913–14 after the sacking, in 1911, of General Victor-Constant Michel, his more defensive predecessor, also seemed the best way to respond to the limitations of much of the French (and other) officer corps, as well as to maintain morale and to answer to the preference for traditional and simple tactics. The French emphasis was on breaking through opponents at their weakest point, as opposed to the German emphasis on envelopment.[6] The latter placed a stress on speedy manoeuvre, and a very different operational geography.

Technological change had altered the nature of space on land and at sea, not least the capability to use it and speedily. This was the case with steam power: both rail and steamships. The latter were not dependent on wind patterns, and that transformed the possibilities for naval operations. In 1845, Sir George Cockburn, an experienced British admiral, noted:

> 'from the period when the first large seagoing steam vessel was successfully completed, it became evident to everybody that a facility never before existing must be afforded thereby for sudden invasion of this country [from France].'[7]

Steam also increased the inshore manoeuvrability of warships, as with the successful Austrian bombardment of Venice in 1849. In turn, as part of the development of an anti-tactics that had operational and strategic implications, steam-powered torpedo boats were to provide a deterrent for such action. So also with mines which, from the 1880s, could be placed rapidly and in large numbers, while no longer requiring firing from the shore, which affected the nature as well as location of the threat to navigation. The mine barrages laid in the First World War very much affected the geography of the naval conflict, and the interplay of minelayer and minesweeper became of major significance to the equation of overall strength.[8]

Mechanised advances in the twentieth century were to create an option of moving the front line rapidly, but there was still the need for supplies, and that need provided an umbilical cord to the existing front of operations. Mechanical mobility, indeed, had its own issues in terms of creating new constraints, both physical and human. The latter focused on fuel supplies and the former on the terrain that made such movements possible. So also with the new constraints that affected the move with warships, first, to steam power in the nineteenth century and, then, to oil in the twentieth. Each entailed the need for supplies at the strategic, operational and tactical levels. In naval activity, refuelling was crucial and therefore bases accordingly, but the requirements differed between coal and oil. At the same time, this was an interactive process, as practices of at-sea refuelling were developed and, more significantly, became predictable. In-air refuelling was to follow for aircraft, and also became normal.

The technology interacted with the degree to which the scale of production of resources, as well as their distribution, were each a means to transform the military and political environment and give force to plans, and yet also a source of vulnerability. This was demonstrated from Antiquity by the blockage of trade routes. The *Honest True Briton*, a London newspaper, in its issue of 27 April 1724, commented:

'The old ammunition of bows and arrows, battering-rams and wooden engines, which were to be procured and made in all parts of the world, are now laid aside ... now the materials necessary for carrying on a war must be by the returns made by the foreign trade that one country drives with another ... no nation can resist invasion, or get out of a just and necessary war with honour, but from the stores it either has, or must procure by trade and navigation.'

The reference here was to such trades as the movement of naval stores, notably timber, hemp and iron, imported from the Baltic to Western Europe; but the shift to coal-based manufacturing and transport in the nineteenth century, and then to oil, very much drove home a dependence on distant power sources that contrasted with earlier fixed power sources, notably water and wind power.[9] Moreover, technology that was non-military could have major consequences not just for the use of military units but also for the location. Thus, in 1854, Sir James Graham, the First Lord of the British Admiralty, wrote about plans to defend a major port from amphibious attack: 'I quite concur in the opinion that the permanent presence of a large military force at Hull is not requisite: that inland concentration with rapid means of distribution by railroad, is the right system.'[10]

Technology was not the sole source of change in naval power, but it was important; and yet also such that the geography of the present can be a poor guide to the past. In particular, whereas oceans and seas dominate current attention in naval conflict, in practice for much of history, rivers, lakes, deltas, estuaries, lagoons and inshore waters were more important in terms of movement of goods and troops. In contrast, the oceans were largely empty of maritime activity, and particularly so when far from land. The geography of shallow waters in turn had implications for the draught and range of shipping used, and therefore of the type of conflict that was possible.[11] Irrespective of the technology, moreover, there were still the limitations of naval power, not least of both offensive and defensive maritime economic warfare.[12]

It is normal to adopt an account of technology in which more recent developments are to the fore, and with the emphasis accordingly on sophisticated machines and their capabilities and lethality. That approach is understandable from the perspective of approaching the present, but can lead to an underplaying of past changes, as well as of the differing parameters affecting the diffusion of technological change. Thus, the varied response to firearms should be understood not simply in terms of military progress, administrative sophistication, or cultural superiority, but, rather, as a more complex process, namely the response to the different tasks and possibilities facing the armies of the period, within also a context in which it was far from clear which weaponry, force structure, tactics, or operational method, were better. Firearms, for example, had to respond to the differences between infantry- and cavalry-dominant warfare, and a key technological change accordingly in the seventeenth and eighteenth centuries, one central to human geography, and the ability to adapt to the physical dimension, was the spread of the horse in North America.

Separately, the marked variety of military activity even in relatively common circumstances, for example in Polynesia prior to contact with Western societies,[13] underlines the need to hold determinism, physical, technological, social and/or cultural, at bay. Fitness for purpose, indeed, and therefore how weaponry was used, were conceived in terms of tasks, social systems and institutional cultures. Indeed, the social shaping of technology was very important in weapons' design, procurement and usage, and remains so.[14]

In tactical terms, developments in weaponry were also significant in affecting constraints, and thereby the local geography. At the simplest of levels, a machine gun reduces the value of forest cover, as the bullets are less readily deflected, while more are fired. As a result, the rate of individual strike, although low, ends up with a high aggregate impact, although a higher rate of fire has major logistical implications. In the case of missile weapons, range was a key factor that had to be understood, with practice and doctrine developed for what was considered to be the most desirable range. In contrast, the most effective range is always so close that the opponent can also inflict considerable damage, which therefore lessens its value. There was also the need to assess the desirable angle of fire.

These considerations became more significant when the target could not be seen, and indirect fire was therefore necessarily used, although such fire still benefits from seeing the enemy, because that reduces ammunition wastage. In many respects, indirect fire was an aspect of a different geography, that of the unseen battlefield. This geography became more significant from the late nineteenth century, on land and at sea, but on contrasting timetables across the world, and with reference to particular weapon systems, being more important for artillery than for infantry, and for infantry than for cavalry.

This contrast had always been an aspect of military command, as efforts were made to integrate the contrasting capabilities of units. This process became more demanding as forces grew in size, but also as complexity in composition posed more problems, including of supplies. To address these command issues, there was, at once, the need for the aptly named 'situational awareness' – understanding the situation at particular sites, but also the more general problem of being able to grasp and work with the combination of possibilities; as well as disrupting those of opponents. Thus, different types of spatiality were at issue, and these played through in the deployment and usage of forces, a type of 'geography' that was closely linked to tasking.

Geography as a matter of the disposition of units, down to their detailed configuration, and in both attack and defence, can be matched by another form of geography, that of the layout of fortifications. Again, there was the need to combine the general characteristics of weaponry and fortification, with the particular ones of individual sites; and anew for both attack and defence. Fortification is in large part a matter of damage limitation, and at the tactical, operational and strategic levels. There was also, as with deployment in battle, the psychological geography arising from issues of display and prestige, and in both general and specifics. These issues were affected by those of culture – individual culture, not least past history, as in the French determination to hold Verdun against German attack in 1916 (it had fallen to Prussian attack in 1792), but were also transformed by the impact of weaponry.

In the twentieth century, fortification spread into comprehensive front-wide systems with the First World War. Then trench warfare, to a degree, risked swallowing the strategic and operational dimensions of war in tactical problems, and notably so on the Western Front in France and Belgium. So also with Gallipoli, the Allied attempt, en route to knocking Turkey out of the war by threatening Constantinople, to break through the Dardanelles, from which Lieutenant General Sir William Birdwood wrote in 1915: 'It seems quite ridiculous that we should be within some ten yards of each other, and yet I am unable to get into their trenches.'[15] On the front lines, the logistical requirements of the huge numbers deployed and in particular of unprecedented volumes of firepower created particular pressures on transport systems, as well as the resulting adaptations. These included the British development of light railways, which, however, were vulnerable to German artillery.[16]

In the Second World War (1939–45, but 1937–45, if not 1931–45, in China), in contrast, the fighting was less static in place and method. Location, nevertheless, remained a key issue, not least due to the continual importance of artillery. Indeed, that was a powerful driver for mapping at the tactical level, for the understanding of ballistics demanded a fixing of target location in order that the algorithms that determined the aiming of guns could apply. Mapping therefore was clearly linked with capability, and the related requirement for maps for bombing was in effect another form of ballistics. The precise location of the target, and (unlike with artillery) an understanding of the routes there, were both crucial, which meant that, in part, mapping for air warfare continued in effect to be two-dimensional, rather than focusing on the three dimensions that aerial conflict required. Air warfare for long, for both bombing and aerial conflict, remained a matter of the visual identification of targets, although that changed greatly in the Second World War. Geography provided convenient references to identify and strike targets by aerial bombardment. Targets on land have both coordinates and a geographic feature associated with them.

Separately, radar was a reflection of the new nature of the three-dimensional character of mapping that stemmed from the addition of aircraft to the very different vertical space represented by terrain. As with the use of mapping for artillery, radar was a response to the need to fix position accurately, but, unlike artillery, aircraft posed an inherently dynamic character in location, and thus in the depiction of location. Radar also allowed effective night-fighting. At the operational level, airpower facilitated and could provide mass and concentration on a decisive point regardless of the geography below.

Geography itself was illuminated and re-imagined by technological changes in the ability both to understand environments and to represent them. Thus the technology of printing, and later that of computing, were both of great significance. Neither was a single-shot change. Printing, indeed, became more significant for geography as it became easier to display more information on maps. Notably, in the nineteenth century, map-colouring ceased to be a manual process and was transformed by the onset of colour printing that made it less expensive to convey more information. The density and complexity of information that could be conveyed increased, as with colour-coded contour zones. As a consequence, the publication of battle-plans became more common. They very much focused on the location of units in the immediate physical setting and therefore encouraged the sense that this was the key element in explanation. The 1840s brought James Wyld's *Maps and Plans, Showing the Principal Movements, Battles and Sieges, in which the British Army Was Engaged during the War from 1808 to 1814 in the Spanish Peninsula* (1840) and William Siborne's successful *History of the War in France and Belgium in 1815* (1844), which included a folio atlas that offered an effective combination of contoured battlefields and army positions indicated by colour. In France, Lieutenant General Lieutenant General Jean-Jacques Pelet, head of the Dépôt Général de la Guerre, produced the *Atlas des campagnes de l'Empereur Napoleon en Allemagne et en France* (1844). An *Atlas histórico y topográfico de la Guerra de Africa en 1859 y 1860* was published in Madrid in 1861, and the first American atlas of military history, Henry Carrington's *Battle Maps and Charts of the American Revolution* in 1881. A onetime academic and lawyer, Carrington was prominent in helping to organise Union recruitment and intelligence, and served in the army after the war.

More general changes in printing were also important. In the 1800s, mechanised paper-making became commercially viable, leading to the steam-powered production of plentiful quantities of inexpensive paper.

The steam-powered printing press developed in the same period, transforming the economics and practicalities of scale. Thus the provision of information to the military about geography was itself a consequence of technological transformation.

The range and pace of technological change increased at all levels from the nineteenth century. Challenges, problems and opportunities interacted. For example, totally different types of operational and tactical geography, and the relevant frictions, came into play with submarines and air warfare. In the latter case, alongside issues of space, came those of totally unprecedented speed. More generally, the extent and pace of change in the geography of war was unmatched. In the twentieth century, on which see in particular Chapters 8, 11, 12 and 13, militaries benefited from the very rapid compilation and addition of information and printing of maps. In turn, digital information and computer-presented maps on screen added a transformation in speed and flexibility, not least in the rapid re-centring of maps as new perspectives were presented.

Advances in weapons technology ensured that strategic effect could be 'miniaturised', in terms of single-actions by individual weapons, with the American use of two nuclear weapons in 1945 dramatically ending the war in Asia. With a characteristic difference in terms of deliverability, the Germans, as part to their development of advanced weaponry such as jet fighters, rockets and new-type submarines, considered the prospect of further advances, notably with long range bombers, multi-stage rockets, space bombers, and submarine-launched missiles. These schemes included plans for attacks on New York City and Washington.[17]

Several of these weapons, in turn, were developed during the Cold War. The process of change continues the case, with network-centric warfare providing problems as well as opportunities,[18] while cyberwarfare, including digital fortifications, is increasingly significant. It is a major development that threatens economies and national security. At every point, it is necessary also to consider the viability of anti-weapons, which, for example, will probably qualify current claims about the paradigm shift offered by drones.[19] Moreover, weaponry still has to be positioned in a range of contexts that are not determined by its capabilities.[20]

The consideration of weaponry plays a role in the periodisation of military history, with gunpowder commonly considered a key element of the coming of modernity; and other indicators, from steamships to aircraft, both of which operated on a very different scale, of the more modern or late modern. Time is an important variable in strategy alongside space; and both invite attention in understanding the conceptualisation and perception of warfare. Ideas of modernisation had a long genesis, but the key source was that of the concept of progress as measured in, and by, social development, an approach that put to one side religious notions of time as leading toward a millenarian outcome, and, instead, offered a different geopolitics. If Montesquieu, Smith and Robertson are all major names in this intellectual project, it was in practice one of a longer pedigree, with notions of improvability in human life accompanied by that of social development. These ideas lent themselves to nineteenth-century interest in scientific formulation and application. Darwinism is part of the mix, as evolutionary ideas provided metaphors and concepts, notably what was to be termed functionalism, in the shape of serving goals necessary for survival and, therefore, strength.

These ideas affected new developing sciences, such as sociology, geopolitics and anthropology, and were brought into academic history through a shared concern with modernity and, therefore, modernisation. Rational choice was seen as at play, from biological preference to economic and political practice and military development, but there was a difference between an emphasis on constraints, as with the French sociologist Émile Durkheim (1858–1917), or with contingent outcomes, as with Max Weber (1864–1920), with a parallel to the geographical ideas of determinism or 'possibilism', that are frequently to the fore in this book. Weber's approach to modernity led him to define it in terms of rationality and standardisation, with motivation in terms of instrumental behaviour, as opposed to traditional action. Weber also linked the prudent rationality related to capitalism with Protestantism. Taken into American thought by the American sociologist Talcott Parsons (1902–79), Weber was the forbear of what was to be called the Structural-Functional approach, and modernisation theory became a key tool in the Social Sciences, a theory emphasising both rational abstract principles and, linked to this, an abandonment and/or overcoming of past practices. Major texts included Walt Rostow's *Politics and the Stages of Growth* (1971) and Francis Fukuyama's *The End of History and the Last Man* (1992), the latter a work propounded around the means, goals and modernity of liberal democracy and free-market capitalism. In the 1960s, and again in the 1990s, modernisation was regarded as a form of global New Deal, apparently able to explain the existing situation, and to create a new world order, that overcame the constraints of geography. Information and theory were chosen and deployed accordingly.[21]

Modernisation theory, however, was often advanced with insufficient attention to practicalities, let alone reality, as with the failure to understand Vietnamese society that characterised American strategy in the Vietnam War. As a related, but separate point, the attempt to produce 'modern', quantifiable criteria of military success fell foul of the ability of the Viet Cong and North Vietnamese to soak up heavier casualties and to defy American equations of rationality and success with their emphasis on quantification.[22]

Other elements were also pertinent, notably secularisation, as again analysis, means and goal of development. Dukheim, Weber and many others argued that modernisation meant a decline in religious practice and significance, and this approach affected a broad tranche of writing in the Social Sciences and Humanities, as well as the discussion of historical change.[23] The cult of reason, understood as inherently secular, with faith banished to the private sphere, however, could mean that the present was asserted as necessarily understanding the past better than the latter had done: reason could reveal the prospectus to a better future and a better-understood past. A circularity in thought and selectivity in evidence were inherent to this process, and both, indeed, were very much to be seen in the work by the proponents of ideas of military modernisation. As far as the circularity was concerned, functions were presented in a quasi-automatic fashion, with needs and drives readily ascribed to states, and effects ascribed to functions, while, in turn, those functions were defined by the effects they produced. So also with the alleged relationship between war and geography.

The cult of a modern reason led to a failure not only to understand the military cultures of the past (and even arguably the present), but also to appreciate the nature of development. Failing to perceive the values of the past, and to understand its practices, resulted in a neglect of important factors in the evaluation of proficiency, capability, limitations and success, both individual and collective. For example, honour was misleadingly disparaged as conservative, if not redundant, and practices of aristocratic officership were misunderstood.

Providing both framework and content for the discussion of military history and much else, revolution, the violent break with the past, was a term in more than fashion in the twentieth century, reflecting not only political commitment, but also that it became the standard way to describe, and apparently explain, structural change, including in warfare, not least the overcoming of constraints, which was a way to understand the response to geography. This practice owed much to the industrial revolution, a term first used in 1799, but popularised by Arnold Toynbee in 1881, with significant capitals. This term was much applied thereafter, and its use was to be the basis for the description of other revolutions, as with the Agricultural Revolution.[24]

It was not therefore surprising that the term was deployed in military history. There were precursors, but the most influential argument was advanced in 1955 by Michael Roberts in a work, published in 1956, that liberally employed the idea of fundamental change and the term military revolution, and that closed with a clear affirmation of transformation: 'By 1660, the modern art of war had come to birth. Mass armies, strict discipline, the control of the state, the submergence of the individual had already arrived' and so on, culminating with 'The road lay open, broad and straight, to the abyss of the twentieth century.'[25] In turn, Geoffrey Parker, in his hugely influential *The Military Revolution: Military Innovation and the Rise of the West, 1500–1800* (1988), included the naval dimension, as well as a wider-ranging chronology and an engagement with the world scale, in effect to explain both the rise (and multipolarity) of the West and why it was to provide the most successful of the 'gunpowder empires', to employ a term probed by Marshall Hodgson and William H. McNeill.[26]

Again with relevance to the understanding of the relationships between war and geography, the emphasis on particular notions of military proficiency, and the embrace of the proposition of military change that is fundamental because described as revolutionary, and described as revolutionary because fundamental, can appear qualified at the very least by the very varied presentation of modern warfare that recent decades have offered. Some historians very much took modernisation theory on board, as in 'the Muslim states ... could no longer meet and defeat the expanding repertory of innovations developed by their Christian adversaries, because the Westernisation of war also required replication of the economic and social structures and infrastructures, in particular the machinery of resource-mobilisation and modern finance, on which the new techniques depended.'[27] However, it is also valid to consider the problems faced by the United States in the Islamic world over the last two decades, as well as by Israel in Lebanon.

Instead, it is the specificity of conflict and individual conflicts, and the multivalent character of war, that emerge; and the language of modernity, modernisation, and revolution is too often misleading as an account, narrative and/or analytical, of this phenomenon. Indeed, to suggest some abrupt shift to a modernity of empirically-derived, rational assessments predicated on an assumption of transformation through improvement across time, provides a conventional way to approach modernity, and to locate pre-modernity accordingly, but is both a partial account of the modern, and an underrating of the complexity and achievement of earlier ages.[28] The multiple characteristics of military capability, effectiveness, and achievement come to the fore, as do the conditionalities of success. Change can be seen as integral and overall, rather than separate and zero-sum. Moreover, this approach can counter the too often misleading reading between proficiency at the respective levels of tactical, operational and strategic conflict, again to employ later abstractions.

The problem of Western-centric and teleological accounts of warfare is central.[29] In particular, it is necessary to address the military vitality of non-Western powers and peoples, the success of whom did not, other than in the most selective of readings, depend on adopting Western-style weaponry and organisation. Given that some of the most effective military systems were very different,[30] this approach appears especially flawed.

A key point is that there was no common military-historical space for particular periods. Indeed, rather than a message with a definition and ranking accordingly of significance in circumstances and changes, a chronological and/or geographical period or space becomes a medium, that of an essentially arbitrary classification with no one common trajectory.[31] For example, far from obvious units, continents divide as much as join, with coastal regions often looking not inland across the continent, but more out to sea and to the other side of the oceans, as with the idea of Atlantic worlds.

Nor is there a common theme across periods and spaces, albeit at a different rate, which was an approach that has been employed in military history. Instead, the major civilisations had military cultures that differed, these differences being a key element of the geographies of war, while within, individual cultures, there were variations reflecting, in particular, the interplay of specific challenges with the quality of particular leaders. An action-reaction pattern of development, with fitness for purpose ensuring that successful leaders created opportunities, and sought to respond to deficiencies in a dynamic fashion, meant an inherent variety in development. So also with the linkage to political systems that followed particular patterns of leadership: hereditary command and control was different to meritocratic rulership in terms of the successful warlord seizing power. And so, moreover, with the élites in question.

Geographical and chronological classifications, such as Africa or the nineteenth century, with their search for common experiences within, and divisions without, can be instructive; but, across time, both within and between regions and periods, there was the desire for an edge in battle, and therefore for difference. This is a difference that can be 'mapped' or approached in spatial terms. Furthermore, 'diffusion' can as much entail adaptation and difference, in the shape of anti-weapons and anti-tactics, as copying. Ultimately, killing the enemy with as little risk to one's own life was generally uppermost, even in cultures that emphasised the heroism of the individual warrior in fighting another, in other words the space of the two in the shape of a conflict between champions.

The best answer conceptually is an emphasis on the contingent and subjective characters of causation and classification. Rather than being freestanding in some universal theory, generalisation will best suit the author's ideas of the structures and dynamics of the geographies of war in a given historical situation. This approach may be in a sense simplistic and instrumental, but some measuring stick is required to make sense of the voluminous mass of details that comprises military history. This should entail an abandonment of the misleading conceit that particular approaches, and the geographies, and more especially geographical determinisms, allegedly explicit or latent in them, are definitive. And so also for battles as apparently definitive, as with the Prussian-German usage from the nineteenth century of Hannibal's crushing victory over the Romans at Cannae (216 BCE) as a model of tactical excellence and therefore success, arising from the fusion of weapons-use and a particular manoeuvre in a given space.[32] Of course, we really know relatively little of Hannibal, his plans, allies and resources, how much he had to pay his mercenaries, who financed the army, and where the recruits came from. The sources are lacking; but it is the use to which past examples nevertheless are put that is crucial.

Hans Delbrück's account of Cannae was highly influential, but even more so was that (influenced by his reading of Delbrück) by Alfred, Count Schlieffen, the Chief of the General Staff from 1891 to 1906. This account was intended both to demonstrate manoeuvre warfare and to provide a basis for military education, and thus was studied by Moltke the Younger and others. It was to be translated into English at Fort Leavenworth. Envelopment, very much an imposition on the locational geography of the opposing force, was the key idea, one seen with the usage of independently-operating corps by Napoleon and his rivals, as at Leipzig in 1813, with the Prussian success at Sadowa in 1866, and with the would-be German successes in 1914 and 1941. The Germans triumphed in neither of the latter years, and Cannae, which had a similar culmination for Hannibal, proved a deceptive guide to strategic success.

There were major differences as ever. In the Second Punic War (218–201 BCE), Hannibal ultimately failed because of inadequate numbers of men and siege equipment after Cannae, and a lack of reinforcements thereafter. In the case of 1941, key elements included inadequate intelligence, leading to a serious underestimation of the number and quality of Soviet forces and material; Soviet advantages in troops, space, time, and Allied assistance, Soviet resilience; Germany needing to fight on two fronts; and seriously flawed German strategy and command. Geographical like historical comparisons need to be alive to contexts.

Chapter 7

Leaders, Generals and Geographers

'In my opinion he always had the map of Europe in his head, and in wartime that of France's northern and eastern frontiers.' Philip Mansel of Louis XIV.[1]

The leaders, both civilian and military, of combatants were repeatedly depicted with globes and maps, a depiction which became a pattern in the West from the sixteenth century. The understanding of space in the shape of the globe linked wisdom with knowledge, the first a habit of mind of a semi-sacral or magical character, and the second more directly related to particular requirements and skills, of which direction and command in war were the more important.

Maps could help anchor the spatial dimension and dynamic of strategic discussion and planning, as was seen clearly during the negotiations over ending the War of the Spanish Succession (1702–13), when Jean, Marquess of Torcy, the experienced French Foreign Minister, urged his British counterpart, Henry, Viscount Bolingbroke, to look at a map in order to see the strategic threat posed by the Alpine demands of Victor Amadeus II of Savoy-Piedmont.[2] In his novel *Humphry Clinker*, the satirical journalist Tobias Smollett made the need for cartographic information apparent, by mocking Thomas, Duke of Newcastle, a leading British minister from 1724 to 1756 and 1757 to 1762, with reference to the position at the beginning of the Seven Years War (1756–63):

'this poor half-witted creature told me, in a great fright, that thirty thousand French had marched from Acadie [Nova Scotia] to Cape Breton – "Where did they find transports? (said I)" "Transports! (cried he) I tell you they marched by land" – "By land to the island of Cape Breton?" "What! is Cape Breton an island?" "Certainly." "Ha! are you sure of that?" When I pointed it out in the map, he examined it earnestly with his spectacles; then, taking me in his arms, "My dear C---! (cried he) you always bring us good news – Egad! I'll go directly, and tell the king [George II] that Cape Breton is an island."[3]

In practice, there is no information on how far, and how, Newcastle read maps. Indeed, such information is rare for this and other periods.

During the Dutch crisis of 1787, a map certainly played a role in the detailed advice offered the British Cabinet, then led by William Pitt the Younger, advice provided by Charles, 3rd Duke of Richmond, the Master-General of the Ordnance (artillery), the sponsor of the Ordnance Survey, and Sir James Harris, the experienced British envoy in The Hague. Richmond 'talked of military operations – called for a map of Germany – traced the marches from Cassel and Hanover, to Holland, and also from Givet to Maastricht'. The former would be the route followed by troops from Hesse-Cassel and Hanover sent to help the pro-British Orangists, the latter that anticipated for the French were they to intervene on the side of the rival Patriots. The following day, Harris saw Pitt, who 'sent for a map of Holland; made me show him the situation of the [United] Provinces [the Netherlands]'.[4] A map would also demonstrate the contrast between the distance allied Prussian troops would have to travel from their Rhineland base in Cleves, in order to mount an invasion of the Netherlands, with the greater distance which France's forces would have to take from Givet in order to intervene on behalf of the Patriots. This advice was designed to encourage British support for action on behalf of the Orangists by illustrating its viability. In the event, the British lent naval backing, the Prussians successfully invaded, and French preparations did not result in action.

Five years earlier, in a letter to the Prime Minister, William, 2nd Earl of Shelburne, pressing for a forward-policy in India, Sir John Macpherson, a member of the Supreme Council of Bengal, and later the Acting Governor General, wrote from the base of Calcutta:

'If your Lordship casts your eye upon the local situation of these provinces you will easily trace the boundaries which nature has traced for an Empire of which the annual revenue is about six millions sterling independent of the value of its manufactures. This Empire is as easily governed and secured, nay more so than the single province of Bengal in nearly the same degree that Britain as an United Kingdom is more easy of protection than England in a separate state from the Rohilla Mountains, along the Tibet Hills to the sea at Chittagong... Scindia [Mahadaji Shinde], the Maratta General with his army is not far from the station of our other brigade at Cawnpore. That vicinity shows the necessity of our extension of territory for if you draw back your frontier to Patna, the Marattas would follow or some power equally dangerous as a neighbour. Thus measures have been gradually adopted by what is called the visionary ambition of Mr Hastings which would maintain our empire in India even if the Carnatic [south-east India] was lost...'[5]

The presentation of leaders and generals with maps became more consistently the case in succeeding centuries, and was one in which public image sat alongside command practice. And so with the world wars, more especially the second. Thus, Adolf Hitler was frequently shown giving maps close attention as he spoke with and listened to his military advisers, and notably so when bent over a map-table in his headquarters, which was crucial to his survival in the Wolf's Lair headquarters when he was attacked in the 20 July 1944 Bomb Plot. Photographs include Hitler marking a spot on a map hanging on a wall, and Hitler, Göring and Mussolini all being shown a map.

However, Hitler, who also had not travelled much, lacked any serious education in geography and cartography, and, far from improving, his understanding of the relationship between symbols on the map and relative capability in the field became far weaker with time. That was an aspect of Hitler's increasingly delusional approach to the war; although, from the outset, as with many others, he had always tended to look at maps and see what he wanted to see, rather than reading maps, a process that requires thought, and notably so at the strategic level of war. German field commanders, such as Erich von Manstein, Erwin Rommel, and Gerd von Rundstedt, were also frequently photographed looking at maps, which was presented as the obvious exemplar of the *métier* of command.

The long- and much-travelled Winston Churchill, who held considerably more familiarity with geography than Hitler, used maps constantly and was frequently photographed with them. Churchill's imperial background and naval interest gave him a world-spanning perception of geography, one that made it readily possible to try to assess the interaction of threats and developments in different areas, as well as competing priorities. The key figure for him was Captain Richard Pim, the supervisor of the War Room at the Admiralty when Churchill was its First Lord (1939–40), before heading the Map Room in No. 10 Downing Street and the Cabinet War Rooms for Churchill as Prime Minister (1940–5). Pim saw Churchill on an almost daily basis, and attended many overseas trips in order to set up temporary map rooms. The maps covered every theatre of war and were kept up-to-date with the latest Intelligence reports on the location of military units.[6]

Franklin Delano Roosevelt saw mapping as a device of America's enemies and as a resource for the Allies. In his speech at the Mayflower Hotel in Washington on 27 October 1941, he referred to the Germans mapping a new order in Latin America, a thesis being advanced by British Intelligence. Preparing for war, Roosevelt obtained his maps from the National Geographic Society (NGS) and drew on the geopolitical skill of Isaiah Bowman, who had played a major role at the Versailles Peace Conference in 1919. The President also created a map room in the White House. For Christmas 1942, he was given a huge 50-inch diameter, 750-pound globe, manufactured under the supervision of the Map Division of the newly-established Office of Strategic Services (OSS) and the War Department, and presented to him by the Army Chief of Staff, General George Marshall, a photographed occasion that was designed to show the President's understanding of geopolitics. Observing Churchill's admiration for his NGS maps at Christmas 1943, Roosevelt asked for a set to be made for him.

An understanding of geography was not only necessary for overall commanders, political and/or military, concerned to direct and prioritise, for, in addition, the requirement for situational awareness was readily apparent for any commander who needed to act in a specific environment. Getting it wrong, usually by exposing troops, whether in movement or stationary, to unexpected attack or to opposing firelines, was very serious and could be tactically or indeed operationally disastrous.

Ambush, in whatever form, was a classic instance of such a failure (and conversely success), as with the successful French/Native American ambush of a British force under Major General Edward Braddock advancing on Fort Duquesne (modern Pittsburgh) in 1755. In part, the Japanese air-assault on Pearl Harbor in 1941 was another instance of a different type of ambush, the strategic one of attacking without declaring war, as also with the German assault on the Soviet Union in 1941, the Israeli one on Egypt in 1967, or the Egyptian and Syrian one on Israel in 1973. More generally, a failure to consider how opponents might use terrain could be the basis of serious disasters, as for the Romans at German hands in the Teutoburger Wald in 9, the British retreating from Kabul in 1842 at Afghan hands, the Italians at Ethiopian hands at Adua (Adowa) in 1896, and the Spaniards at Annual in Morocco in 1921, all of which were therefore aspects of over-ambitious strategic commitments and operational plans.

Geographical understanding included an appreciation of what the operational grasp of an entire campaign entailed, and, related to that, of the possibilities presented by a regional landscape. How these fitted into the war as a whole was more properly the field of strategy, but operational skill at the regional level was a key component of strategic success. The ability of generals varied considerably, in large part being a product of factors outside their control, including the supply of reinforcements, the moves of opponents, and the weather.

For most of history, the relevant training of commanders was that from experience and the wisdom passed on by senior officers. Writings provided an opportunity to gain insights, one facilitated with the development and spread of printing. This offered an opportunity to understand the past as when Arthur Wellesley, later 1st Duke of Wellington, en route to India in 1796 on a long sea journey, extensively read military history, for example Julius Caesar's *Gallic Wars*. Another form of experience was accompanied by peacetime manoeuvres, by visits to battlefields, and by the institutionalisation of the 'staff ride', a translation of *Stabs-Reise* which testifies to the role of Helmuth von Moltke the Elder in developing the practice in the late nineteenth century. Landscape-based exercises were joined by map-based ones once cartography proved able to engage accurately with terrain features.

Landscape was not taught in a value-free fashion. For example, there was a turn-of-the-century fascination in Britain with the American Civil War (1861–5), in part because it appeared to show how a society without the background of conscription could rapidly create an effective army. Army staff candidates being taught at Camberley were expected to study *Stonewall Jackson and the American Civil War* (1898; 3rd edn, 1902) by the

Professor of Military History, Colonel George Henderson (1843–1903), and to know the minutiae of Jackson's Shenandoah Valley campaign of 1862, in which a mobile Confederate force had outmanoeuvred and defeated larger Union forces, a lesson that was believed to be relevant to the British military which, because it did not have conscription but also had a large navy, would have a smaller force than Continental rivals. So also with the use of the Civil War in 1929 by Basil Liddell Hart, the leading British military commentator, in order to demonstrate his thesis of the value of the 'indirect approach to the enemy's economic and moral rear', and subsequently by J.F.C. Fuller, another British commentator.[7]

Trends, however, cannot account for the particular strengths and weaknesses of individuals in understanding the geographical context. These have existed from the outset, Julius Caesar presenting himself, notably in his *Gallic Wars*, as good at tactical and operational generalship; but are easier to discuss critically when biographical information is more plentiful and can more readily be applied as a result in discussion of particular generals, as with Napoleon, whose grasp of geography, however, proved highly inconsistent, being especially weak for Spain, or three prominent British generals in the late nineteenth and early twentieth centuries. Sir Frederick Roberts, later Earl Roberts, knew India inside out from the British perspective and, before going there, also had a knowledge of Afghanistan from his father, General Sir Abraham Roberts, an East India Company army general, who fought in the First Anglo-Afghan War of 1839–42, and, to a greater extent, from Henry Durand's history of that war. Durand's son Mortimer, who had put together the history, published in 1879, was, as Political Secretary at Kabul, with Roberts when he marched there in 1879 during the Second Anglo-Afghan War. This information was not just geographical in a physical sense, but also general as in the sectarian nature of particular tribes. Roberts, moreover, had Afghans working with him.

Herbert, Earl Kitchener had mapped parts of the Middle East, and his work was highly regarded. As a young officer, he scouted Sudan trying to open communications with General Gordon besieged in Khartoum in 1884–5. Kitchener's later Director of Military Intelligence, Lieutenant Colonel Reginald Wingate, had extensive knowledge of Sudan, partly from operations on the Sudan frontier and partly from prisoners escaped from the Mahdists, and, in 1899, was in command of the force that defeated the

Mahdists. In the First World War, Kitchener's strategic grasp, reflecting the linkage of different fronts, required geographical knowledge.

Henry, Lord Rawlinson, who was Commander-in-Chief in India in 1920–5, had read extensively about recent events in India and the fighting in Waziristan, which required background knowledge of terrain and roads, or of a lack of roads. He also read William Wilson Hunter's *A Brief History of the Indian Peoples*, chapter one of which outlined the geographical setting. Hunter was a Vice-President of the Royal Asiatic Society.

Knowledge related in large part to particular areas of strife, as for Britain with the North-West Frontier of British India. Kitchener's knowledge of the Middle East was less common. So also with the French army: whereas commanders in the early sixteenth century would be familiar with Italy, where the French frequently campaigned from 1494 to 1559, their counterparts from 1830 would more commonly have knowledge of Algeria. Although West Point devoted much attention to fortress architecture and gunnery, American officers in the nineteenth century tended to have knowledge of Native American warmaking and culture, and of how this interacted with the terrain and seasons.

Military knowledge about geography had its counterpart in geographical interest in war, which was far more pronounced in the nineteenth and early twentieth century than is the case now. Geographers gained much of their employment from the state, and the latter was frequently linked to military matters, not least as a result of imperial expansion as with the French in Algeria in the mid-nineteenth century, whereas now the state role is via higher education. Moreover, wartime in the case of the two world wars, saw a wholesale mobilisation of society that included geographers, one that was inherently competitive. This mobilisation was carried on in liberal societies during the Cold War. In comparison, their totalitarian counterparts, whether Nazi Germany or the Soviet Union, were apt to see everything, in both peace and war, as a branch of conflict, and treated geography accordingly. The idea of a geographical world free from such influences, not to say constraints, is one that is far less normative than its protagonists might suggest. The concern of Marquess Pombal, Portugal's leading minister, that mid-eighteenth-century French scientists in its leading colony, Brazil, were spies[8] was one that was expressed more insistently in the twentieth century as espionage was institutionalised. Furthermore, the assessment of the human environment as a landscape opened up to surveillance by aircraft and spaceships encouraged a resistance to such locational knowledge being enjoyed by potential opponents.

There were multiple linkages between geographical works and the military; and publications helped make these links normative. For example, the *Atlas physique, politique et historique de l'Europe* (1829) by Maxime-Auguste Denaix was published in Paris by a graduate of the École *Polytechnique* who had gone into the army before moving to the *Dépôt Général de la Guerre*. It was engraved by Richard Wahl, who had been trained at the *Dépôt Général*, and published under the sponsorship of the Vicomte de Caux, the Minister of War. By the time of the 1836 edition, which was published with the approval of Caux's successor as Minister of War, Denaix was head of the administration at the *Dépôt*. An important continuity in expertise had developed there, and comparable continuity looked toward the creation of General Staff systems. Cartography was the fundamental tool for planning by such systems, the maps important for a systematic process of effective and rapid decision-making, and for the implementation of strategic plans in terms of timed operational decisions and interrelated tactical actions.

Founded in 1816, the land survey section of the Prussian General Staff trained its officers in trigonometrical, topographical and cartographical skills, and all officers in the General Staff were expected to work there for several years. War games and manoeuvres required a knowledge of landscape. Prior to the attack in 1866, Moltke sent staff officers into Bohemia posing as landscape artists. They painted the fortress works at places like Königgrätz, and did the same sort of Intelligence work in France in 1870.

Other countries followed suit. In France, the Army Geographical Service established in 1887, had sections on geodesy, precision surveys, topography, cartography, the construction of relief models, and precise instrumentation. The Japanese army founded the Imperial Land Survey within the General Staff in 1888, German influence led the Turkish General Staff to create a cartographic section in 1895, and the Chinese Military Survey Institute followed in 1902.

In the world wars, there was a recruitment of geography for the cause of war as there had not been earlier to the same degree in wars in Europe, for example the Napoleonic Wars. Thus, in the First World

War, leading French geographers, Paul Vidal de la Blache, Emmanuel de Martonne, Albert Demangeon, Lucien Gallois, Emmanuel de Margerie and Louis Raveneau, were recruited into the *Commission de géographie* established in January 1915, to prepare, in concert with the Army Staff, material on the geography, both physical and human, of campaign areas.[9] For Britain, the Royal Geographical Society (RGS) played a significant role as a cartographic agency closely linked to the intelligence services, producing maps at the request of the government. In 1914, the RGS urgently addressed the tasks of producing an index of the place names on the large-scale maps of Belgium and France issued to the British officers sent there. In addition, a four-sheet wall map of Britain at the scale of 1:500,000 was produced in order to help the War Office plan home defence strategies in the event of a German invasion, which was feared in 1914. The RGS then pressed on to produce a map of Europe at the scale of 1:1 million. By the end of the war, more than ninety sheets had been prepared, covering most of Europe and the Middle East.[10] The Ordnance Survey and many commercial businesses also played a major role in British mapping.

The militarisation of information during the Second World War greatly involved geographers, as it had earlier done in the First World War. Indeed, from 1942 to 1945, the American government employed two out of every five geographers who were members of the three national geographical associations. Information was not only necessary in determining how to understand spatial relationships in the world, but also in assessing how best to produce the necessary *matériel*, and when it was likely to become available; and thus in turning conception into possibility.

For example, Armin Lobeck, who had worked in the Geography Section of the American Versailles delegation in 1919, going on to become a professor of geology at Columbia University, New York, was employed by the Military Intelligence Service of the General Staff and by the Army Map Service, and produced a set of topographic maps for Europe, as well, more specifically, as maps and diagrams in preparation for Operation Torch, the successful invasion of French North Africa in November 1942; for Operation Overlord, the invasion of Normandy in June 1944; and for an invasion of Fascist Spain if it was judged necessary, as was not in practice the case. Other works by Lobeck included *Southeastern Europe: Strategic Map of Climatic Types* (1943) for the Army

Map Service, and, with others, *Military Maps and Air Photographs: Their Use and Interpretation* (1944). One of his co-authors in this, John K. Wright, had brought out in 1941 (with other co-authors), *The European Possessions in the Caribbean area; a Compilation of Facts Concerning Their Population, Physical Geography, Resources, Industries, Trade, Government, and Strategic Importance.* Lobeck's *Geomorphology: An Introduction to the Study of Landscapes* (1939) was important in its use of scientific graphic representation, notably physiographic and block diagrams.[11]

The NGS was highly active during the war, both in creating maps, not least using new projections, such as the azimuthal equidistant projection, and in distributing them. In addition, the War Department ordered over one million maps from the NGS, while the NGS's Pacific map was widely used by military and civilian agencies, and that of Germany played a role in military planning.[12] American cartographers also played a role in planning new industrial capacity for military production; thus, they charted the best places for the new shipyards and for the inland manufacture of components, and took part in planning relevant road and rail links.

As the war became global, so it became more important to understand it accordingly, which the Americans and British did more successfully than the Germans and Japanese. Aside from the interest in globes, aerial views, and orthographic projections (a depiction as if from outer space), there were also concerns to improve cylindrical maps. Samuel Whittemore Boggs, the chief cartographer at the US State Department, commissioned Osborn Miller, the head of the Department of Technical Training of the American Geographical Society, to do so and he repositioned the Poles in the Mercator projection, providing a worldview similar to the latter, but with a reduced aerial distortion in polar regions, a change valuable as trans-Atlantic air movements became more common, with American aircraft flown to British bases. As a reminder that people and work are not in compartments, Miller, a British artillery officer in the First World War, was also an expert in the use of oblique air photos for making small-scale reconnaissance maps and published a contribution on 'Topographic Mapping from High Oblique Air Photographs' for the first *Manual of Photogrammetry* (1944).

Geologists were used extensively in order to understand and map terrain, both for military operations, as with German preparations for the planned invasion of Britain in 1940, and for utilising resources. Geologists of the Geological Survey of Great Britain provided advice on obtaining water and building materials for the military, and sand for sandbags, and also on underground storage opportunities. There was also reports by the Survey on mineral resources on the Continent as well as on dust storms in North Africa.[13] Such activity led directly into the extensive Cold War use of geographers and related specialists, for example oceanographers, by the competing powers. Repeatedly, geographical understanding, especially mapping, was important to planning for war.

Chapter 8

The Need to Map

The significance of geography is such that commanders require an understanding of mapping. For most of history, and still to this day, the relevant maps have overwhelmingly been mental maps, the understanding of place in the mind's eye, which were really means to help consideration and exposition. Thus, the plan of an ambush or a fort might be drawn with a stick, a finger in the earth (dirt) or in powdered sand, sketched in the air, or described with words. These methods did not leave records, written or otherwise, that survive, which is a crucial point when looking at the geography of war, and notably so for pre-modern warfare, with changing types of information apparently a key instance of modernity. Nevertheless, rather than being unfit for purpose, pre-modern armed forces carried out complex operations that would have required a foreknowledge of terrain, routes, climate and supply possibilities, and a reasonable assessment of timing.

How that knowledge was conveyed is less clear, but oral report was the key means. Thus, in Roman sources, although there are not references to the use of maps on campaigns, there are many references to scouts being sent out to learn about the locality, which suggests that an aural and visual approach to geography was employed, rather than a written system. So also more generally for ancient, medieval, and early-modern warfare. Reconnaissance was both about the terrain and concerning opposing moves, the two for long run together, whereas now the former is generally apparent in advance through the availability of maps, or, at least, many aspects of it and notably so of the physical terrain.

Oral report went on being significant in the last two centuries, but sometimes with disastrous effect, as during the Crimean War (1854–6), when, as a result of misunderstanding verbal orders, the cavalry of the British Light Brigade charged directly into Russian cannon at Balaclava in 1854, taking heavy casualties accordingly. Oral report was very differently used in the forward-control of artillery by spotters.

Any emphasis on mental mapping and oral report can lead to the conclusion that the alternative standard approach to war and cartography is teleological, in that it adopts a progressivist account, one predicated on the assumption that producing maps in physical copy is the desirable outcome and, indeed, a necessary means for war. Instead of this approach, a needs-based assessment to mapping is appropriate, one that considers the idea of fitness for purpose in terms of the maps, their formats, and their usage.

Such an approach, moreover, valuably complements that of considering the survival of artefacts, not least by asking what purpose is served. For maps in this context, there is the question not only of why they were retained, but, in particular, linked to that, their potential value on a recurrent and/or long-term basis, which is a crucial dimension of fitness for purpose. The military is especially focused on the question of usefulness.

So, indeed, with the issue of accuracy. That was not a fixed quantity, but again a relative one focused on use. Accuracy necessarily involves both effort and time, and, therefore an element of fitness for purpose. Therefore accuracy is dependent on the need, or rather varied needs, for mapping, as well as the opportunities that exist. Such a contextual approach provides the background to a consideration of the specifics of the subject.

First, and most obviously, not all places were, are, or will be, equal in coverage and significance. Indeed, that is a major difference between, on the one hand, the mapping of the world, in whole or part, and the use of such maps for war; and, in contrast, on the other hand, more specific and detailed mapping for particular military purposes. The latter process is integral to the point about places not being equal in mapping, in terms of which places are mapped, to what detail in both scale and content, and with what anticipated usage.

Linked to that issue comes that of purpose *and* timing, in particular the contrast between maps produced prior to the period of immediate need, and those arising from the latter, with all the relevant pressures of need, production, and timing. Indeed, in the second case, there was a collapsing of the distinction between map and photograph, with the photograph serving as a form of map, and for immediate tactical purposes. Thus, the trench maps of the First World War were substantially based on aerial photographs. This point underlines the difficulty of defining a map, but also, as a related point, the question of means versus ends in mapping.

Returning to the point that not all places are equal, sites to be fortified attracted particular attention for depiction, and, more especially, in order to plan how best to defend them. In this case, there was again an overlap with other forms of illustration, notably in the shape of diagrams and pictures. That contrast, however, although very important, was not as clear as might be presumed, as many maps included pictograms as devices. Moreover, some maps were simultaneously diagrammatic and pictorial; and each was regarded as enhancing the other. This was not only a characteristic of the past but can also be seen with the combination of views in some modern maps, for example for aircraft navigators.

At a very different scale, the degree of spatial understanding at the strategic level was increased from the ancient era by the spread, through trade, travel, conflict and other means, of interaction between societies. Thus, the major extensions of the world readily known to Western Classical commentators (thanks to the conquests of Alexander the Great and, later, the Romans, and to trade links between the Roman world and South Asia) provided geographers, such as Eratosthenes and Strabo, with much fresh material and ideas, the two frequently being linked. Eratosthenes (276–194 BCE), chief librarian at the Library of Alexandria, was the first to calculate the circumference of the Earth and the tilt of its axis, and created a grid system to help map it. Strabo (c. 63 BCE-23 CE) produced a descriptive geography. Geographical information was produced in the Ancient West in part in lists, in part in maps: a high proportion of early maps was in the form of linear itineraries and, therefore, lacked the measured space and coordinate geometries we now associate with mapping.

So also with China, where information obtained from Chinese overseas expeditions and from border wars fed into a long-established practice of assembling geographical material. Under the Han Dynasty (206 BCE-220 CE), there was an official dedicated to surveying in preparation for war. Chinese colonisation of steppe lands to the north and north-west, a colonisation closely linked to defence and forward-defence against nomadic attacks, relied heavily on an understanding of topography and invasion routes. Later, the Northern Song empire (960–1279 CE) accumulated, mapped and stored geographical information on the empire.

Subsequently, further west, the Ottoman Empire used frontier surveys to provide information on key frontier areas. The first, of the province of Buda, compiled in 1566 when Suleyman the Magnificent campaigned there, reflected the military sensitivity of the Hungarian frontier at a time of conflict with the neighbouring Habsburgs.

In Christian Europe, there were significant developments in mapping from the fifteenth century, notably the application of mathematical proportionality to the known world and, secondly, the impact of printing. The linear perspective mirrored cartography in its attempt to stabilise perception and make it more realistic. In both, there was an emphasis on accurate observation faithfully reproduced, and this was important to the presentation of terrain and other geographical features. Furthermore, the use of mathematics to order spatial relationships provided a visual record of measured space. In place of idealised and formulaic representations, came a desire for topographic specificity in the shape of an understanding and presentation of the distinctive.

The Western perception of geography was enhanced by advances in trigonometry and, critically, in the dissemination of practice and perception across a broad range, which were intertwined with a major change in the geographical imagination, in the shape of being able to consider the spatial dimension without necessarily seeing the physical object or being in that particular space. Maps were particularly significant as they presented knowledge at a distance, and did so in a fixed form and one that was readily understood by more than one observer and over a period of time, all of which were/are points crucial for military planning. A self-reinforcing linkage between learning and visualisation, on the one hand, and book- and map-learning on the other, was, in turn, made dynamic as the application of knowledge became a process responsive to changing information. Geography thus was precise, complex and dynamic. Improvements in map production further encouraged their use, notably woodblocks giving way to engraved copper plates, and the change from the screw press to the rolling press.

Peacetime preparation was an aspect of a desired wartime mastery of geography. Thus, under Henry IV of France in the 1600s, the *ingenieurs du roi* produced detailed manuscript maps of the major frontier provinces, one, Jean de Beins (1577–1651), who was also a fortification expert in the province of Dauphiné, drawing maps based on his surveys of the different valleys in the Alps which he then linked into a master map. These surveys revealed the value of the individual valleys as invasion routes into Italy and their vulnerability to attack from that direction.[1]

Developments in French mapping in the seventeenth century were a significant aspect of the relationship between geography and war. In the early years of the reign of Louis XIV (r. 1643–1715), before he took personal control of the government in 1661, military mapping was pretty basic: a few good sketches and ground plans were one-offs because of a particular siege during the war with Spain from 1635 to 1659, and were not part of a systematic programme, and, as a result, there was no comprehensive basis for consulting maps. In contrast, provincial officials were instructed in 1663 to send all available maps and geographical information to Paris, and these were then used by Nicolas Sanson, the Royal Geographer, to devise a series of maps of France. Moreover, a permanent collection of maps for military purposes, the *Dépôt de la Guerre*, was founded in 1688. The records of fortifications there included the *Recueil ds plans des places du roi* compiled in 1683–8.

Relief models of fortified towns were another form of conveying information, including on the impact, or at least input, of terrain and waterways. These models survive in Lille and Paris and indicate the tactical geography that was thereby offered. They were even cautiously displayed to foreign ambassadors as a means to deter foreign enemies. Relief models went on being used, for example by the British for the Western Front during the First World War,[2] and in the following world war.

In the case of Sweden, one of the most dynamic military powers of the period, the marked change in acquiring and displaying spatial information occurred between the sixteenth century and the first half of the seventeenth, with the start of military map-making and naval cartography, both by collecting maps and by the training of professional map-makers. The Swedish war archives contain a collection of maps from the Thirty Years War (1618–48), which Sweden under King Gustavus Adolphus entered in 1630, and from later, reflecting the army's need of maps for planning and information during operations in foreign countries. Furthermore, the National Land Survey of Sweden, which began in 1628, mapped not only Sweden at a large scale, but also lands occupied and annexed by the Swedes, such as Western Pomerania, thus providing a vital tool in planning defences.

By the eighteenth century, detailed information was more commonly used in Europe at the operational level to plan foraging and marches. Maps and staff planning both became more significant. Maps meant that commanders could move beyond experience and guesswork. Mapping projects were frequently focused on military needs, while the development of accurate and standard means of measuring distances made it easier for cartographers to understand, assess and reconcile the work of their predecessors, and the establishment and use of accurate values for longitude ensured that it became possible to locate most places accurately.

Maps also became more predictable as mapping conventions developed. Even at the end of the seventeenth century, there was no standard Western alignment of maps, which was an aspect of a more general lack of standardisation and, even, precision. However, in the eighteenth century, the convention of placing north at the top was established, while an increased awareness of cartographic distinctiveness and change encouraged the idea that maps could, and thereby should, improve and respond to new and more accurate information. The correct relative location of features was expected, as was accurate proportionality and keeping to scale. In addition, aside from specific improvements in mapping techniques and concepts, maps were increasingly created not only for particular purposes but also for general reference, a process that enhanced their use.

The military were the major source for mapping across much of Europe. The long-standing surveying and charting facilities and interests of Western armies and navies varied greatly, but proved very important in the eighteenth century. In terms of scale, comprehensiveness and accuracy, the surveys then were in a different class to those a century earlier.[3] Drawing on the cartographic traditions of their varied possessions, particularly Italy and the Austrian Netherlands (modern Belgium), the Austrians were especially prominent in this mapping, in their far flung possessions of Sicily, Lombardy, Austria, Bohemia, Hungary and the Austrian Netherlands. Ruling Sicily between 1720 and 1734, the Austrians employed army engineers to prepare the first detailed map of the island, while, as an aspect of Austrian defence preparations against Prussia, a major military survey of Bohemia (the western, major, part of the modern Czech Republic), already surveyed in 1712–18, was begun in the 1760s and completed in the 1780s; the Prussians had invaded

Bohemia in the 1740s, 1750s and 1770s, and were to do so again in 1866. In turn, Frederick II (the Great, r. 1740–86) of Prussia had his conquest from Austria of Silesia (now South-West Poland) mapped.

The resulting detail was often considerable. The maps of the Austrian Netherlands drawn up in 1771–4, supervised by Joseph-Johann-Franz, Count of Ferraris, the Director-General of the Artillery, were based on military surveys and comprised 275 leaves. At this stage, there was no equivalent in Britain and, had the Austrians remained in control of the region, instead of losing it to French invaders in 1792 and then lastingly in 1794, then this mapping might have established a tradition that enjoyed the prestige of the later (British) Ordnance Survey.

Military engineers from other countries were also important. In Piedmont, the *Ufficio degli Ingenieri Topografi* was founded in 1738 with four topographical engineers recruited.[4] Following the suppression of the 1745 Jacobite rebellion with William, Duke of Cumberland's crushing victory over 'Bonnie Prince Charlie', Charles Edward Stuart, and his Jacobite army, at Culloden in 1746, William Roy of the British Royal Engineers between 1747 and 1755 carried out a military survey of Scotland, which served as the basis for an accurate map. Six surveying parties were employed. The map was produced at a scale of one inch to 1,000. The survey and maps were designed to help in the military response to any future rebellion, and to assist in the process of the governmental reorganisation of the Highlands. This was a key aspect of a longer term extension of central control that included roadbuilding and the establishment of fortified positions, notably Fort Augustus, Fort William, Ruthven Barracks, and the still-impressive Fort George near Inverness.[5]

Moreover, the French military engineers of the period, especially Pierre Bourcet (1700–1780), who rose to be a general, tackled the problems of mapping mountains, creating, as a result, a clearer idea of what the Alpine frontier looked like. His work on the Alps was continued by Jean Le Michaud d'Arçon (1733–1800), a general geographer and military commentator. The mapping helped the French Revolutionary forces in their successful campaigns there in the 1790s, notably those of Napoleon, although this mapping does not itself explain why the French were more successful than in the 1740s when they had last contested this area. Bourcet also mapped Corsica, as part of the brutal imposition of French control there in the face of a bitter rebellion in 1768–70 after the island was purchased from Genoa in 1768. Success in overcoming this rebellion, a process demonstrating the far greater resources of the French monarchy, ensured that Napoleon was born a French subject in 1769. He was to be an enthusiastic commissioner and user of maps which he regarded as a necessary operational tool. In 1809, Napoleon created an Imperial Corps of Surveyors with a staff of ninety, and, in his very frequent criticisms of his subordinates, he often commented that they would see the error of their ways if they simply looked at a map.[6]

War repeatedly led to an increased demand for geographical information, and at a number of levels. Thus, the silk maps printed for military use in northern Italy at the Milanese press of Marc' Antonio Del Re in the 1730s and 1740s, during the Wars of the Polish (1733–5) and Austrian (1740–8) Successions, for example *Italiae Septentrionalis* (1735) and *Nuova Carta Corografica, o sia centro del gran teatro di Guerra in Piemonte Savoia l'anno 1744* (1744), were very useful for route planning. In his *Pensées sur la Tactique, et la Stratégique* (1778), the Marquis Da Silva, a key Piedmontese military thinker, pointed out, however, that, because maps could be defective, generals still needed to gain personal knowledge of the terrain.

In Britain, the Trigonometrical, later called Ordnance, Survey, began in 1791, the year in which the Corps of Royal Military Surveyors and Draughtsmen was founded. A double chain of triangles was completed from London to Land's End by 1795, and a one-inch-to-the-mile map of Kent, a key potential invasion area, published in 1801. After 1801, the surveyors moved to the south-west of England, another likely area for possible French invasion, which was covered by about 1810.[7]

Geographical knowledge, notably maps, were in much demand for the annual training manoeuvres of conscripts and reservists that were increasingly significant in Europe in the late nineteenth century, as preparations were made for war.[8] There was consideration as to how best to present cartographic information to help military planning and operations including discussion about how much information to convey. The influential Baker Committee on the Military Map of the United Kingdom reported in 1892 in favour of coloured maps, with contours, road classification and the use of symbols, and not names, in order to achieve less clutter.[9] These methods became more common as uniform maps that were readily understandable and thus useful were required. So also with charts at sea, with navies again playing a key role. For the United States, as for many other states, the nineteenth century proved a crucial period in the development of surveying, map production, and ocean charting.[10]

In turn, the twentieth century was also crucial. Although trigonometry is an ancient branch of mathematics, its refinements, such as the retriangulation of Britain in the 1930s, and, more recently, digital mapping have enabled the production of more accurate maps permitting more precise targeting of enemy installations.

The world wars saw a particular need for mapping. That of the Second World War, on which see also Chapter 12, looked also to the post-1945 situation, not least due to the significance then of air power and the role of the United States. As a response to the outbreak of war in Europe in 1939, the Army's Map Section was expanded prior to American entry into the war in December 1941. This section was responsible for the Air Corps as well as for land operations, and efforts were made to extend its geographical coverage, a process accelerated by a survey of the existing situation which suggested that only a tenth of the world had been adequately covered, and that some of this coverage was out-of-date, which was indeed the case. In 1941, again prior to the war, work began on aeronautical charts for the Americas, long-range charts for the world, and then planning charts for the world at 1:5 million, and charts at the same scale for presenting meteorological data.

Aside from producing new maps, the lack or limitations of available information could greatly enhance the value of purchasing and capturing maps. German preparations for an invasion of Britain in 1940 included large-scale town plans marked with strategic locations, and copies of Ordnance Survey maps, with overprints highlighting sites which were targets, the shoreline marked in terms of cliff, sand, steep and flat, and photographs to help with selected invasion beaches; yet another instance both of the value of a variety of perspectives and of the significance of photography for mapping. In 1941, the Germans systematically looted the Yugoslavian Military Geographic Institute, and also benefited in the early stages of Operation Barbarossa, the invasion of the Soviet Union launched that June, from the capture of the Minsk, Kiev and Kharkov map factories.

In response, the Soviet Union moved fast to complete the 1:100,000 map of the state west of the River Volga, the area exposed to German attack, a task that entailed 200 new sheets and that was completed by the end of 1941, a major achievement in a short period of time. Moreover, the Red Army developed a flexible production system in which maps were prepared and printed in order to meet immediate operational needs, which entailed the overprinting of maps with specific tactical information. Underpinning this activity for the Soviet Union was a more general attempt to improve the training for mapmaking and the production of maps, including the introduction of a uniform geodetic (coordinate) system.

Even more than with the usual military cartography, secrecy was at the heart of mapping for war, and, aside from producing their own maps, governments also restricted the distribution of existing and new maps that might help enemies. Thus, the United States restricted topographic maps produced by the Geological Survey, as well as the nautical charts created by the Coast and Geodetic Survey. Partly-justified claims that the Germans had used Soviet maps in their invasion greatly affected access to the latter in the Soviet Union. Moreover, information on industrial activity in those maps that came into use was restricted. Conversely, espionage often focused on gaining access to secret plans and maps.

An important element of the strategic nature of mapmaking was provided by alliance co-operation. Thus, in 1942, under the Loper-Hotine Agreement, named after those responsible, the American Army Map Service was given full responsibility for mapping the Americas, Australasia, the Pacific, Japan, the West Indies, and the North Atlantic; and the British for the rest. This allocation accorded with the systems the British had already in place for overseas production, most significantly centres in Egypt and India. As during the First World War, the Survey of India extended its activities beyond the British Empire. The Survey was given the task of mapping Iraq, Iran, Afghanistan, Burma (Myanmar), Thailand, French Indochina, China, Malaya (Malaysia), and Sumatra, with most sections under direct military command, and air surveying, which was a means to acquire information about hostile territory and to map at speed, increased.

As part of a broader pattern of co-operation, the Geographical Section of the British General Staff and the American Army Map

Service exchanged map and geodetic material. The interoperability of geographical information between allies was a major requirement. The Western Allies also initiated the World Aeronautical Chart, a 1:1 million scale map series using the Lambert conformal conic projection which provides maps on which straight lines approximate to a great-circle route between endpoints.

The British and Americans, moreover, used the maps already produced by the cartographic agencies of European states, the British Geographical Section of the General Staff and the American Army Map Service, in their topographic maps, seeking to homogenise different mathematical base data and geographical contents from the numerous source maps, sorting out the complications of name spellings, and bringing the maps up to date in order to increase their reliability and usefulness.[11]

By the 1940s, mapmaking for war had to engage with land, sea and air across much of the world, and was not only reactive to specific requirements but also proactive in the sense of where it might be necessary to operate. This very much remained the situation in the post-war world, on which see Chapter 13.

Chapter 9

American Wars, 1754–1865

Trans-oceanic campaigning was not common prior to the sixteenth century. The Ming Chinese naval expeditions did so in the Indian Ocean in the early fifteenth century, but, thereafter, China did not, although the situation would change considerably in forthcoming years. Instead, with the exception of some Ottoman sixteenth-century operations in the Indian Ocean, such campaigning was as matter of Western European activity. Portugal and Spain were the key powers in early expansion, but the entry of other European forces from the mid-sixteenth century increased trans-oceanic conflict. The war between Portugal and the Dutch in the South Atlantic from 1602 to 1654, especially from 1630 to 1654, was the major instance, but, from the 1750s, there was a greater emphasis on trans-oceanic campaigning, with Britain and France in conflict from 1754 in North America. There the operational theatre in 1754–60 spanned from Cape Breton Island to the Ohio Valley, with the Lake Champlain corridor between Canada and the Hudson an important invasion route, alongside the maritime route into the St Lawrence.[1]

In a way that is well-nigh inconceivable today, British and French forces had to traverse vast distances, often through wild, inhospitable terrain. This made large armies vulnerable, as with the British advance on Fort Duquesne in 1755, to enemy tactics of *petite guerre*, by which small, highly-mobile detachments carried out fleeting attacks and ambushes on the flanks of their larger adversary. Commanders therefore required maps that both gave an account of routes and terrain suitable for planning and which conveyed very practical knowledge that would allow their forces to move quickly without being over-exposed to enemy action.

They accordingly ordered the preparation of both reconnaissance and route maps. The former involved the rapid production of information, and the resulting maps were generally crude. For example, in February 1775, just weeks before the battles of Lexington and Concord on 19 April launched the War of American Independence (1775–83), General Thomas Gage, the British Commander-in-Chief, North America, dispatched two amateur surveyors to reconnoitre the countryside around Boston which was the key British garrison point and the centre of political contention.

Route maps, which were of more particular significance, were usually executed by professional military surveyors. While they may have incorporated intelligence gleaned from reconnaissance maps, these maps laid out specific routes for the army to take, often also drawing on information from (sometimes already existing) topographical surveys conducted under scientific conditions. This mapping was frequently undertaken with specific reference to an intended itinerary, and considered both the desired daily progress and the most appropriate sites for encampments and for the resupply of the force. As a result, an accurate and formal detailing of distances and features of the landscape was crucial. In October 1760, the highly talented Lieutenant Colonel James Montresor wrote to General Jeffrey Amherst, the British Commander-in-Chief, North America, a master of planned, methodical campaigning:

'I think it my duty to acquaint your Excellency that I have got in great forwardness a general map of that part of North America which has been the seat of war wherein is distinguished the roads that have been made by the troops, the navigation of its rivers, its carrying places, the new forts and posts constructed, the several hospitals, barracks and buildings for the soldiers, the marches of the army, the places where have been engagements, attacks, sieges and camps, interspersed with useful remarks. The most part laid down by actual surveys with geographical and military observations made in that country from the year 1754 to 1760. As this map will show at one view what has been done in that country, I hope that it will be very acceptable, as well to the ministry as to the military, as your Excellency's march from Albany to Montreal, and Brigadier General Murray's from Quebec is only wanting to complete it.'[2]

Montresor sought information on the details of these successful advances earlier in 1760 while Amherst himself collected maps. Montresor's career showed the significance of British imperial conflict and expansion for cartography, and the central role of military appointments in this context. His father, James Montresor, a French Protestant, had served in the British army, eventually as Lieutenant Governor of Fort William in Scotland. James Montresor himself (1702–76) served in the army before becoming a practitioner-engineer, gaining a reputation as a draughtsman. Having served at Gibraltar and Minorca, he became Chief Engineer at Gibraltar in 1747. From 1747 to 1752, Montresor produced twenty-six plans of various parts of Gibraltar's defence works, with sections of the fortress and barracks of Gibraltar and of the Spanish lines and forts. In 1753, he produced a plan of the fortifications. Montresor became Chief Engineer of the Braddock expedition on Fort Duquesne in 1755. After its disastrous defeat, Montresor prepared plans and projects, surveying and mapping part of Lake Champlain, a key area of operations where the British finally succeeded in 1760 after initial failure in 1758. Becoming Director of the Royal Engineers in 1758, Montresor played a leading role in operations until 1760.

In turn, Montresor's eldest son, John, a lieutenant, serving with his father on a frequent pattern, was wounded on Braddock's expedition in 1755. In 1758, he became a practitioner engineer, before constructing a chain of redoubts near Niagara in 1764 and producing linked plans. Montresor was appointed Chief Engineer in America in 1775 and constructed the defence lines near Philadelphia in 1777–8 after it was captured in 1777 by General William Howe following the British victory at Brandywine. From this stage of his career, Montresor produced plans of Boston, New York, and the battle of Bunker Hill in 1775.

The scale of operations in the War of American Independence was less extensive than might seem because, and, notably prior to 1780, most occurred within areas of significant settlement or relatively close to them. Nevertheless, there were problems in assessing the practicalities of campaigning both within and outside these areas. Whether or not accompanied by maps, or by maps that have survived, the planning of itineraries was a key element of military activity. Perhaps the finest set of route maps produced during the century were those by the Comte de Rochambeau's engineers that painstakingly charted the route of the French army from their American base at Newport, Rhode Island to attack that of a British army at Yorktown, Virginia in 1781, a significant distance.[3] This carefully-chosen route afforded the army the speed and stealth which allowed it to arrive at its objective at an ideally opportune moment, while avoiding British detection. As a result, George Washington was able to bring overwhelming force to bear against the British under Lieutenant General Charles, 2nd Earl Cornwallis at Yorktown, and, under heavy pressure on land and without the prospects of evacuation by sea, the besieged Cornwallis was forced to surrender.

In this case, the geography of British maritime-based power-projection had been temporarily trumped by a concentration of Franco-American forces; but such a temporary trumping was all that was required. In this combination, the French navy played a key role, as it ended, temporarily, the British advantage Washington had noted in August 1777 when commenting on the British army then sailing under General Sir William Howe from Staten Island towards the Chesapeake:

> 'They have stood out to sea again, but how far, or where, they are going remains to be known. From their entire command of the water they derive immense advantages, and distress us much by harassing and marching our troops from post to post. I wish we could fix on their destination. In such case, I should hope we would be prepared to receive them.'[4]

Whereas, in the nineteenth century, British naval capability was to lead to a heavy emphasis in the United States on coastal fortifications in doctrine, force structure and allocation, and expenditure, the military geography was very different during the War of Independence. There was then no equivalent network of forts, while those that existed, such as Fort Washington near New York, were in practice a source of vulnerability, as they fixed garrisons, which also happened for the Americans with Charleston in 1780. To win, the British had to force defeat on the Americans, and sieges provided them with an apparent means to do so. In the event, the fall of Charleston did not bring the British sufficient regional control to provide a safe area from which to further counter-revolution.

Once the Thirteen Colonies forced recognition of their independence in 1783, their geopolitical situation in North America was key to their expansion, and not simply the opportunities provided by the physical geography. The disunity of Native Americans was crucial, but so also was the extent to which in the foundational early decades they enjoyed only limited support from Britain and Spain. Yet the limited number of American regular troops meant that there were insufficient forces for any widespread garrison policy. Indeed, garrisons could only work as part of an expansionist policy if they were accompanied by the 'pacification' of areas brought under control earlier in order to provide operational and strategic depth for fresh advances. If not, expansion simply brought the need for more garrisons.

The War of 1812 with Britain (in fact 1812–15) was the key conflict in this period. It was fought across a range of regions each with very different physical and human geographies, from the Canadian frontier to the Atlantic coast, and the Gulf coast to the interior conflicts with Native Americans. Both the last and the Canadian frontier, especially to the west, were not well-known, other than by local people. During that war, the geography pressed on both sides hard in terms of the frictions of climate, communications and logistics.[5]

The War of 1812 was followed by a process of strategic fortification designed as a pro-active response to vulnerability, with the perception of risk focused on Britain, and not on Native Americans. The latter were to bulk large in the public memorialisation of American strategic geography in the shape of the conquest of the West, one frequently presented as relatively more difficult for the Americans than in practice it generally was. However, this memorialisation of a past geography of war left out the landscape of potential in the shape of possible conflict with Britain, which dominated the defence budget in the shape of the construction of coastal fortresses. The firepower required to stop attacking ships entering ports was formidable. Eased relations with Britain in the 1850s and, even more, from 1871, led, however, to a different priority.

As far as the American interior was concerned, environmental factors were important, notably in permitting rapid expansion, which, in turn, provided geopolitical advantage. Furthermore, moving from the forests of the east into the Great Plains, and developing mounted forces for operations there, permitted a lower density in fortifications than would otherwise have been necessary when the reliance had been on infantry columns. This lower density was also related to the scale of the area that had to be covered, while there was not the clear pattern of routes to be protected provided by river valleys and passes through wooded regions and uplands further east.

The admission of Texas to the United States in 1846, and then the Mexican-American War (1846–8), an expeditionary conflict not waged in the United States, were followed by a major extension of the fortification imprint.[6] This was not a matter of random building, as the forts reflected a series of politico-strategic objectives, including the needs of settlers for reassurance. In contrast, the War Department preferred to see troops concentrated in large forces, which was regarded as the best way to maintain discipline and training in the army, and also to intimidate opponents. In practice, the forts were not so much defence-focused as mustering points for offensive campaigns against Native homelands, although the strategic, operational and tactical geographies were such that both roles played a role, as did that of reassurance.[7]

During the American Civil War (1861–5), there were the usual contextual geographical issues, including the impact of resources, climate, weather, topography and cover, on military potential and moves. There was also the influence of conflict on the environment, both human and physical.[8] Command responses were an aspect of the contextual impact. Poor planning, an inability to implement plans, especially the coordination of units and the interaction of moves with a planned time sequence, repeatedly emerged. They had a particularly serious impact on offensive operations as it made it difficult for units to provide adequate levels of mutual support, a flaw readily apparent in Union conduct at the battle of Antietam in 1862. The field commanders on both sides were seriously hampered at the outset by a shortage of adequate maps, which contributed to the 'loose command arrangements'.[9] Commanders sought to use maps for strategic, operational and tactical reasons, not least for devising overall strategy and because of the scale of operations, the need to coordinate and move forces over considerable distances, within and between individual campaigns, the unfamiliarity of much of the terrain, and the need for detail.

Aside from at the level of campaigns, the scale of battle was such that it was no longer sufficient, tactically, to rely completely on the field of vision of an individual commander and his ability to send instructions during the course of the engagement. Instead, it was necessary to plan far more in advance, especially so in preparing artillery positions, in mounting and responding to frontal attack, and in coordinating attacks from a number of directions. It was also necessary to understand terrain in order to control and use it. Specific factors brought this to the fore, notably the interplay of rail links and field operations, and the best use of water routes. At a more detailed level, the heavily-wooded nature of much of the terrain posed a particular problem for the understanding of battles as they developed, most prominently with the Wilderness in northern Virginia in 1864. At the same time, that situation did not dictate an outcome but, rather, made it harder to control the flow of a battle and thus ensure that numbers would have a decisive impact. Skills in combat and command were therefore even more significant.[10]

The Union forces had a particular need for maps as they were advancing south into the Confederacy, with which they were not familiar, and also seeking to make best use of their more numerous reserves. Tasking and needs drove mapping. Commercial cartography, however, could not produce sufficient maps. As a result, the Confederate and Union armies turned to establishing their own map supplies. By 1864, the Coast Survey and the Corps of Engineers were providing about 43,000 printed maps annually for the Union army. The production of standard copies was crucial given the scale of operations and lithographic presses produced multiple copies of maps rapidly. Surveyors and cartographers were recruited for the military. In 1864, the Union's Coast Survey produced a uniform ten-mile-to-the-inch base map of most of the Confederacy east of the Mississippi. The scale and detail was very different to the mapping of the 1750s.[11]

The geography of the war was changed by rail, but more particularly at the organisational (especially logistical), strategic and operational levels, than at the tactical one.[12] Indeed, the role of railheads, such as Marietta, Georgia, near Atlanta, indicated the interaction of very different transport capabilities at operational and tactical levels.

At the strategic level, geography set the basic parameters in terms of which states seceded, and notably among what became the borderland states. The defection of the Upper South from the Union was crucial: Virginia, Tennessee, and North Carolina were each more important in economic and demographic terms than any state in the Confederacy, while it became easier to think of the Confederacy as a bloc of territory that could be defended in a coherent fashion, and that therefore required a coherent strategy in order to bring it down. The secession of Virginia and North Carolina in particular greatly altered the location of the likely field of operations in the east, pushing it far northwards. However, in turn, the Union being able to retain Delaware, Maryland, Kentucky, Missouri, and what became West Virginia, blocked invasion routes into the north, and exposed the South, notably Virginia and Tennessee, to attack. Because Maryland stayed in the Union, the central battleground lay between the two capitals, heavily-fortified Washington and Richmond, which helped give a geographical focus to the conflict, cut across the potential expansiveness derived from the scale of the Confederacy, an area of more than 750,000 square miles, and held out the possibility of a quick end to the war, one, however, thwarted by Union failure at the battle of First Bull Run in 1861.

Because the war continued, it was necessary to reconcile the conflict west and east of the Appalachians and, within each, in turn, to deal with competing priorities. Despite the presence of the capitals, there was no geographical determinism, and indeed the Eastern Theatre became important in part due to the role of the commanders there, notably the influence of Major General George B. McClellan in 1861–2 as both commander of the Union's largest field army and overall strategic director. The possibility of amphibious attack, however, suggested a significance for the Eastern Theatre that was not brought to fruition due to the failure of the Union's Peninsula Campaign in 1862, a failure both to take Richmond, the vulnerable Confederate capital, and to fix the Confederate forces.

Further west, there was a very different force-space ratio, with the resulting requirements and opportunities, notably for mobility. Rivers, such as the Mississippi and the Tennessee, provided invasion routes, but did not ensure success. The latter was clearly shown with the Union's ability to capture New Orleans and move northwards up the Mississippi, and also take other coastal positions, but, repeatedly, not then find exploitation easy. More positively, the Union, strengthened the blockade by coastal expeditions, obliged the Confederacy to fight a two-front war in the Western Theatre, and strangled the essential overseas trade in cotton.

Yet, as a reminder of the difficulty of evaluating strategic choices and consequences, and thus geographical factors, the lack of an effective integration of expeditionary operations within the larger context of Union grand strategy can be regarded as mistaken and as helping commit the Union to a lengthy war of attrition in Virginia;[13] one that exposed it to the risk that war-weariness would lead to a change in leadership and policy in the 1864 Presidential election. Abraham Lincoln was concerned about this possibility.

The focus on Virginia in the end forced the Confederates, with their northward advances checked in 1862, 1863 and 1864, onto the defensive. Here, although trench warfare developed near Petersburg in 1864–5, part of a more general significance for field fortifications in the war,[14] there was no equivalent to the First World War, as the battlespace and the force-space ratio were both very different to the Western Front. As a reminder of the need to understand geographical contrasts, the Atlantic in the Civil War did not act like the English Channel in the First World War was to do, as Union forces were able to mount amphibious assaults beyond the front line. However, these assaults did not provide a war-winning capability on the Virginia Front. On the other flank there was no equivalent of the relatively short distance to neutral Switzerland, but instead land to beyond the Mississippi. Yet the Appalachians provided a marker for that particular battlefront. Comparisons and contrasts can be made between the Civil War and other conflicts, but the geography of individual wars proved highly specific, in both physical and human terms.

Turning away from the Civil War, Americans did not tend to see their expansion as imperialism, but the British academic Hereford George noted the significance of population density as a key geographical factor, writing of the Americans and Canadians having 'before them the prospect of indefinite expansion, at the cost of getting rid of the aborigines, thinly scattered over the whole area, whom they were neither able nor desirous to convert into slaves'.[15] The institutional framework for mapping America was provided by the army's Corps of Topographical Engineers, which was created in 1838 when the Topographical Bureau was expanded and organised under army control. The Topographical Corps played an important role in providing maps for the war with Mexico (1846–8) as well as in the exploration and mapping of the West. Military surveyors used native maps and geographical information, but only to a limited extent. They were concerned to locate, understand and utilise the lands they surveyed in the context of an expanding state. Localities acquired meaning with reference to the project.[16] Force was a powerful factor in this mapping. In 1849, James Simpson's exploration and mapping of what was to be north-western New Mexico and north-eastern Arizona was undertaken as part of the punitive expedition against the Navajo by John

Washington, the Governor of New Mexico. Simpson was able to explore the Canyon de Chelly only after Washington had overawed them.

This pattern was more generally the case in the American West. The ability of Native Americans to use the often difficult terrain, notably the Seminole in waterlogged Florida, and their effective fighting practices,[17] were countered by winning allies, fortification and the overcoming of the environment. The latter included winter campaigning, as in late 1868 in north Texas. Mounted infantry provided both mobility and firepower. This was also the case with other areas of imperial activity, for example for the British in southern Africa, as with the Bechuanaland Field Force.

Returning to the United States, not only the Native Americans posed a problem. Concern about the possibility of war with the Mormons in Utah in 1858–9 led to efforts to find first a river route to the Great Basin via the Colorado River and then to explore the route from Santa Fé. In the first attempt, the prefabricated paddle steamer USS *Explorer* rapidly fell victim to the rocky bed of the Colorado River. However, Lieutenant Joseph Ives led the expedition up the Colorado and, via the Grand Canyon, to the Painted Desert and then Fort Defiance. The army also played a major role in developing transport links to the West. Thus, in the 1850s, the American presence in Minnesota was consolidated by a network of roads which were surveyed and built through the War Department. Railways served for military purposes, settlement and economic integration. It was not only through war that the military played a key role in the development of the United States. Instead, it was more generally significant in the relationship between the land and its use.

Chapter 10

Geography and Empire

'[T]hey had now to deal with a foe capable of bursting through the great mountain barriers in which they put their trust, and of violating the integrity of territory which they believe to be incapable of access by organised troops... For the enemy had learned that an Anglo-Indian army could force its way into these fastnesses, could seize their crops, destroy their defences, burn their villages, and could, after making its presence felt in every ravine and nook, get out again; and that settled the matter.'[1]

C harles Callwell (1859–1928), a very talented British officer, in his *Small Wars: Their Principles and Practice* (1896), captured the determination of imperialism to control geography and, in particular, to overturn the limits that might seem to be defined by physical features, and to use harsh measures to that end. Callwell had served in the Second Anglo-Afghan War (1878–80) and the First Boer War (1881), the former very difficult for Britain and the latter a failure. It is not surprising that, in seeking to overturn geographical limits, he, and the army as a whole, therefore adopted assumptions about need and prudence, assumptions that were military-political, a term employed to indicate the extent to which these two elements should not be distinguished.[2] Callwell's work achieved widespread recognition, and that was to be renewed in the 1990s, with a new edition in 1996, because it was to be seen as a guide to asymmetric warfare. Callwell went on to serve in the Boer War of 1899–1902 and in 1902–7 as Assistant Director of Military Operations, going on to be Director in 1914–15 and a Major General. In an instructive critique of many assumptions, Callwell saw the need for strength on both land and sea, and for co-operation between them.[3]

Geography came to the fore with empire, as occupation, preservation and rule all posed major requirements: for conquest, for maintaining power in the face of opposition, and for giving a shape to the territories over which sovereignty was asserted and enforced. This shape, both understanding and organisation, was a matter and process of knowledge, physical and human, as well as a response to it, not least in terms of the interplay of the two.[4] Thus, in 1849, James, 1st Marquess of Dalhousie, the Governor-General of India, argued, with reference to the North-West Frontier of (British) India (now of Pakistan), where he was pressing for punitive raids:

> 'with a population so long inclined to turbulence as the border tribes, and so little accustomed to show submission to any of the governments under which they have successively passed, I conceive that we must be prepared to expect from time to time risings among the tribes over whom our rule has been proclaimed, and plundering inroads by those which lie close to our frontiers.'[5]

This was the area about which Callwell was to write, and also Winston Churchill in his *The Story of the Malakand Field Force: An Episode of Frontier War* (1898), which described an episode the previous year.

Similar challenges were faced by non-Western empires,[6] and not only in frontier areas. Thus, the distribution of garrisons is a key instance of geography, one studied for imperial powers from Ancient Rome to modern America. In the case of China in the late seventeenth century, the Emperors regarded their Bannermen, a major element of the regular forces, as more reliable than their more numerous and recent Han Chinese Green Standard troops. The Bannermen, who included Manchus, Mongols and Chinese, were stationed in northern China, around the centre of authority, Beijing, and down to the River Yangzi, and the garrisons lived in segregated walled compounds, an important geography of immediate location that kept them separate from the local population and their sympathisers. The first permanent Banner garrison was not established in the south-west (below the Yangzi) until 1718, and this development reflected the severity of the crisis for China caused by the conquest of Tibet in 1717 by the Zunghars of Xinjiang, and the Chinese failure in 1718 to drive them out. The Green Standard troops were stationed all over the country, but with many in the south. There was also a difference in function, with the Green Standard troops focusing on dealing with rebellions, while the Bannermen, preponderantly cavalry, were the vital troops in confronting challenges from the steppe, and did not have a tradition of infantry warfare. Similar geographies can be seen elsewhere, including in garrison locations[7] and in command patterns. Such patterns cross-cut with others, from ethnic, factional and institutional links, to career patterns based on particular skills, for example cavalry skills.

Imperial military activity owed much to the determination of potential combatants to fight. For example, in the case of China, the Kangxi (r. 1661–1722) and Qianlong (r. 1735–96) emperors put much more of an effort into overcoming the Zunghar challenge on the steppe than into expanding into south-east Asia. Environmental factors played a role in this choice, not least the distance from Beijing to the latter, but greater significance rested on the steppe origin and identity of the Manchu dynasty and on the significance to it of the struggle with the Zunghars over the Khalka (eastern) Mongols. At the same time, there was a repeated determination by the Chinese to control indigenous people, not least in borderland areas, and there was military activity accordingly.[8]

The history of empires suggested that there were no necessary geographical limits to them. This was very much the case with India, as some empires based in the north of India ranged much more widely, but others did not. The key contrast was political. Thus in Mughal India from the 1710s, the viceroys of the Deccan and Oudh became autonomous and were not to be brought back under its control. The earlier centralising policy of Aurangzeb (r.1658–1707) had alienated many of the key groups, and they did not rally to the throne as the Mughal empire, came to face potent challenges.

For all empires, adaptation could help in facing the challenges of the environment, both physical and human. Fortifications were a classic means to do so, providing security, in resources and protection, against the physical and human environments. Thus, creating a new geography, the Russians constructed fortified lines both to provide a way to establish themselves on the steppe and so as to thwart the large-scale northward raiding attacks by the Crimean Tartars. The construction of successive lines, such as the Belgorod Line (1635–53) from Akhtyrka to Tambor, each farther south, also provided a way to consolidate and demonstrate the Russian position in the steppes. Thus defensive lines served as a substitute for natural features when, as in the steppe, they were not available, and acted to even the situation with attacking cavalry, and helped elicit consent through intimidation.

Very differently adaptation was shown in 1761–6 when the Dutch in coastal Ceylon (Sri Lanka) fought the interior kingdom of Kandy which, earlier, had successfully seen off the Portuguese in 1594–1621 and 1638. Columns sent out against the capital, Kandy, in 1764 were unsuccessful due to disease, difficult jungle terrain, heat, humidity, an absence of maps, and effective guerrilla opposition. In contrast, in 1765, the Dutch replaced swords and bayonets with less cumbersome machetes, provided troops with a more practical uniform as well as new maps, and moved fast which helped lessen the impact of disease. The Dutch captured the deserted capital, but the Kandyans both refused to engage in battle and sapped the Dutch with raids, leading the Dutch in 1766 to agree a peace that did not leave them in control of the interior. At the same time, as with the Portuguese, this was a case of Dutch forces in Kandy, and not vice versa. So also with the British, both when unsuccessful against Kandy in 1803 and when definitively victorious in 1815.

Adaptation was found across the range of activity. For example, it was shown in the building material used for fortifications, as with the emphasis on timber, stone or other materials. More generally, fortification was a cross-cultural phenomenon, but with many geographical variations, reflecting both the human and the political environment. Thus, Spanish fortresses in Florida, such as *Castillo de San Marcos* in St Augustine, built in 1672–95, were constructed of a concrete-like mixture made up primarily of oyster shells.

The amphibious range of Western powers, in the shape of the distance across which effective amphibious operations could be mounted, was significant, both in terms of capability and in meaning that there had to be adaptation. Combined, for example, with the island nature of the Philippines, this capability helped ensure that having established, from their colony Mexico, a base on Cebu in 1565, the Spaniards by 1573 were in control there, as well as in the islands of Leyte, Panyam, Mindoro and the central plain of Luzon. Yet far more than geography was at stake. There was no powerful political entity able to mobilise resistance in the Philippines, the nature of local fortifications were limited, and cultural assimilation was aided by the animist nature of local religion, and the willingness of Spain to encourage effective Christian missionary activity.

In the First Anglo-Burmese war in 1824–6, the British also displayed amphibious range and effectiveness. They did not need to fight only in the difficult jungles of the frontier zone, instead, in 1824, capturing Rangoon with a force sent from the Andaman Islands. In 1824–5, the British launched successful amphibious attacks on targets in the region of Tenasserim, and, in 1825–6, successfully advanced up the Irrawaddy River to Mandalay, just as, in 1842, a British force was to advance successfully up the Yangzi River to Nanjing.

However, terrain away from coasts and rivers proved more difficult. The physical environment there was the battleground of two rival human environments. Native resistance could be most effective when it was practised by apparently 'primitive' peoples using dispersed warfare; not possibly or probably (and the distinction is significant) as a consequence of deep reasoning, but because they were skilled in hunting. Such techniques were successful in frustrating more sophisticated, cohesive and concentrated European formations, although more infrequently beating them. If the peoples were nomadic or had scattered settlements, they obviously presented the Europeans with fewer or poorer fixed assets to threaten, no central target to defeat or conquer, and opposing forces that were difficult to fix, a situation that faced the Americans in the Philippines in the early 1900s, and encouraged their use of harsh policies in suppressing resistance. The British in India found this as a fundamental problem: the more sophisticated 'civilized' peoples were easier to conquer than the 'primitives'. However, the latter too were eventually generally 'contained' or 'controlled,' if it was worthwhile for the Westerners, those words reflecting the norms of the imperial power.

Lieutenant Colonel Frederick Lister complained in 1850 of resistance in the India-Burma borderland in the 'Chin Hills': 'the facilities which their jungles afford, both in materials and position, for throwing obstacles in the way of an advance or retreat'.[9] Lieutenant Hugh Pearce Pearson, who wrote in 1858 that Indian rebels were elusive 'owing to the intense thickness of the jungle',[10] was offering a reflection that could have been made of many other imperial wars. As a result, particular techniques were devised to subjugate the local environment. Donald MacAlister, who served with the 'field force' sent in November 1901 against the Aro Confederacy in south-east Nigeria, an area that was to see much more deadly conflict in the Biafran War of 1967–70, wrote:

'We have to break through the jungle in single file. In order to prevent flank attacks flankers are sent out who cut paths through the jungle parallel (22 November) ... Our carriers and bushmen have cleared the bush all round and everywhere trees are being felled and the ruins of the huts pulled down ... We had the Maxim [gun] pouring into the bush this morning (25 December).'[11]

Armies both benefited from imperial geography, requiring for their operations the information thereby obtained, and also helped provide it, although other agents and agencies of imperial states also played a role. Thus, in British India, army officers played a key role. Lieutenant Colonel William Lambton, a veteran of Yorktown and Seringapatam, began the triangulation of India in 1800, and became Superintendent of the Trigonometrical Survey of India established in 1817 and largely completed in 1890. Colonel Colin Mackenzie, another veteran of the capture of Seringapatam in 1799, became first Surveyor General of India in 1819. An aspect of control was that brought by naming positions, and then recording and disseminating these names.[12]

In Britain, alongside the existing institutions and posts of the Ordnance Survey and the Hydrographer to the Navy, the Depot of Military Knowledge was created in 1803 within the Quartermaster General's Office at Horse Guards, London. Maps were also printed by the Quartermaster General's Office at Dublin Castle, by the relevant office at Colombo, where a Ceylon Survey Department had been established in 1800, and, later, by the Quartermaster General's Department in Simla, India. When he died in 1873, John Arrowsmith, an active map-maker prominent in the Royal Geographical Society, was working at the India Office in London on a map of Central Asia on the scale of about ninety miles to an inch. By 1881, the key agency in London was the Intelligence Department of the War Office, but their maps could be faulty and with dangerous consequences, as with some of those used during the Boer War of 1899–1902.[13]

Beyond the bounds of imperial control, it was necessary to rely on other means, including secret agents. From 1863 to 1893, Britain sent Indians to Tibet and Central Asia, trained as surveyors but disguised as pilgrims or traders. They were provided with concealed instruments as well as strings of prayer beads containing eight fewer than the usual 108 beads in order to help establish distances. The information from these 'pundits' led to the mapping of the major routes, although not of surrounding regions. This mapping greatly helped the British when they sent an expedition that captured Lhasa, the capital of Tibet, in 1904, the first such expedition from the direction of India as opposed to that of China.

Because mapping was associated with imperial conquest and control, it was frequently highly unwelcome. In New Zealand, the Maoris often resisted British surveying, and, partly as a result, violent clashes occurred in 1843 and 1863. A triangulation survey of the country began in 1875, but again with Maori opposition.

Maps, atlases and globes also brought imperial conflict home to audiences in the metropole. The sixty-foot high, gas lit model of the globe built by James Wyld, at the time of the Great Exhibition of 1851 in London, was exhibited in a large circular building in Leicester Square in 1851–62. In his accompanying published *Notes*, Wyld emphasised both the need to move beyond traditional continental divisions and to appreciate the opportunity to understand military resonances:

> 'A vicious class of school-books, parcelling out the world into antiquated divisions, and representing it principally under its physical aspects, affords no adequate idea of political geography, still less of the vast empire of the English race, scattered over the regions of the globe.... The Indian hero [by which Wyld meant British not Indian soldiers] will fight his battles over again.... The veteran, fresh from the Atlas of Battles, will ... show how the great Duke [Wellington] prepared and carried out each successive enterprise ... he may illustrate the science of war, the campaigns of Alexander, the march of Hannibal, the labours of Hercules.'

Atlases and newspaper maps threw light on recent and current warfare. Alexander Keith Johnston's popular *Half-Crown Atlas of British History* (1871) had a map of part of China to illustrate the Opium Wars, while the 1891 edition included maps of Afghanistan, and, West, South, and North-East Africa to illustrate recent British conflicts, and that of 1902 three maps to illustrate the Boer War of 1899–1902.[14]

The choice of terms, such as 'civilized,' 'primitives,' 'contained' and 'controlled,' by Western contemporaries and their use indicated the cultural contrasting during and about imperialism and conquest. Aside from the normative languages of the period in question comes the nature of subsequent scholarship, of which this book of course is a part. There is a tendency to regard those who suffered imperialist expansion as weakened by the 'bounds of culture…. The constraints of their culture and its time-honoured formula for glory.'[15] That approach creates a new geography, a cultural one focused on the apparent responsiveness in the past (and present) to what is seen as modern warfare, and a geography that is delimited accordingly. However, there are conceptual, methodological, and empirical flaws with this approach, not least its judgmental tendency about the automatic supposed tendencies of what is presented as cultural conservatism, and also an assumption that it would fail.[16]

The debate over the supposed early-modern Western military revolution and its global impact is an instructive instance of this issue, and is important because this thesis has been the standard Western one in explaining a capability gap that permitted Western imperial success. Light is cast on this subject by considering the subsequent period, for there was a major transformation in global geopolitics and military potential in the nineteenth century, one that continued into the early twentieth century, culminating with the extent of Western empires after the First World War. Thus, in so far as it occurred, the early-modern European military revolution did so later than generally argued.[17] All the criteria advanced are seen better not with aspects of the utilisation of gunpowder, a truly slow-moving process, but rather with changes in the nineteenth century and, notably in its second half.

If one century of change has to be discerned, it is 1850–1950. In part, this is a case of weapons and delivery systems, culminating in bomber offensives by large air forces, naval conflict beyond the horizon, submarine campaigns, and the atom bomb. The use of new elements for warfare, notably air power beyond the earlier, pre-1850s, range of limited ground-based rocketry, was certainly in a different league to anything seen earlier. State mobilisation of manpower, economic and financial resources was magnified in its potential by population growth, industrialisation, growing wealth, urbanisation and transformative changes in communications. Railroads and steamships were important to power projection and logistics.[18] The rise of nationalism was part of the process of nineteenth-century change. With characteristic complexity, the conjunction of these trends emerged at different times in particular areas, but the relevant spread in time between areas was far less marked than over previous centuries.

The global dimension was also very much changed. By 1800, in total contradistinction to any focus on the percentage of the world's land surface occupied by Europeans, most of the population was not under European control, nor threatened with it. Russian sway over the Siberian wastes logged up the square miles, but not much else. The dominant external challenger in northern India were the Afghans, not the British, and, aside from the Afghans, the key players there during the eighteenth century were the Mughals, the Marathas, and the Persians. The Russians had neither retained nor regained Peter the Great's conquests of 1722–3 in Iran. The Chinese still controlled both Taiwan and the Amur Valley, whence the Dutch and Russians had been driven respectively in 1661 and 1685–9. Much of North America was under the claim, but not the control, of European or European-settler powers. In Africa, the Europeans were essentially in a few coastal enclaves, and the Portuguese attempt to go further in Morocco was crushed in 1578, Spanish attacks on Algiers in 1775 and 1784 were repelled with serious losses, and the headline success of Napoleon in Egypt in 1798 was defeated by the British in 1801 only to be followed by British failure in Egypt in 1807. Portuguese expansion in Angola and Mozambique had long stalled.

This situation was transformed in the century from the early 1840s (when there were British successes in China and Sind, and against Egypt, and French victory in Morocco in 1844) to 1936 (the Italian conquest of Ethiopia). It was in the years from 1860 to 1936 that European forces entered Beijing, Lhasa, Baghdad, Damascus and Addis Ababa, all for the first time, and Jerusalem for the first time since the Crusades. Independent states of European origin, from Argentina to the United States, overcame Native Americans. Traditional enemies of European power were defeated, from the Sumatran Sultanate of Atceh to the Ottoman Empire. Africa was totally partitioned, while Russia took over most of Central Asia.[19]

For these and other reasons that draw on a geographical assessment, it would be appropriate, if using the term 'military revolution,' to redate it as part of a new drawing of chronological boundaries. This also circumvents the somewhat ragged idea of a military revolution that ends in 1800, an idea that sits uneasily with the notion of another beginning with 'peoples' warfare' from 1775 and/or 1792. That was not an issue that was satisfactorily addressed, except maybe with the subliminal notion that revolution occurred all the time as if it was a condition of modernity and vice versa. In practice, any reading of Napoleon's campaigns suggested no real sophistication or effectiveness absent from Han China or the Roman Empire, and it was understandable that nineteenth-century commentators should look back for exemplary lessons about warfare.

Redating 'military revolution' serves not only better to understand the history of war in the broadest sense, but also contributes to a reconsideration of the earlier period usually referred to as early-modern. There is a tendency, in which intellectual, academic and other strategies and goals interact, if not combine, to emphasise the modernity of this age, but that is misleading. In many senses, notably organisationally, socially and economically, the period should more appropriately be put with 'the Middle Ages,' leaving 'modernity,' which is growing lengthier and more complex with the continuing passage of time, to begin in the nineteenth century.[20] That redating certainly might help explain why the model of Hannibal's victory over the Romans at Cannae in 216 BCE subsequently served the Germans poorly in the First World War. Moreover, the Soviet Union in 1941–2 thwarted Germany despite losing major battles, as Rome had also done at Carthage.

Alongside the allegedly transformative change of modernisation, however defined and whenever dated, there were repeatedly similarities in military affairs. This was understandably so, as fitness for purpose was the motivation for essentially *ad hoc* responses by existing forces and institutions to particular needs and opportunities. Thus, the very use, in the late nineteenth and early twentieth centuries, of reservists and of large-scale expansion in army size for wartime was another version of earlier practices. Or, consider the following:

> 'their young men from their past observations express no very respectable opinion of our manner of fighting them, as, by our close order, we present a large object to their fire, and our platoons do little execution … though they acknowledged our troops thereby show they are not afraid, and that our numbers would be formidable in open ground, where they will never give us an opportunity of engaging them.'

Afghanistan 2020 in response to the Americans, or Germany in 9 to the Romans? No, Governor William Bull of South Carolina in 1761 reporting on Anglo-American prisoners released by the Cherokees.[21] So often, it is the recurrences and continuities that are of note.

In practice, the general process of Western developments, considered in terms of imperialism or other factors, did not presume a certain military geography, nor any particular tactics, operational method or strategy, or response to them. Nor is it appropriate to see one strategy, operational method, and tactics as characteristics of Western or non-Western conflict, as there were a wide variety of environments and circumstances, so that, although the standard image of Western ordered free-power formations against non-Western fluidity and, in particular, shock tactics, was not without some basis, it was not a valid description of the wide variety that pertained. Nevertheless, such an image accorded with the cultural requirements of many Western commentators, and military observers shared these values, Major General Stockley Warren feeling that the battle of Mazina in 1880 showed 'the immense superiority of controlled volley firing, over independent blazing away,' with the Afghans losing out to the 'heavy volleys' of the British.[22]

Such techniques entailed the particular spatial presentation of Western forces outside the West. They advanced in columns, but, in battle, generally relied on massed formations that provided controlled firepower, notably hollow squares and close-packed lines, a method very different to that in conflict within Europe. Thus, in 1912, artillery and machine guns helped a French square of infantry repel a larger but poorly-armed Moroccan attack at Sidi Ben Othman, with more than 2,000 Moroccans killed, before the French pressed on to occupy nearby Marrakech and annex southern Morocco.[23]

It was necessary for imperial powers to try to adapt to the environments present, many unfamiliar, as for the Chinese in Burma in the late 1760s. Lieutenant General Sir Frederick Roberts in 1885 stressed the problems caused for the British use of artillery by the absence of roads in Afghanistan where he had commanded. Rudolph, 10th Earl of Cavan, Chief of the (British) Imperial General Staff and a veteran of the Boer War, and the Western Front and the Italian Front during the First World War, argued in 1924: 'so much of our work has to be done in uncivilized parts of the world that it is a mistake to pin faith to a type of unit largely dependent on civilized conditions, good roads and open country.'[24] A lack of good maps could be a major problem, as notably for the British in the

Boer War in South Africa in 1899 and in the Gallipoli operation of 1915. Field Marshal Slim, the British commander in Burma in the victorious campaigns of 1944–5, remarked later 'The British army fights all its battles uphill and usually on the junction of four map sheets,'[25] which in part was possibly an ironic reference to the marginal nature of Burma from an Indian perspective.

At the same time, efforts were made by these powers to establish a geographical infrastructure, first by the building of roads and railways, and then by the use of airpower. Roadbuilding, for example, improved the British position on the North-West Frontier of India.[26] In Sudan, the British found it easier to maintain control in the north than in the forested south, and the armoured cars of the machine-gun batteries in the Sudan Defence Force proved effective.[27] Airpower proved a major form of imperial policing in the interwar years,[28] but, as also for the Americans in Nicaragua, it was only patchily successful, mostly as either a deterrent (operationally) or against convenient targets (tactically).

Whatever the firepower available, key elements included the presence (Afghanistan for opponents of British on the North-West Frontier) or not (Morocco 1925–6) of neighbouring areas of support and refuge, and, separately, the determination of the two sides. Defining imperial borders and politics generally entailed ignoring pre-existing boundaries and conflicts between ethnic groups and kingdoms. There was also the practice of openly assigning different levels of privilege to these groups, thus helping to sustain rivalry. Divide and rule in this fashion was frequently a conscious process. However, had the imperial powers made different use of the human geography of the areas they conquered to form state boundaries, then at least some subsequent post-imperial conflicts might have been avoided, because the imperial boundaries proved particularly durable.

The effort to preserve empire encountered opposition within territories, albeit to very varied degrees. The resulting conflicts could also reveal the limitations or precariousness of new military means to overcome geographical constraints, as with those vulnerable to aircraft using cover and travelling by dark. In the case of the rebellion in Waziristan on the North-West Frontier that broke out in 1936, the tribesmen cut telegraph lines, which led most signalling to be carried out using coloured flags, the heliograph and dispatch riders as only the largest bases had radios.

Such tactical and operational issues sat alongside the strategic questions of the relations between geography, control and prestige. There was an understanding that the latter was significant, and to a degree that can be underplayed by a focus on realist factors, including physical geography. Thus, the recapture of colonies conquered by Japan was regarded in 1944–5 as important to British prestige; and this involved planners, including Churchill who, as a result, wanted a focus on Malaysia before units were sent to help in the assault on Japan. In September 1944, Admiral Sir Geoffrey Layton, Commander-in-Chief of Ceylon [Sri Lanka], wrote of:

> 'the vital importance of our recapturing those parts of the Empire as far as possible ourselves. I would specially mention the recapture of Burma and its culmination in the recovery of Singapore by force of arms and not by waiting for it to be surrendered as part of any peace treaty … the immense effect this will have on our prestige in the Far East in post-war years. This and only this in my opinion will restore us to our former level in the eyes of the native population in these parts.'[29]

Admiral Louis Mountbatten, Supreme Commander of South-East Asia Command, strongly agreed.[30] In the event, these views, which, despite British preparations for just such an offensive in August 1945, were probably redundant anyway, were trumped by the Japanese surrender after the American use of two atom bombs dropped from aircraft flying from recently-conquered American bases in the western Pacific. A new age of war and a new geopolitics had emerged.

Chapter 11

The First World War, 1914–18, and the Interwar Period, 1918–39

The role of geography in war was unprecedented in the successive world wars. In part, this was because of their hitherto unique geographical range, with the resulting issue of reconciling commitments on particular fronts. It was also due to the nature of the fighting on land and at sea, and the fact that it now included the impact of conflict in, and from, the air. The range of weapons and of platforms was new, a result of the use of aircraft (which had only been very limited hitherto) and, eventually, in 1918, early aircraft carriers. At the strategic level, an understanding of the distribution of resources was important, as with the German need, in both world wars, to seize and retain Romanian oil supplies. Developing prior to the First World War, military Intelligence greatly expanded during it, with cartography a key element.[1]

To focus on the very new, aircraft, first used in war by the Italians in Libya in 1911, permitted an understanding and presentation of the geography of conflict very different to those hitherto available. Poor at the outset of the war, reconnaissance was rapidly transformed, with reports from pilots and observers given new accuracy by cameras, which were able to record details and to scrutinise the landscape from different heights and angles. Instruments for mechanically plotting from aerial photography were developed, and a flight over part of Italy by Wilbur Wright in 1909 appears to have been the first on which photographs were taken. Aerial photography was to prove valuable in both mobile and static sections of the First World War, overseeing the landscape in a way that previous reconnaissance could attempt only in a more limited and slower fashion: by hilltop observation or scouting patrols or from balloons with their more limited manoeuvrability and speed. At this stage, however, night and cloud remained key limitations.

In the mobile stage at the start of the war, aircraft could provide information on advancing forces. Indeed, the landscape had to be read in light of how swiftly the opposing forces were able to move, which only partly depended on the terrain or topography, and on how difficult they would find it to mount an offensive. The French, for example, could, as they did in 1914, readily use their rail system to move troops from eastern France. There, with great loss of life, they had been unsuccessfully attacking German troops. The troops moved to support the defence of Paris, did so successfully.

The Germans, on the other hand, as part of a broader problem of strategic conception and operational implementation,[2] faced the problems of taking over the rail systems of conquered areas of Belgium and France, including different gauges of track, an issue that was also to face them in Russia. The use of maps did not necessarily cover such issues, while planning did not prevent a serious operational incoherence on the advancing German right flank in France in 1914 nor provide a way to deal with the consequences.

Planning had sought to capture the issues of geography, but failed to overcome its possibilities in the shape of the 'friction' of circumstances; although that flaw was even more the case in terms of a failure to note wider strategic circumstances in the shape of political responses, notably the significance of Britain's entry into the war in response to the German invasion of Belgium. As far as conflict was concerned, geographical assumptions needed to note the expanded range of modern weaponry which, combined with the slow pace of unmechanised forces, limited the possibilities of flank movements and attacks. This made envelopment more difficult during the mobile phases of the war and thus made it more likely that defeated forces would be able to retreat, avoiding both destruction and a speedy enforced peace. The limitations of field leadership in rising to the challenges of controlling large numbers of troops and confronting the implications of new technology within a given space-time unit were also a major problem.

On the Western Front, the mobile stage, with its possibilities of breakthroughs if not envelope, was followed by deadlock, trench positions and frontal attacks, which forced a different geography to the forefront. At the same time, larger troop numbers altered the parameters of conflict, lessening the constraints against the casualties of frontal attacks, a point noted by Colonel W.H.W. Waters, a member of the British Military Mission with the Russian army in the Russo-Japanese War of 1904–5:

'Frontal attacks were a very conspicuous feature of both sides during the late campaign in Manchuria. In some instances, they could have been advantageously omitted, and flank attacks made in their stead, but when armies, each numbering say a couple of hundred thousand combatants, cover the whole of the ground available for a battlefield, as on the Shaho, frontal attacks cannot be avoided.'[3]

Aside from the numbers, the space to be overcome created an additional factor. In January 1915, Arthur Balfour, a (civilian) member of the British Committee for Imperial Defence, wrote:

'I agree, and I fear that everybody must agree, that the notion of driving the Germans back from the west of Belgium to the Rhine by successfully assaulting one line of trenches after another seems a very hopeless affair, and unless some means can be found for breaking their line at some critical point, and threatening their communications, I am unable to see how the deadlock in the West is to be brought to any rapid or satisfactory conclusion.'[4]

This problem helped lead to the search for an alternative. Drawing on the geopolitics of the British and French empires, naval superiority in the Mediterranean offered a force multiplier, apparently providing an opportunity, in the Gallipoli campaign of 1915, to attack the centre of Turkish power, one that was not geographically possible for the Allies in the case of Germany, Austria or Bulgaria. This search for an indirect approach focused on combined operations appeared to conform to British strategic traditions, notably in the Seven Years War (1756–63) and the Peninsular War (1808–13), traditions formulated by Julian Corbett in *Some Principles of Maritime Strategy* (1911). Such a focus would permit Britain to achieve success with its strong navy and relatively modest army.[5] In the event, a mishandled campaign left this strategic geography in the lurch, and in the case of the attack on Turkey in 1915 it was anyway problematic.

The particular needs of trench warfare, for both defenders and attackers, infantry and artillery, created a new geography, and, therefore, new demands for mapping that had not been anticipated by military cartographers. Location was one issue. The French had concentrated their military mapping on the German-French frontier and on fortified positions, such as Belfort, which was the protection against any German advance into Franche-Comté and a totemic site after its successful defence during the Franco-Prussian War; only for the French to discover that much of the fighting took place nowhere near these positions, but, instead, close to the Belgian frontier.

Moreover, detailed trench maps became necessary in order to be able to plan both effective defences and successful assaults on them. Effective infantry-artillery coordination was important to success in attack and defence. The complexity of defence positions was enhanced by barbed wire, and by defence-in-depth. The new geography was tactical, operational and strategic.[6]

With time came more static military positions, as well as concealed locations to protect the guns, and a need, on the part of attackers, for heavier and more precise artillery fire. These developments led to the use of maps as the key means of precision and planning. For the battle of Neuve Chapelle on 15 March 1915, the first major British trench warfare attack on the Western Front, the plan was based on maps created through aerial photographs. Improvements in photogrammetry (mapping by means of photography) reflected the importance of aerial information as a means to change the geography of battle. At first, the system was more *ad hoc*, the *Times* [of London] noting on 27 December 1914:

'The chief use of aeroplanes is to direct the fire of the artillery. Sometimes they "circle and dive" just over the position of the place which they want shelled. The observers with the artillery then inform the battery commanders – and a few seconds later shells come hurtling on to, or jolly near to, the spot indicated. They also observe for the gunners and signal back to them where their shots are going to, whether over or short, or to right or left.'

Aircraft became a key form of real-time data collection. The replacement of glass-plate negatives by film-based cameras was also highly important. Moreover, the invention of cameras able to take photographs with constant overlap, proved a technique that was very important for aerial reconnaissance and thus surveying, notably with the development of three-dimensional photographic interpretation.[7]

The evolution of artillery tactics made linear defensive lines, including systems several lines deep, vulnerable, if not unworkable, during the second half of 1916; and this, instead, led to defensive networks focused on mutually-supported strongpoints, with the first line only a series of thinly-manned outposts. The purpose was one of containing break-ins and preventing them from becoming breakthroughs. In 1917, the Germans pulled back to the shorter *Siegfriedstellung* or Siegfried Line, known to the Allies as the Hindenburg Line, which was up to fifteen miles deep. The new geography was made more deadly and specific by the clearance of the area between the new and old lines in order to create clear fields of fire. Vast amounts of concertina wire were employed to funnel attackers into zones covered by machine guns, artillery, and mortars.

Due to the nature of trench warfare, maps were produced for the military at a far larger scale than those with which they had been equipped for mobile campaigning. Thus, the British army replaced its 1:80,000 scale maps with 1:10,000 scale maps, a formidable task of both map-making (in the midst of war) and production. These maps needed to be up-to-date and required a high degree of accuracy in order to permit indirect fire, as opposed to artillery firing over open sights. This accuracy came in part from better guns, but mostly from improvements in photogrammetry. Maps worked to record positions, as well as to permit the dissemination of the information.

Very immediately, the relationship between war and geography was changed with the proliferation of shell craters, while the battle-space had expanded with the depth of defence provided by multiple trench lines. Zonal defences, in turn, required a new offensive geography, not that of linear formation advancing against linear defences, but, rather, focusing on opponents' strong points in order to destroy the cohesion of their defence. The necessary techniques of surprise attack, infiltration, and focus on particular points, were to be called storm-trooper techniques because of the German term *Stosstruppen*, but were also developed by the British, French and Canadians, and helped greatly in tackling defences in depth.

It was necessary, furthermore, as part of this precision in attack, to locate the position of artillery in a precisely measured and understood triangulation network, which permitted long-range artillery fire that was directionally-accurate by means of firing on particular coordinates. This made 'deep battle' possible. Lieutenant Colonel Percy Worrall, a British infantry officer, noted of the Western Front in April 1918, when the German Spring Offensive was being resisted: 'The artillery and machine-gun corps did excellent work in close co-operation … it was seldom longer than 2 minutes after I have "X-2 minutes intense" when one gunner responded with a crash on the right spot.'[8]

Standardisation and precision were aspects of the engagement with the particular geographies in question. Military maps came to show north points, magnetic declination, and grid deviation, and the grid systems aided the precise use and coordination of the increasingly precise information they presented. Each element of precision was important. Accurate surveying and mapping reduced the need for the registration of targets by guns prior to attack and, therefore, allowed an element of surprise, which was important to the success of offensives. For long-distance targeting, the French *Service Géographique ds Armées* had to change the projection they used in the past for the *Carte d'état-major*, the Bonne projection devised in 1752 and adopted in 1802, and switch to the Lambert projection which they did in 1915. *Canevas de tir* and *Plans directeurs* were created for indirect firing.

Meanwhile, the scale of map-production increased greatly. When the British Expeditionary Force (BEF) was sent to France in 1914, one officer and one clerk were responsible for mapping, and the maps were unreliable. By 1918, in contrast, the survey organisation of the new much larger BEF had risen to about 5,000 men and had been responsible for more than 35 million map sheets. No fewer than 400,000 impressions were produced in just ten days in August 1918.

After-action reports made clear the way in which artillery helped plan the battlefield in terms of space and time. Thus, for the British in the Battle of the River Selle on the Western Front in 1918, a major success for them in late October as they forced the Germans out of a new defensive line and helped precipitate crisis of confidence in the German leadership:

'The 5th Battalion Machine Gun Corps and 5th Divisional Artillery put down a magnificent barrage – 4 minutes on railway – jump to road beyond and rest for 8 minutes – creep forward 10 yards in 4 minutes arriving at protective line … smoke shells were used to denote the beginning and end of each pause, and thermite shells to denote boundaries and to help guide advancing infantry… [Later] The five minutes bombardment demanded by the C.O. undoubtedly saved the battalion many lives.'[9]

Aside from the need for precise information for artillery, the size of the armies, the proliferation of new weapons, and the extent of entrenchment, all forced commanders to consider the coordination in time and space of fire, manoeuvre, obstacles, reserve positions, and so on, largely sight-unseen, and accomplishing such coordination by topographic maps, aerial photography and enhanced communications. These skills, and the related infrastructure, were important in conceptually confronting the detailed geography of the battle-zone, and as also more broadly, for example in developing the understanding of the necessary transport systems.[10]

Combined operations proved particularly significant. Thus, although sometimes decried, the maps produced for the Gallipoli campaign in 1915 could employ several layers, with information for the army and the navy, using different projections and different symbols, including tracing paper to update maps with Intelligence, thus offering a dynamic character to situational awareness. During the campaign, both British and French map makers provided blank maps to aerial reconnaissance in order to spot enemy lines and then update the maps that were produced. The mapping entailed the collection, compilation and synthesis of information in a demanding time schedule.[11]

An appreciation of geography and a use of maps were crucial in order to produce coherence in command, especially the implementation of strategic plans in terms of timed operational decisions and interrelated tactical actions. Without an adequate grasp of maps, and what they meant in practice on the ground and in terms of practicality, command practices were unsystematic and inadequate, encouraging incoherent operations, battles without effective overall plans, and piecemeal tactics. As always in war, it was necessary to excel in the midst of uncertainty, a situation that required an understanding of the specifics of the tactical environment.

Maps, watches and telephones helped the coordination of manoeuvre with artillery, as much synchronisation had to take place to carry an army through an enemy's defences. General Sir Douglas Haig, the BEF commander, was critical in July 1916 of his French counterpart, Marshal Joseph Joffre: 'The poor man cannot argue, nor can he easily read a map.' However, training in mapmaking and map use became common so that maps in part became a mindset crucial to shaping and sharing information.[12] Alongside tactical success, it was necessary to coincide and sustain attacks along a broad front in order to prevent the opponents' sealing of any breakthrough by means of concentrating their reserves in that specific area. The Germans crucially failed to do so in their Spring Offensives of 1918 on the Western Front.

The range of demands for maps increased greatly as the war continued, not least as there was a search for advantage by the warring powers. New requirements included air navigation maps for the rapidly-growing number of aircraft, hydro-geological mapping,[13] transport planning maps,[14] and maps for the extensive underground mining that was used to plant explosives beneath opposing positions.[15]

In turn, the geographical span of mapping reflected the wide-ranging nature of campaigning. For example, the British used aerial photography and sketch maps on the Palestine Front, in the Hejaz, and in Mesopotamia (Iraq),[16] with the Surveys of Egypt and India respectively responsible for the bulk printing of maps. Not all combatants, however, developed wartime cartography at the same rate. Thus, facing operations across a wide extent of relatively poorly-mapped territory, and with its limited resources under great pressure, Russia did not see a comparable production of aerial photography or the use of the resulting information for artillery targeting. The same was the case for Austria.[17]

It proved necessary in the war to transform static into manoeuvre warfare, and, at the tactical level, combined-arms operations was the best way to do so, notably well-aimed, heavy, indirect fire benefiting from aerial reconnaissance, ably coordinated with rushes by infantry carrying supplementary firepower in the shape of mortars, grenades, and light machine guns. Fitness for purpose meant a particular understanding of the spatial dynamics of trench systems, and this was rapidly acquired as experience was distilled and diffused. There was, however, the question of where to devote resources.

Considering 'the geography that was not,' in the shape of plans for campaigns that were not brought to fruition, is instructive, but also throws light, by extension, on the need to assess a range of factors in terms of choice for, or against, action. Thus, plans for an amphibious assault on the Belgian coast in 1916–17 reflected the potential for combined operations, the need to lessen the costly vulnerability of the Allied position in the Ypres salient by gaining territory, the German lack of commanding defensive, surveillance, and artillery positions in the low terrain, and the problems created by German submarines sailing from Flemish bases. However, the strength of German defences, with the added mobility offered them by the railway, were important in discouraging such an assault. Moreover, there was the important political point that lessening the commitment to the Western Front itself, by withdrawing and/or allocating troops for an amphibious assault, would increase the pressure on France, part of the army of which had uncertain morale in 1917. Repeatedly, in this and other conflicts, the significance of geographic factors owed much to the particular dynamics of alliance politics, and at specific moments.

Geography provided challenges in many forms, for example the appalling and unseasonal wet weather that hit the British Passchendaele (Third Ypres) offensive in 1917,[18] the *Times* on 21 September noting: 'All shell-holes are full of water. Every man I saw was coated with mud, some only to the knees, but many to their very throats, and it is to be feared that some wounded must slip into the holes and never get out again.' As a reminder of the multiple and interactive nature of circumstances, this wet weather was particularly challenging due to the terrain and soil structure of the area under contention.

Yet a human geography was also involved, as the war led to a marked alteration of the geography of the theatre of combat.[19] Thus, the proliferation of trenches, bunkers and shell craters, as well as the destruction of vegetation and drainage systems during the three battles of Ypres, in part due to shell damage, made even worse by the torrential rain of 1917, changed the topography dramatically. The reclaimed marshland was returned to an expanse of pockmarked swamp and muddy mires. Moreover, attacks on enemy strongholds by a frequent bombardment of shells destroyed built environments. The worse example was the levelling of Ypres.

The Interwar Period

The return of mobility seen on the Western Front in 1918 looked toward the conflicts that followed the First World War, notably civil wars in Russia, China and Spain, and the Greek-Turkish war. The spatial dimension, however, was different to the 1918 campaign, as the assault on well-defended positions was no longer the key element.[20] As so often, it was what humans contributed to the geography that was crucial.

The civil wars were shaped by the need to control key positions within the far less well-fortified interior of countries, especially rail nodes. In the

Russian Civil War of 1917–22, the Communists benefited greatly from their central position and interior lines of communication and, to a degree, were able to mount sequential offensives, but there was no comparable success for the Republicans in the Spanish Civil War of 1936–9.[21]

The warfare of the 1920s and 1930s suggested a far greater mobility than that of the recent world war. However, there continued to be attempts to contain this, notably by means of defensive systems, most famously the French Maginot Line, but also the German West and East Walls, the Dutch Water Line, the Finnish Mannerheim Line, and, in Tunisia, the French Mareth Line. The situation was far harder across most of the world, with equations of space and resources affected by different priorities.

Nevertheless, the establishment of garrison positions and fortifications in an attempt to contain the situation remained a common feature of rule. Thus, facing insurrection in Syria in 1926, French forces successfully encircled Damascus with barbed wire and machine-gun posts, while, facing a graver challenge, the Nationalist (Kuomintang) government of China used blockhouses to try to seal the Communists into mountainous areas, notably in the 1933–4 campaign against Mao Zedong in the region of Jiangxi. The difficulty facing regular forces was captured in an account in the (London) *Times* of 3 January 1928 about the ambush of an American Marine unit by Sandinista forces in a mountain pass in Nicaragua: 'Finding it useless to fire at the hidden enemy he hurried his men forward through the Pass ... to the outskirts of Quilali where he deployed and engaged the enemy in the open. The insurgents then retired.'

Meanwhile, looking ahead, a key theme in military speculation in the 1920s and 1930s, focused heavily on the potential of aircraft to provide a totally different geography of military decisiveness. Brigadier General Billy Mitchell, the vigorous protagonist of American air power, very much took that view in *Winged Defense: The Development and Possibilities of Modern Air Power* (1925). It began:

'The world stands on the threshold of the "aeronautical era". During this epoch the destinies of all people will be controlled through the air.... Mountains, deserts, oceans, rivers, and forests, offer no obstacles. In a trice, aircraft have set aside all ideas of frontiers. The whole country now becomes the frontier and, in case of war, one place is just as exposed to attack as another place.'[22]

This very much looked ahead to the expectations of a new form of military geography in the next major war, and paralleled J.F.C. Fuller's presentation of the potential of tanks. The institutional setting was particularly significant for air power. Thus, the establishment in the United States in 1939 of the Army Air Forces provided a basis that was more adroit at command and planning than in the previous more inchoate situation.[23]

Speculations about the next war related practically, not only to the issue of what weapons systems could achieve, in absolute and relative terms, but, also what they would be expected to achieve in light of specific tasks and the related geography.[24] In a situation made more dynamic by technological change, strategic uncertainties surrounded the prioritisation of planning.

The interwar period was also one in which, taking forward prewar works such as Ellen Semple's *American History and its Geographic Conditions* (1903), there was extensive work on the interaction of environment and history. Key examples include O.G.S. Crawford's *Man and his Past* (1921), Thomas Griffith Taylor's *Environment and Race* (1927) and *Environment and Nation. Geographical Factors in the Cultural and Political History of Europe* (1930), Charles Paullin's *Atlas of the Historical Geography of the United States* (1932), and Gordon East's *The Geography behind History* (1938). There was criticism of environmental determinism, notably that of pre war writers, the German Freidrich Ratzel and the American Ellen Semple, criticsm for example by the French historian Lucien Febvre, the American anthropologist Franz Boas, and the American geographer Carl Sauer. The result was a *'possibilisme'* – in Febvre's term, in which human and physical integration were to the fore.[25] Human behaviour in this account was not determined solely by the physical environment, because humans were/are an active element in the human-environmental partnership. That was a reasonable conclusion also for the role of geography in war.

The dimension of human geography was readily seen in the degree to which confrontation was increasingly contextualised in the 1930s by a tension between aggressive, revisionist powers, notably Japan, Italy, Germany and the Soviet Union, and, on the other hand, those which sought to preserve stability and the *status quo*. This contrast provided very different strategic drives and perceptions of territory, and these differences were to be taken forward into the Second World War.

Chapter 12

The Second World War, 1939–45

The geographical dimension of this war was pushed to the fore by the interaction of campaigning or possible campaigning across much of the world. The range of possible campaigning was accentuated by the degree to which there was no fixity in sides until the very close, with the Soviet Union not attacking Japan until August 1945. This situation helped underline a fluidity that was compounded by the uncertainty of the effectiveness of recent and new weapons systems, and also concerning the resilience, adaptability and skill of individual combatants. In particular, while keen to secure its food, fuel and mineral resources the Germans had crucially failed conceptually to confront the space of the Soviet Union, which they invaded in 1941. This space proved a force-multiplier for the defensive and, as such, an aspect of the reserves. This Soviet advantage was accentuated by the degree to which German war-making, with its emphasis on surprise, speed, and overwhelming and dynamic force at the chosen point of contact, was designed for an offensive strategy that was most effective against linear defences, but not against defences in depth.

The mobility of forces on land, sea, and in the air meanwhile carried with it not only specific requirements, notably for fuel, but also an expanded capability that ensured that the defender faced the risk of being obliged to defend areas of interest against attack to a greater depth than in the previous war. This became more significant due to the Allies fighting not only Germany but also Italy from June 1940 and Japan from December 1941. As an aspect of preparations, the British, in 1940, mapped the border areas of Kenya in preparation for campaigning against Italian East Africa (Ethiopia, Italian Somaliland, and Eritrea). In the event, the Italian invasion of Kenya was restricted to the capture of the border post at Moyale. The threat of a Japanese invasion of Australia in 1942 led to the production of large-scale maps for coastal areas, notably of Queensland, New South Wales, and Victoria, and near the cities of Adelaide, Darwin and Perth; these maps linked to the location of artillery, for example to protect the naval base of Freemantle near Perth and also the sea approaches to Melbourne.

Such a geography of response to invasion was very different to that of concern about subversion, a concern that tended to focus on areas of alleged political and/or ethnic dissidence, with paranoia often playing a role. In February 1941, when Australia was at war with Germany, and the latter allied to the Soviet Union, the Australian War Cabinet was anxious about Communist subversion, specifically 'the continued state of industrial unrest in the community.'[1]

Magnified by the range permitted by technological developments, mobility provided the attacker with a range of opportunity that encouraged defenders, naturally reactive, to prepare defence over a great area. This extent of area created problems in 1941, both for the British on the island of Crete when, overcoming the advantages of defending an island, it was successfully invaded by the Germans in an airborne assault of unprecedented scale, and for the Americans on the Philippines: the Japanese initially landed with far fewer troops, but kept the Americans guessing where they would land their main forces. In the Philippines, as in the Dutch East Indies in 1941–2, the Japanese accentuated this situation by successive amphibious assaults leapfrogging the defenders, assaults that were concerted with air support. Sequential cumulative pressure helped rapidly overcome the defences of a vast area of operations.

This system of overcoming the friction of defended geographical distance was to be repeated by the Americans in 1943–5. The time taken to defeat the Japanese on the island of Guadalcanal in the Solomon Islands (August 1942–January 1943), the large number of islands they continued to hold, and the casualties, time-loss, uncertainty and risk that the Japanese might thereby impose on an American advance, meant that the Americans needed to mount at sea the equivalent of the Soviet bypassing on land of German 'hedgehog' positions which were left isolated and irrelevant by cleaving blows. As a result, in each case, the war became one that was far from linear in terms of a clear front line.

This might seem to be modern, in contrast to the situation in the First World War; but that contrast which draws in the discussion on the potential offered by mechanised warfare on land, at sea and in the air, has to be handled with a degree of care as there had been a similar bypassing of defended strongholds in earlier eras of warfare when there were different forms of combat. In the Second World War, in 1943–5, island-hopping was crucial to the strategic context of American joint operations in the Pacific. Maps of American advances tend to ignore the Japanese positions that remained, but these bypassed positions, even those such as Rabaul and Truk with large garrisons, once without significant, or any, naval and air support, lacked strategic relevance and operational point.

The notion of a broad-front advance anyway meant less when it was a case of islands in a vast ocean (as opposed to an inland sea such as the Mediterranean), and notably so in the contexts of American air and naval superiority; although that superiority was not fully secured until 1944, more particularly the battle of Leyte Gulf of 23–26 October, a heavy defeat for the Japanese fleet. In contrast, resistance and vulnerability on the flanks were far more of an issue on land, although it could be lessened by their use of tactical air power, as by the Allies in their advance across France in 1944.

As in other wars, strategic geographical factors, such as the significance of Britain, India and Australia as bases for Allied operations against the Axis, were played out in terms of particular campaigns, and were in turn affected by them. For example, a British strategic review of August 1941 noted: 'Iranian oil and the Abadan refinery are essential to us. Our present positions afford a defence in depth to the shores of the Indian Ocean and Persian Gulf.'[2] Indeed, the establishment of a regional command reflected this concern, while also helping to fix attention and resources.[3] This was part of a more general process in which such commands were established, and their divisions, roles and military resources then contested. Similarly, the pursuit and security of economic resources was important to all the combatants, notably oil, coal, iron and food. This helped explain the determination to control particular areas, including them from which resource-sources could be bombed, such as Crimea which to Hitler was a threat to the Romanian oilfield, his principal source of non-synthetic fuel.[4]

Separately, resources alone could be less than certain in their consequences, as in 1944 when the Allies arguably had, at least to a degree, too many, both for the narrow front of operations on the eastern part of the Normandy battlefield, and for the logistical strain posed by the subsequent broad-front advance. The operational geographies of campaigns saw the response of combatants to resource issues and the interaction of combatants with each other and with the physical geography. The interactive nature of the resulting relationships imposed frictions and, more seriously, shattered plans. Thus, the German ability to advance a large mechanised force through the Ardennes, which became a key episode in the Fall of France, was a cause of great strategic surprise to the Allies in 1940. It underlined the need for geographical awareness of the possibilities of the terrain, as well as the geographical significance of the Intelligence war. These points were fully understood when the Cold War was planned for in Germany from 1945.

Aside from defensiveness, space posed a challenge to the speed of operations, and fatally so for the Germans in the Soviet Union in 1941. They could not bring enough force close to their principal targets to overcome Soviet resistance before winter set in, although, looked at differently, the Germans simply could not defeat the Soviets. In contrast, although there were failures, the Soviets made considerable progress in developing and sustaining 'Deep Operations' that both seized and used the initiative. The operational dimension of offensives in the Soviet army in 1943–5, notably Operation Bagration in 1944, which took forces westward across Belarus to near Warsaw, while inflicting very heavy losses on the German Army Group Centre, hinged on an ability to seize and retain the initiative, including by bringing forward supporting units, and to the resulting capability to outmanoeuvre opponents by advancing in depth rather than adopting the linear approach of advancing along the entire front. This ability depended on staff officers being well-informed about the distances and locations involved.

This capability was finally demonstrated in Manchuria in 1945 when the Japanese underrated Soviet mobility and speed, and inaccurately assumed that the Soviets would need to stop for re-supply after about 250 miles, providing the Japanese with an opportunity to respond to the Soviet advance.[5] The Soviets crucially were able to move faster than the Japanese had done in China in Operation Ichigo in late 1944–early 1945, when, in an offensive from both directions, the Japanese successfully opened the land route from areas of China already under control to Vietnam. Achieving scale, speed and distance, American operational art also improved, notably integrating different arms.[6] In contrast, one German, explaining in June 1945 his compatriots' defeat on the Eastern Front remarked: 'Because our lines of communication were too long.'[7]

At the tactical level, the spatial dynamics for all powers were frequently those centred on combined-arms operations and, in particular, the ability to bring together tanks, infantry and artillery, in order for them to maximise their capabilities, and to condition men to machines. Spatial understanding, of weapons and terrain, were the aspects of the relevant training. The Americans, for example, favoured 'triangular' operations in which the opposing force was frontally engaged by one unit while another turned its flank, and a third, in reserve, was poised to intervene where most helpful.

Precision about location was necessary given the issues of coordination essential to ensure tactical success in specific circumstances. This concern with location was also an aspect of the more general role of terrain. Thus, on a long-standing pattern, open flat lands proved far easier for operations including combined-arms than their marshy, forested, mountainous or urban counterparts. In the first case, the Pripet Marshes were a key instance, in the second, the Hürtgen Forest, in the third much of Italy, and in the fourth Stalingrad. In the Hürtgen Forest in late 1944, the trees themselves became part of the German defences against the costly American advance because of the way they splintered under artillery bombardment, with the splinters as deadly as shell fragments.

Further north, the Anglo-Canadian clearing of the *Reichswald* Forest from 8 to 22 February 1945 was an equivalent to the Hürtgen Forest operation, but in flooded terrain that thwarted tanks and wheeled vehicles and necessitated the use of Buffalo amphibious vehicles. In preparation, the Allies repaired the few roads and built bridges, but a rise in the temperature led to a thaw that turned the terrain into a quagmire. The Germans opened dams on 9–10 February to increase the flooding, while the shortage of roads caused an enormous traffic jam on 9 February. The flooding, another instance of geography being altered by war, certainly hindered the Allies, but also the Germans, making their field defences pointless and isolating their troops, who were thereby more vulnerable to attack.

With Italy, the peninsula nature of the battlespace meant that the Allied search for an open flank was dependent on the potential for amphibious operations, but the attack on Anzio in 1944 did not develop as intended. Moreover, fortified positions that could be held, such as Leningrad, Stalingrad and Tobruk, when first besieged by the Germans, provided, or helped anchor, defences that curtailed, and even could help determine, campaigns of movement; and if they could not be held, these positions could still impose costs in terms of time, casualties and units and resources committed, as with the German capture of Sevastopol in 1942 and the American capture of Manila from the Japanese in 1945.

The geography, both physical and human, of the defensive was therefore brought into play in response to the 'offensive geography' of the plans of the attacker. These plans reflected resource-availability as well as available Intelligence on the defender, but also a sense of the practicality of mastering space by means of specific plans and particular techniques. The latter can be seen with the debates over Allied strategy in 1942–4, notably the relationship between offensives in the Mediterranean and in north-western Europe, as well as in 1944 with disagreements over how the campaign in the latter should proceed. The disputes then, and subsequently, between advocates of broad and narrow front approaches to Germany (the latter pushed by Montgomery for the Lower Rhine and by General Jacob Devers, the commander of the 6th Army Group, for the Upper), were in part about known factors, such as acute and increasingly serious Allied logistical strain, in part about unknowns, notably likely German resistance, and, in part, expressions of views about the use of space in war, for example the very danger of an advance with open flanks, and thus the risk of flank attack.

Alongside the strong Soviet resistance on the direct route to Moscow, this risk had helped account in 1941 for the Germans deciding to send units from Army Group Centre south to attack the numerous Soviet forces in Ukraine. This entailed both taking advantage of an opportunity, but also addressing a challenge. Indeed, repeatedly, the psychological weight of the fear of flank attack sat alongside the practical. At any rate, in different, but both difficult, contexts, the Western Allies arguably did not demonstrate a grasp of the operational dimension of offensive warfare in 1944 comparable to that of the Soviets.[8]

More specifically, in 1944, the sequence of fresh attacks during Soviet breakthroughs prevented the Germans from falling back in order, thus preserving a continuous front. Defensive 'hedgehogs' had been regarded as a response to the potential of new techniques. General Claude Auchinleck, the perceptive British Commander-in-Chief in the Middle East in 1941–2, drew up instructions in October 1941 in which he offered a guide to the new geography of conflict made apparent by German mechanised advances, as well as specific aspects of the defended environment that had to be provided accordingly. Auchinleck stressed the value of engaging the Germans in manoeuvre warfare, but also offered 'general principles governing all the strategy of the defence', principles that reflected the strain on the classic geography of defence posed by the greater mobility of attacking forces:

'All main communications, road or rail, will be denied to the enemy by a series of defensive areas sited astride of them, and arranged in depth.

These defensive areas will be made tank proof, and capable of all round defence, and stocked so as to make them self-supporting for at least 60 days.... In no circumstances will a garrison abandon its area, unless ordered to do so by a superior commander.

Adequate air support for these defensive areas is essential and whenever possible they will contain one or more landing grounds to enable communication to be maintained with them by air and, when feasible and desirable, to enable air forces to be operated from within their perimeter.... It is essential that all idea of maintaining a linear defence in the face of superior enemy armoured forces be abandoned. Penetration between the defensive areas ... must be expected and accepted ... so long as these areas hold firm and thus deny to the enemy the use of the main arteries of communication, he can not continue for long to press forward with large forces.

The garrison of each defended area will include anti-aircraft artillery and should, if possible, include infantry tanks for counterattacking purposes, but the bulk of such armoured and motorised forces ... will be held ... to bring the enemy to battle on ground of our choosing and to make the fullest possible use of the defensive areas as pivots of manoeuvre.'[9]

In practice, while such 'hedgehogs' had an importance on narrow-front campaigns, channelling the advance and also challenging its flanks and rear, these 'hedgehogs' were less significant in resisting broad-front attacks, as used by the Soviets in 1944–5; especially when the 'hedgehogs' could not rely on armoured counteroffensives nor on the supplementary geography of air support.[10] Under the pressure of offensive capabilities, notably the development of mechanised warfare, a continuous front ceased to be a necessarily valid defensive mechanism, unless the front was restricted, as in Italy in 1943–5. However, the same drawback was true of these 'hedgehogs,' which had already been of only limited value to the Germans in the face of earlier Soviet offensives. They could be readily bypassed.

The multi-layered situational understanding necessary in the First World War had become even more essential in the Second World War as more factors had to be integrated in a conflict in which air power played a more intense role while land warfare was more mobile. Long-range intelligence was seen as a key means to success. 'The nation with the best photo reconnaissance will win the next war', declared Colonel-General Werner von Fritsch, Germany's army commander in 1938,[11] and aerial photography, notably by Do-17Ps and He-111Hs, indeed helped the dramatic and successful German invasion of the Low Countries and France in 1940. The German attack on the Soviet Union in 1941 was preceded by long-range reconnaissance missions by aircraft flying at high altitude, and the Soviets failed to prevent this, although the Germans did not grasp the size of the Soviet military.

The Germans were not alone in aerial reconnaissance. A chart of Pearl Harbor captured from a midget submarine attacking Pearl Harbor on 7 December 1941 showed that the Japanese, who had some very good reconnaissance aircraft, could have reasonable prior knowledge about locations. The Philippines were reconnoitred before the Japanese landings in December, while, in May 1942, the Japanese created a sketch map of Port Moresby in New Guinea drawn from aerial photographs; but maps of the Pacific produced before the war for Japanese forces were heavily derivative of the limited colonial mapping by the Western imperial powers attacked by Japan in December 1941: Britain, the Dutch and the United States. Moreover, the Japanese were aware of the deficiencies of their information, being worried for example about coastal reefs and other navigational obstacles off New Guinea which they invaded in 1942, but on the nearer north coast rather than sailing round to Port Moresby on the southeast one.

Once the Japanese had conquered widely, they prepared more maps in order to support fresh offensives and to protect against Allied counterattacks, notably in Burma, New Guinea, and the Solomon Islands. Produced in a hurry and often without much, or any, benefit from aerial reconnaissance, the Japanese maps were inadequate as operational tools, let alone for tactical purposes with the precision the latter required. In contrast, on those islands further from the Allies, for example the Philippines, which the Americans did not invade until late 1944, the Japanese had more time for mapping, although their maps still lacked the degree of cartographic accuracy and information seen in their Allied counterparts. The Japanese aeronautical maps of China were good, as was mapping of parts of the Soviet Union, but cartography did not have high standing in the Japanese army, and Intelligence analysis was inadequate in content or application, as shown in both China and Burma. However, in terms of preparing defensive positions, the situational awareness was fit for purpose.

The doctrine as well as technology of aerial reconnaissance advanced during the war, and each operated in a positive relationship with the other.[12] The focus can readily be on the technology and, in particular, on how Britain and the United States produced simpler and much less heavy cameras than their German counterparts, which, in large numbers, could therefore be carried by smaller and faster aircraft, such as the British Spitfire and the American Mustang, than those of the Germans. The British eventually used the Mosquito PR-34 which, with its speed and service ceiling, was less vulnerable to ground fire and aerial interception than other aircraft, as well as having the considerable range important for aerial reconnaissance. This process was further helped by the wider use of colour film as a consequence of Kodak's 1942 development of Ektachrome reversal film. Colour much increased the information that could be accessed. Aerial photography, moreover, improved significantly during the war, thanks to better cameras that offered enhanced magnification.

Technological enhancements were significant, in part because they made a doctrinal transformation possible, notably in the shape of a deliberate focus on repeated photographs of the same site, which thereby provided more information on the extent to which the Germans were using and changing a site. Equally important, photo-interpreters greatly improved their analysis of the resulting film. They had to respond to dispersion and disguise procedures in order to ensure that targeting remained appropriate, and, with their focus from the outset on long-range strategic bombing, in which the cost and risk were justified by the effectiveness, the British and Americans put more of an emphasis on this than the Germans or Japanese.

Air photos were not only crucial for planning and assessing bombing missions and the damage they had caused, but also important for operations on land and in shallow water, by providing information on topography, beach gradients and water depths, including over coral, which was a key point in the Pacific. The scale and sophistication of aerial photography, which was generally organised by index maps, was such that there would have been adequate American mapping for the large-scale invasion of Japan planned for late 1945. In contrast, other commitments and the total loss of the air war, ensured that the Axis powers progressively suffered from a lack of adequate up-to-date aerial photography, not that that prevented attacks, notably the Bulge operation in December 1944.

During the war, the need to coordinate air and land, air and sea, and land and sea, operations, especially true for tactical ground support from the air, and for airborne attacks by parachutists and glider-borne troops, as by the British at Arnhem in 1944, resulted in the increased complexity of many maps, so as to help with planning in three dimensions. Moreover, the development, explicit and implicit, of what has been termed the operational dimension of war, that between strategy and tactics, was significant, encouraging demands for mapping at a certain scale, and for planning for a standardised scale for all maps to make them comparable. Indeed, an understanding of the spatial dimension and of the terrain of the battlefield, as well as appropriate maps, were crucial to the German mission command system or *Auftragstactik*.

The place of air warfare, which was increasingly given operational and strategic roles, helped drive a new geography of war. Thus, in the Pacific, the decision, first by Japan and then by America, to seize islands was in part a function of providing airfields to expand the air support envelope across the Pacific. For air warfare, precise knowledge that could be reproduced on maps was required, and this knowledge was a matter of conditions as well as locations. While being kept secret, weather data, which both the Germans and the Allies sought to acquire in the North Atlantic, establishing manned or unmanned weather stations in Greenland and elsewhere, was mapped. As was necessary, notably for joint operations, meteorological mapping and analysis became increasingly important and sophisticated, especially with the depiction of air masses and the fronts between them. There was important standardisation by the Americans from 1942, in part in order to help prediction, while, by 1944, the Americans and British were employing radar and radio direction finders to track the weather, and hydrogen balloons were used to indicate wind speed and direction.

To help bombers, existing printed maps were acquired by all powers, and supplemented by the products of various surveillance activities. To guide their bombers to targets in Britain from 1940, the Germans used British Ordnance Survey maps enhanced with photographic information from aerial reconnaissance. More generally, as part of the process in which the war saw increased preparation for a total struggle, as well as technical improvement, aeronautical charts for aircraft became increasingly sophisticated, and were tailored to different tasks and speeds, especially in the United States, where five basic, standardised charts, each with a distinctive scale, were developed during the war: for flight planning, cruising, descent, approach, and landing and taxiing, and target perspective charts provided the view from the cockpit.

During the war, non-stop flights became far longer, and especially so for the Americans and British, not least due to larger bombers and to the use of fuel-drop tanks. The issues accordingly, for navigation encouraged the pursuit of more comprehensive aeronautical maps, notably the Western Allies' 1:1 million scale World Aeronautical Chart map series using the Lambert conformal conic projection, which provides maps on which straight lines approximate to a great-circle route between endpoints. Long-range bombing, such as that of Japan by the Americans in 1944–5, necessitated particularly accurate maps as it pushed the limit of the bombers' flying range which affected the bomb load and, as a trade-off, defensive armament that could be covered. The National Geodetic Survey's map of Japan, which was issued in April 1944, provided an azimuthal equidistant projection (all points on the map are at proportionally correct distances from the centre point) that depicted straight line routes converging on Tokyo.

With maps, the general direction of travel was, where possible, away from the use of existing sources and, instead, to the upgrading of existing maps thanks to air reconnaissance and to the creation of new maps. Thus, in the Soviet Union, the geodetic survey service switched to focus its aim on providing the military with maps and lists of coordinates, and to carrying out surveys where required. As most of the large-scale Soviet mapping envisaged in 1938 had not yet been done, immediate need was the priority. Similarly, the German military mapped Europe, western Asia, and North Africa, at the scale of 1:1 million between 1941 and 1944, which was the same scale as a new Soviet state map on which work was begun in 1941.

Alongside the production of completely new maps, there was a republication and updating of others. Thus, the Anglo-Soviet occupation of Iran in 1941, both in order to facilitate supply routes to the Soviet Union and to thwart possible German influence, led to the upgrading of existing British maps, followed by new maps of parts of Iran by the India Field Survey Company in 1943. In Egypt in 1940–2, the British benefited from operating in an area they had controlled and mapped prior to the war. The allocation of manpower and, in particular, aircraft in a situation of shortage was important to new mapping, as in North Africa where the British only had sufficient air reconnaissance after the deployment in late 1941 of the aircraft of the South African Survey Company once the conquest of Italian East Africa (Ethiopia, Somalia, Eritrea), in which it had been involved, had been completed. In North Africa, a key challenge was the need to cover part of the Sahara Desert, as the Italian mapping of Libya, while good, was largely restricted to the coastal strip. This need was increased by Allied attempts to advance a distance into the interior, not least to turn the flank of Axis coastal positions, a practice that matched the Japanese outflanking of British positions in Malaya in 1941–2. There was also a need for more detailed local maps.

In their campaigns in North Africa in 1940–3, the British also adapted Italian and French maps for their colonies of Libya and Tunisia respectively, as with the maps for the Mareth Line in Tunisia which the British, advancing from Libya, as the French had feared the Italians would do, overcame in March 1943. Original Italian maps of 1936 and 1940, with the addition of contours added by the South African Survey Company and aerial information supplied by the RAF, were the basis for the maps of Tripoli in Libya published by the War Office in 1941 and 1942.[13]

The operational flow and needs of the war very much affected the development of mapping, as did changes in the scale and structure of mapmaking, and at every level. With time, the Allies built up their capacity, in part as the Soviet Union recovered from the disruption caused by the German invasion and the move east, to escape the Germans, of production facilities. In turn, as the Soviets advanced westward beyond their pre-war borders in 1944, so they had to redraw local maps to create ones that matched Soviet specifications. Their extensive annexations in 1939 and 1940, of eastern Poland, Karelia (from Finland), Estonia, Latvia, Lithuania, and Bessarabia (from Romania), had already posed an issue for Soviet mapmakers, but this became more urgent once they moved westwards. This was a process that matched the earlier one faced by the Germans as they advanced in 1939–42, but one in which the more methodical Soviets displayed greater thoroughness, and to which they devoted more resources.

The Americans created new and renamed organisations, notably the Army Map Service, built new facilities, and recruited far more staff for mapmaking, including many women. In 1942, American activity was in part *ad hoc*, as bold plans drawn up in 1941 for new mapping were necessarily superseded by immediate demands, under the pressure of Japanese advances and attacks in the Pacific. As a result, existing maps were rapidly and simply revised, especially by adding a grid. In contrast, in 1943, new maps were compiled, often on a smaller scale and incorporating different and new material.

In addition to maps produced in the United States, there was much activity in the field. Each American army division had a Topographical Battalion able to carry out field surveys to produce maps and to print them, which aided the process of the rapid dissemination of appropriate maps to platoon-level units. The British had lorry-mounted map printers in France in 1939–40; lost at Dunkirk in 1940, they were replaced. Rapid mapping in large quantities meant that it was readily possible to record progress and adjust and adapt to new targets, so that, in North-West Europe in 1944–5, the Twelfth American Army Group produced daily situation reports, showing its position, and that of adjacent Allied forces and German units, with information overprinted on the base maps, and each sheet was accompanied by a report giving detailed material on troop positions. Particularly large numbers of maps were produced by the Allies in advance of major attacks, such as Operation Veritable, the Anglo-Canadian clearing of the *Reichswald* in February 1945.

Dependent on combined arms operations, the Western Allies proved particularly good at creating and using maps of a number of types, especially for invasions. As part of a longer-term improvement in such mapping,[14] aside from the very extensive and frequently updated maps of the landing sites, with a valuable, indeed fundamental, distinction drawn between adequate and incomplete Intelligence, there was much provision for the subsequent campaign. This included not only conflict but also the provision of facilities. Produced in 1943, a 'Geo-Topographical and Airfield Map,' for use in selecting sites in North-West Europe for rapid airfield construction, depicted existing airfields, alongside a colour-based grid: 'Blue rulings (horizontal) refer to density of possible sites in an area, judged on levelness and closeness of country,' while 'Red rulings (vertical) refer to soil types which govern permeability and drainage.' The categories were 'Granular Soils (permeable); Loam Soils (fairly permeable); Clay Soils (impermeable); and Marsh (waterlogged).' Very different criteria were covered by a July 1943 map of theoretical beach and port capacities.

Operation Overlord, the invasion of Normandy in 1944, launched on D-Day, 6 June, was preceded by precise study and mapping of climatic conditions, as these directly affected the troops' ability to land. As well as predicting average weather conditions, there was also work on five-day forecasting. Furthermore, tides and moon-phases were significant. The invasion was preceded by more than two years of aerial photography, and the resulting maps were highly-detailed. British COPPs (Combined Operations Assault Pilotage Parties) collected, mostly at night, information on hydrographic and beach conditions. The resulting maps had to include tidal levels and coastal defences. The nature of the German gun positions were carefully graded, for example:

'Fixed coast gun, in open position
Medium battery, in open position
Heavy battery in casemate
Medium, fixed coast howitzer
Light, mobile gun or gun-howitzer
Anti-tank gun, less than 50 mm
Light, machine gun'

and so on.[15]

Reflecting the geography of prioritisation and commitment for each power, there were 'cinderella' areas that had received less attention. The British had to produce new maps for south-east Asia, a task made more difficult by the major impact on aerial reconnaissance of the seasonal extent of low cloud cover, notably in Burma (Myanmar), with the same problem for the Americans and Australians in New Guinea. In 1943, the Geographical Section of the General Staff produced a new map of Burma and, in 1944, followed up with a series of maps of the region showing airfields in Japanese-occupied territory. In south-east Asia and the far-flung Dutch East Indies (Indonesia), where distances were far greater, Allied mapping, for example of Borneo, depended on advances that led to the capture of airfields from which aerial reconnaissance could be made, in this case in the Moluccas. As the British planned its recapture, the survey of Singapore, first made by the Federated Malay States Surveying Department in 1938, was updated by the War Office in 1944 and then re-issued again in 1945.[16] In the event, Japan's surrender ensured that the operation was not mounted.

As with 1898 with operations in Cuba and the Philippines,[17] but now facing the need to operate in the poorly-mapped Pacific, much of which had been in British or Japanese hands prior to the conflict, the Americans made extensive use of photo-reconnaissance, not least for mapping invasion beaches. Amphibious attacks required maps both of the islands and of the coastal waters. The American navy had the old Royal Navy Admiralty charts, but most dated from the late nineteenth or early twentieth century. While pretty good, their use posed problems, such as shoals created by subsequent storms. For the Solomon Islands, there were some Australian maps and charts, but relatively few, and the American landing force on the island of Guadalcanal in August 1942 lacked adequate maps, a problem that indicated the need for special landing maps. Moreover, the American naval raid in October 1943 on Wake Island, which before Japanese capture had been an American possession, encountered the problem of inadequate charts for the surrounding waters, and so also for the Australians with northern Australia and New Guinea.

However, as the Pacific islands, bar New Guinea and the Philippines, were small, aerial reconnaissance allowed the army and marines to make up maps quickly to issue to the troops, and this was done down to the platoon level. Very different in scale, the Philippines, an American colony prior to the war, had been surveyed by the Coast and Geodetic Survey, a civilian agency under the Department of Commerce. Its 1933 map of the Philippines as a whole, a map with depths shown by soundings, which greatly clarified sailing routes, was reissued in 1940, and the Survey's data and charts were used for the successful American invasion of the Philippines in 1944–5. In 1944, moreover, the Army Map Service published maps of the individual islands and cities, for example Cebu, with the necessary depths of the coastal waters and location of the coral reef, both of which were important to amphibious operations. The Service also published maps for other areas of potential operations, notably southeast China, West Java and Borneo. Some of these maps were reproduced for the Aeronautical Chart Service. The Australian Navy Hydrographic Service, surveyed New Guinea from 1939, pressing on to produce surveys for elsewhere in the South Pacific, in part using material from US Coast and Geodetic Survey mapping, especially of the Philippines.

The American Marines incurred heavy costs in the capture of Tarawa Atoll in the Gilbert Islands in November 1943. The landing was greatly hindered by the coral reef, the depth of which had been misunderstood in part due to a reliance on aerial photography. This exposed the need for proper advance reconnaissance and beach surveys. As a result, the Americans created Underwater Demolition Teams for the Pacific, pressing forward an initiative begun in late 1942. The recent development of the open-circuit scuba system allowed divers to swim in and out and actually go ashore at night to do the surveys, collect sand samples, plot the location of reefs, obstacles and defensive arrangements such as mines, and determine the beach gradient, all prior to the landings. There was a widespread use of fathometers for inshore navigation.

In the final year of the war, the American Naval Hydrographic Office printed more than forty million charts. Indeed, some survey ships were equipped with presses that could print 2,000 sheets an hour. This was an aspect of the cumulative experience and capability that was important to American operations. That the Americans could plan where they wanted to operate and where to mount an invasion, increased the demand for maps and charts, as did the inherently fluid style of their operations. Similarly, the supply of, and need for, charts was more problematic for Britain than in the First World War due to the pressures created by the far greater range and speed of operations, and the resulting number of tactical possibilities, leading to increased demand. In part, this demand was met by the use of rotary offset printing machines. Indeed, in the final run-up to the invasion of Normandy, the Hydrographic Office provided documents to over 6,000 vessels and authorities.

There were also new technological requirements and opportunities. The first experiments with radar involved detecting surface ships, and the ability to direct gun-fire by radar developed. The role of location at sea changed, reflecting the extent to which surface ships engaged at beyond visual range, as well as the growing significance of aircraft carriers and submarines. Aerial reconnaissance and radar were each of great importance. The latter included the use of radar-controlled fire, as on 14 November 1942, off Guadalcanal in the Solomon Islands, when the radar-controlled fire of the American battleship *Washington* wrecked the Japanese battleship *Kirishima*, a night engagement that was crucial to the American success in fighting on land on the island. Until reliable, all-weather day-and-night reconnaissance and strike aircraft were available, which was really only in the 1950s, surface ships provided the prime means of fighting at night, although the highly-successful British carrier attack on Italian warships in the harbour at Taranto in November 1940 was mounted at night. Moreover, some carrier aircraft carried radar.

Submarines were less vulnerable than surface ships to blockade, detection, and destruction, could be manufactured more rapidly, more cheaply, and in large quantities, and required smaller crews. Both submarines, and the warships and aircraft hunting them, faced grave difficulties given the vastness of the oceans and the problems entailed in finding and engaging targets, particularly, but not only, in poor weather and low visibility. A key part of the struggle involved the attempt to decipher the naval codes of opponents, in which the British and Americans proved particularly successful at the expense of Germany and Japan respectively, although also having to respond rapidly to changes in these codes.

The British overprinted Admiralty charts in order to clarify the submarine threat and the possible response, including the range of submarine patrols between refits, the range of British destroyer escort groups, and the likely limit of convoy routes. The Weekly diagram of U-boat Warfare produced by the Admiralty's Anti-Submarine Warfare Division recorded the estimated average of German submarines in an area, the anti-submarine vessels, the convoys, and the Allied shipping sunk. Coastal Command monthly reports used a chart of the waters round the British Isles to record submarine sightings, attacks on submarines, anti-submarine patrols, anti-invasion patrols, and convoy escorts, and therefore showed changes in the range of German and British operations. Charts were also used to record the sinking of U-boats, for example when crossing the Bay of Biscay, and thus to gain an insight into their likely movements. In addition, diagrams of attacks on particular convoys also aided subsequent analysis, and plans were produced depicting the submarine threat to a convoy.

In contrast, radar offered little against a submerged submarine, whereas ASDIC-SONAR [Sound Navigation Ranging] would be very useful, complementing the use of signals interception to fix the general area of submarine presence. However, the vulnerability of submarines on the surface ensured that radar played a role, being important in finding surfaced submarines, and in detecting periscopes. Aircraft rapidly came into the picture against submarines.

Capabilities were related to problems: radar was in part a reflection of the novel nature of the three-dimensional character of mapping that stemmed from the role of submarines at sea and from the addition of aircraft as a dynamic element to the vertical space already partly represented by terrain. The likely significance of air power and submarine attacks made radar a major factor as a defensive capability. Indeed, as with the use of mapping for artillery, radar was a response to the need to fix position for accurate fire.

In 1942, there were marked improvements in Allied capability, including the increased use of shipborne radar and better sonar detection equipment, and this very local locational information powerfully supplemented that from Signals Intelligence, notably Ultra, which was less specific in its locating of U-boats. In turn, enhanced weaponry, especially effective ahead-throwing, depth-charge launchers and more powerful depth-charges, as well as accumulated experience, gave effect to this information and capability. Similarly with anti-submarine air resources: again, very local target-finding was important, including ASV MK II radar and better searchlights. Radar sets small enough to be carried by aircraft, a key feature of applied capability, and yet capable of picking up submarine periscopes at five miles, were a crucial tool. As a reminder that locational identification was part of a struggle between applied technologies, this radar lost its potency when the Germans were able to introduce detection equipment on U-boats. In turn, in March 1943, the MK III radar, which could not be detected by these receivers, proved a crucial addition.[18]

However, unlike artillery on land, which generally fired from a stationary position, aircraft and submarines (like tanks) posed an inherently dynamic character in location and, thus, the depiction of location. So also with naval artillery which fired from a highly-mobile platform. Thus, radar, which looked ahead to what was to become a key element in the recent depiction of the battle-space, that of the GPS (Global Positioning System), was a response to faster moving elements on the battlefield, although, to increase effectiveness, it was necessary to develop systems and practices to handle atmospheric features. Radar, and eventually GPS, came to help forecast atmospheric (weather) features, that, in turn, were of enormous assistance to the armed forces in times of war.

Artillery very much depended on the precise location of guns and their targets within a clear and accurate set of coordinates. Artillery boards were the means, with slide rules, of working out the firing data. British artillery would be sent grid references, usually a two-digit Alfa prefix (to confirm which map), and then a six figure number of Eastings and Northings, which was computed at the gun battery command post, and the elevation and azimuth sent to each individual gun. Aircraft, in contrast, at the tactical level, would eyeball the target employing their navigator and a map. However, firepower was enhanced when support could be more speedily integrated through the use of radio by trained forward observers.

Bombardment plans were particularly important for invasions, not least to ensure the coverage of all defended positions. For the successful American invasion of Iwo Jima in February-March 1945, a 'Special Air and Gunnery Target Map', produced as an annex to the operation plan, contained a grid system to be used for pinpoint designations, and an arbitrary target square system to be used for area designations. The detailed defence symbol key indicated the extent of prior information provided by aerial reconnaissance.[19]

The needs-based aspect of mapping took many forms. In the Soviet Union, there was a need, not for oceanic mapping, but for marine navigational-artillery charts for the Baltic and Black Seas which were designed to help warships bombard targets inland in support of ground forces. Detailed inland information and a kilometre grid were supplied accordingly. This task very much matched the general doctrines and practice for the use of Soviet warships, which were largely a matter of support for land operations.

Terrain remained a major factor in conflict[20] and terrain evaluation maps were significant for infantry, artillery and vehicles operating off-road, both military and logistical. Such maps were major additions to topographical maps. German terrain evaluation maps were impressive and effective, covering a range of needs, both offensive and defensive, and regions, including the Libyan Sahara, and appeared at a number of scales. Colour was a key aspect in helping make the maps readily accessible. Aerial photography was important in providing data, but alongside ground information such as bridge weight limits. The material offered in German terrain evaluation maps included not just ground suitability, but also forest composition (type of tree), which was important to a number of aspects of close combat, and density, slope gradients unsuitable for armoured vehicles, and important viewpoints with their field of view.

The British in the autumn of 1940 established the Inter-Service Topographical Division which carried out terrain analysis to supplement topographical maps, leading to the printing of information on maps in order to make them more useful for troop movements, for example with the notation 'Irrigation ditches' on the maps prepared for the Salerno landing in Italy in 1943. Other remarks printed on the map included 'slopes generally unsuitable for widespread deployment' and 'limited deployment possible after reconnaissance'. Tactical needs led the British to develop what were termed Goings maps which were designed to display the nature of the terrain and used colour to provide readily-grasped analysis. In addition to the terrain, metalled roads were presented differently depending on their width.

The Americans created a Military Geology Unit in June 1942. Led by Wilmot 'Bill' Bradley, a member of the Geological Survey, the Unit produced valuable and plentiful material for operations, notably Operation Husky, the invasion of Sicily in 1943. For that, they showed areas favourable for invasion, as well as water-supply maps depicting wells, both perennial and non-perennial (a key distinction in Sicily), springs, aqueducts and reservoirs. These maps were typically printed with tables giving the estimated maximum yield of sources shown on the map. The value of this material in turn led to an increase in the Unit's work in Europe.[21]

There was also coverage of Pacific operations. Thus, the Unit produced Strategic Engineering Studies that included areas for potential airfields, for example on the island of Leyte in the Philippines. The necessary data included the degree of flatness as well as conditions for clearing, foundation, drainage, construction materials, and water supply. Based on existing geological maps, there was also the mapping of the type and distribution of construction materials, such maps usually accompanied by tables summarising the suitability of the material mapped for a variety of purposes.

Mapping information was related to need, so that the American 1945 map of southern Okinawa, included roads, the boundary of the area suitable for airfield sites, and the suggested runway, to scale. The key included construction requirements, classed as minimum, moderate or maximum; the number of possible runways suggested; the length of longest suggested runway, in terms of 6,000 feet or not more than 5,000; and reported existing Japanese airfields. Such airfield-construction maps were usually accompanied by tables that summarised ground conditions, grading and drainage problems, accessibility, and the availability of water and construction materials. For all powers, the rapid forward-deployment of aircraft was important at the tactical and operational levels, but it took on particular significance for the Americans due to the distances that had to be covered in the strategic bomber offensive against Japan, and the significance of this offensive. In effect, the same was to be the case during the Cold War.

There were also maps more specifically for campaigning. Thus, the American map of Kikaigashima Island, north-east of Okinawa, was graded accordingly, for example with:

'4   Terraces. Movement and road construction moderately difficult.
4a. Movement impeded only by scarps; friable clay soil; terrace surfaces even.
4b. Movement impeded by sticky clay soil; surface rolling.'

Such material was fed into the maps produced for Intelligence summaries, such as that for Operation Anvil, later Dragoon, the American-French landing in Provence on 15 August 1944, for which the area within 200 miles of Toulon was subdivided into seventeen regions described on the key in terms of their terrain. There was more detailed consideration of the target areas for amphibious and airborne forces. There was also an overprinting of existing French maps with detailed information on defences, bridges, the likely capacity of harbours, and the general topography: 'Tree and scrub covered hills with steep slopes, numerous streams, peat bogs and swamps will prevent widespread deployment of tracked and wheeled vehicles in this area.'

American terrain evaluation maps covered a range of topics, including not only the impact of the terrain on troop and vehicle maps, but also additional material on slope, soil, vegetation, climate and geological features. 'Trafficability', the suitability of the terrain for cross-country movement, was the key element, and the Americans became adept at producing such material rapidly, as, in January 1945, in preparation for the successful invasion of Germany. The material was made more valuable by being accompanied by charts showing, per month, the expected number of days of 'trafficable ground'.

The information available to American troops was formidable. Thus, the 'Stop Press Edition of 20 May 1944' for Isigny-sur-Mer in Normandy, a map to be used for briefing ground troops, which was an update of the basic edition of May, a map at a scale of 1:25,000 or 2.53 inches to the mile, included information on the softness of the ground, and on bridges: their overall length, the width of the stream at water level, the width of the road, and the load classification of the bridge. For roadsides, the existence of banks, ditches and hedges was recorded, and whether they were on one or both sides of the road. As an instance of the cumulative nature of geographical information, the information drew heavily on aerial photographs, with the contours interpolated from spot heights on the French maps as amplified by photographs. The information on magnetic declination was followed by 'compiled from Air Photographs on a control provided by existing French Triangulation'.[22] Despite plentiful Intelligence, there was still to be a shock from the nature of the *bocage*, the hedged Norman countryside, with the possibilities it offered the defensives.

Reliable maps and mapping encouraged planning to reach a specific point on a map at a certain time, planning already seen in the First World

War; but that crucial planning goal was now linked to greater mobility, which required the mapping of more terrain. In addition, the use of maps within the military was more widely extended. Whereas most ordinary soldiers (unlike officers and senior non-commissioned officers) did not use maps extensively during the First World War, they did so in the Second World War, and developed spatial awareness accordingly because maps were extensively employed at the tactical level to record both location and plans. Situation overlays were frequently employed, although the means varied: from pencil or pen to a printed overlay. Such maps were produced at a variety of scales, to cover units and combat at many levels. Hand-drawn maps were often part of the situation at the tactical level. For this reason, German officers and NCOs were taught map-drawing.

Maps were only one element in overcoming the problems of geography. Thus, for the Americans in the Pacific, the ability to overcome geography at the strategic level reflected the full effectiveness of the combined-arms naval forces the Americans deployed, including capacity, preparation and doctrine, notably carrier operations, landing craft, amphibious doctrine, fleet supply trains, floating dry docks, and rapid airfield construction. At the same time, in order to confront the problems of geography at the tactical level, notably the defensive possibilities of jungle-covered mountainous terrain, coastal cliffs, and caves there was the need to develop weaponry and technique accordingly, including sustained bombardment, combat engineers, armoured bulldozers, mounted and hand-held tank-flamethrowers and napalm. Underground Japanese defences, as on Peleliu (1944), Iwo Jima (1945), and Okinawa (1945), provided effective interconnected firing positions. Geography had another implication, as on most of the Pacific islands the Japanese lacked room and capability to manoeuvre and retreat, and, linked to this, had a greater density of troops and fortifications than on New Guinea and Luzon.

The ability to lessen geographical constraints was differently understood and seen at sea. Thus, German plans for an invasion of Britain in 1940 suffered from the lack of an appropriate force structure including the absence of proper landing craft, an absence for which the proposal to use towed river barges able to travel at only three knots was no substitute. This proposal was an instance of the *ad hoc* planning and make-do expedients that have frequently been so important to combined operations across history. Another geographical aspect was that it was deemed necessary to invade before mid-September, when the weather was likely to make sea conditions hostile, but this timetable could not be met: aside from the problems involved in assembling landing vessels, the army needed to be resupplied after the Battle of France and moved to the embarkation zones. While a geographically-based time-space matrix might appear to explain the failure to mount this invasion, in practice, as so often, military politics was an element. In this case, it in part was a context for a failure of planning and combination in which there was a lack of clarity between invasion and the *Luftwaffe* conviction that it could win by air assault alone.

Precision locational and navigational information, including on the weather, was necessary for air as well as naval warfare. This information became more significant for air warfare as strategic bombing offensives were launched. Target identification faced problems in assessing significance, and, while raids were anticipated by careful briefing using target maps and photographs, there were also serious problems with accuracy. The British wished to destroy industrial targets in Germany, but the Butt Report on night raids in June-July 1941 showed that they were not doing so. Nevertheless, concerned about the daytime vulnerability of their bombers, the British focused, from March 1942, on night-time area bombing, helped by the Fire Hazard Maps produced for German cities, maps revised in the light of aerial reconnaissance, with the cities ranked on their economic importance as targets.

The capacity of bombers increased thanks to the use of four-engined aircraft, but, although the most significant American one, the American B-17 'Flying Fortress', was a steady platform that could carry a large bomb load, precision bombing was not easy until the use of guidance systems from the 1970s. Radio navigation in wartime was far more difficult than during peace due to an emphasis, in the face of resistance, on the night-bombing of defended targets, an approach for which the use of landmarks as navigation tools was not possible unless under moon-lit clear skies when, however, aircraft were most vulnerable. There was a lack, over enemy territory, of ground-based radio aids, notably directional beacons providing bearings. As a result, hyperbolic navigation systems developed, which employed receivers on aircraft and ships to fix location using the difference in the timing of radio waves received from land-based beacon transmitters. Thus, location could be plotted from synchronised signals emitted from a considerable distance in order to guide bombers to the target.

With OBOE, a targeting system first used in December 1941, and Gee-H, a radio navigation device introduced in 1942, the British developed accurate radio navigation systems which ensured that weather, darkness, smog and flying close to the ceiling, were less of an obstacle to bombing that had hitherto depended on visual sighting. The Germans used the comparable *Knickebein* system. While radio navigation charts presented information from transmission stations, radar recognition charts to facilitate target recognition were produced, for example of the North German coast by the British. Given the problems of using charts during night bombing conditions, particular colour schemes were adopted.

Locational information, the instant mapping of a raid as it proceeded, by navigators working with precise maps, was important, but there were problems for the Allies with identifying the target, even in cloudless daylight and without anti-aircraft guns or enemy fighters; and accuracy remained heavily dependent on the skill of the pathfinder aircraft that preceded the bombers in order to identify targets. However, thanks to incremental steps, notably the role of airborne control at the target, Allied accuracy and precision improved and was significantly better in 1944 than for 1943, with the ability to mount attacks on a number of targets at the same time increasingly characteristic of Allied bombing.

The geography of airpower was fixed in part by strategic choice, for that affected the goal and location of air attack. Even if one particular form was pursued, for example strategic bombing as opposed to battlezone isolation, there were still different targeting geographies, for example against industrial plant, or with society as a whole as the object of attack in order to wreck morale. These targeting geographies were guided by practicality, and thus technological development and force structure, but also by doctrine and the concepts it refracted.

Mapping was crucial for defence against air attack, as well as for attack. This was more than simply about technical developments, as mapping is a product and aspect of information systems, both a creation of them, and a means to their success. This was clearly shown with the Battle of Britain in 1940, when, in a serious Intelligence failure, the Germans underrated the size, sophistication, and strength of the British defence and, in particular, failed to understand the role of British radar and radar stations, and their place in the integrated air-defence system, a system of information, analysis, and response. This control system, with its plotters of opposing moves and its dedicated telephone lines, was an early instance of the network-enabled capability seen in the 2000s, with its plasma screens and secure data links: in each case, the targeting, sensors and shooters were linked through a network that included the decision-maker. In 1940, on the British side, but, crucially, not the German side, able command decisions and good Intelligence were thus linked through a system that was effective for rapid analysis and prompt response.

In turn, in reaction to the subsequent Allied air offensive, the Germans developed a complex and wide-ranging system of radar warning, with long-range, early-warning radars, as well as short-range radars that guided night fighters (which also had their own radars) toward the bombers. Air defences were organised in a spatial fashion, with the particular requirements of interception and the control of units being made more dynamic by radar. This system helped cause heavy Allied losses, and led the British, in turn, to map the areas and organisation of German night fighters. German radar-defence systems could be wrecked by the British use of 'window': strips of aluminium foil that appeared like bombers on the radar screens, which were, in effect, maps. In the autumn of 1943, the Germans adapted their radar to circumvent this, but, in turn, that November, the British began to fly electronic countermeasures aircraft. Allied navigators used radar charts, on which Intelligence officers inked in German flak belts. The maps also marked the IP, the initial point where the formation was to begin its visual bomb run.

The German ability to 'map' an Allied raid as it was proceeding was not matched by Japan, which lacked the integrated nature of the German defence system and had to protect a larger area with fewer resources. Japanese airfields were often without protective radar. This situation helped ensure that Allied aircraft were able to mount successful raids, for example, crucially, on the New Guinea airfield at Wewak in August 1943, after which Allied ground operations in New Guinea were rarely threatened by Japanese aircraft. In this, as in other respects, effectiveness across the geographical range was set in part by relative capabilities.

A variant for air power, and another attempt to overcome geography in the shape of distance, was the use of a spatial reference system to guide long-range missiles, most significantly the German V-rockets, for missiles did not have a pilot who could direct them. In planning routes for the V-1, which was launched from 13 June 1944, the Germans came to appreciate that there were discrepancies between British and Continental data sets, although V-1 (like V-2) targeting was so imprecise that this was not a crucial problem. Indeed, due to the lack of a reliable guidance system, a key element in the tactical proficiency necessary for operational and strategic effect, the missiles, although destructive, and notably so in the London and Antwerp areas, could not be aimed accurately. The use of missiles reflected the inability of the Germans to sustain air attacks on Britain, as well as Hitler's fascination with new technology and the idea that it could bring a paradigm lead forward in military capability and satisfy the prospect of retaliation for the British bombing of Germany.

Very differently, there was map production by Resistance movements in Europe, based on existing topographic maps that were supplemented by their observations. At the same time, local Resistance activity reflected in part the mental grasp of a landscape, one that was more aware of possibilities for concealment or ambush than anything provided by a map. Resistance groups used highly accurate mental maps of their hideouts, and of their locations where they operated, so that the Germans would be less able to find them. Separately, there was also a spatial pattern to Resistance activity arising from both physical and human geography. Mountainous, swamp and forest regions were far more conducive, for both base areas and raids, than those that lacked natural cover. Yet this situation, as in Yugoslavia and the Soviet Union, was greatly complicated by ethnic, religious and political factors, as well as the nature of occupation.[23] Regular forces lacked that complexity of adaptability.

Meanwhile, atlases offered to the public included information necessary not only to follow the flow of campaigning, but also other factors, not least the role of economics in explaining strategic interests. Thus, natural resources and trade played a large part in J.N.L. Baker's *Atlas of the War* (1939), while in George Goodall's *The War in Maps* (1940), maps and text stressed factors such as the Lorraine iron deposits. A map of 'Belligerents and Neutrals' in September 1939 carried the caption, 'Though the map presents the appearance of "encirclement" of Germany, Poland was a negligible factor, and could not be helped by Britain and France.'[24]

The Second World War provides an opportunity to think about the geographies of war with closer access to the relevant sources than for other major conflicts. The war indicates clearly the degree to which participants sought to understand and overcome the constraints of geography, and devoted major efforts to that end, with the war of production having major environmental constraints and consequences.[25] The conflict reflected the complexity and multi-layered decision-making of war, and how a race towards better geographical knowledge and mapping, aided by continuously improving technology, was important to eventual success, notably, but not only, in naval and air warfare. In turn, particular theatres of war were transformed by action, thus creating opportunities[26] and also the need for more geographical knowledge.

Chapter 13

The Cold War and the Sequel, 1945–2000

The Cold War, the struggle between the Communist and Western blocs from 1945 to 1989, was consistently understood and presented in geopolitical terms, both for analysis and for rhetoric. A sense of geopolitical challenge was used on both sides to encourage support for readiness. The spatial dimension of threat was propagated across a number of media and was readily apparent in the standard American Van der Grinten map projection, which continued the Mercator projection's practice of exaggerating the size of the temperate latitudes. Thus Greenland, Alaska, Canada, and the Soviet Union appeared larger than they were in reality. In contrast, the would-be equal-area Peters' projection presented in 1973 made the Soviet Union appear less of a threat.

There was the question, however, whether new technology had completely overturned the established geography of war. In 1949, Omar Bradley, Chairman of the Joint Chiefs of Staff, told the US House of Representatives Committee on the Armed Services that atomic weaponry had made the large-scale amphibious assault anachronistic,[1] an analysis that was unwelcome to the navy and the marines. Indeed, a geography based on strategic nuclear bombers developed. For the United States and Britain, both nuclear powers, a range of bases were designed to target the Soviet Union, from Leningrad round to southern Russia, with the bases in England and Iraq respectively, although the Iraqi revolution of 1958 ended that strategic alliance.

In turn, the threat to the Soviet Union was extended into the Arctic and eastwards, with bases in Greenland, Iran and Pakistan. The significance of particular bases reflected not only their intrinsic potential in terms of location, but also the political context, both of those states and of alternatives. Thus, Cyprus and Aden became more important to Britain in the 1950s after the loss of bases in Palestine (1948), Suez (1954), and Iraq (1958) and this encouraged unrealistic attempts to retain them.[2] In addition, the development of Soviet long-range nuclear bombers led, in a new strategic geography, to construction in the 1950s of early-warning radar systems in Canada that were designed to protect the United States from bombers attacking over the North Pole.

Subsequently, the delivery of atomic warheads by long-range rockets led to the consideration of targeting that would have killed in the hundreds of millions, producing a geography of risk from nuclear devastation. Local geography played a role. Thus the destruction of Hiroshima, which occupied a saucer-type plain, was more widespread than that of Nagasaki, which was situated among hills and ridges that reduced the atomic blast. The geography of risk brought new geographical parameters in terms of the rocketry, although, as earlier with bombers, range remained a factor. It varied depending on whether strategic, intermediate-range, or tactical rockets were involved. This factor was seen in the case of American concern in 1962 about the location of intermediate-range Soviet rockets in Cuba, the basis of the Cuban Missile Crisis in which a form of spatial control, in terms of a naval blockade of Cuba, was used to thwart this threat.

More mundanely, the availability, on both sides in Europe, of tactical nuclear weapons affected the thinking about front-line operations, not least the need to protect troops from the threat of radioactivity. As earlier with poison gas, radioactivity had tactical, operational and strategic spatial implications, the first extending to the breathing, and thus kit, of the individual soldier.

Other factors in creating new geographical requirements and understanding included both blocs having major requirements for interoperability. Thus NATO advanced a geographical policy that introduced the Universal Transverse Mercator grid on NATO maps, and, later, it encouraged digital information exchange among its members. At another level, NATO was an aspect of the regional geopolitics of the war, with regional commands, on the pattern of the recent world war, having particular implications for strategic prioritisation, operational planning, and force allocation.

With its emphasis on the containment of the Soviet Union, a geopolitical rationale for a strategic goal, the Cold War for the Western powers meant military commitments to unfamiliar environments, most prominently Korea and Vietnam. In contrast, the defence of South Asia, which had been the earlier focus of British concern and knowledge, was of slight consequence, as the 1962 Chinese attack on India was only brief and was not repeated. In Korea, in contrast, it was as if the late nineteenth-century Japanese concern about Russian expansion had been taken on by the American-led United Nations coalition.

The shrinking of distance entailed more rapid and far-flung force deployment, for both time and space were involved. This shrinking and deployment accentuated the need to consider the constraints of new environments without lengthy, if any, prior acculturation. As a secret British War Office publication, *Warfare in Undeveloped Countries. Part 1. Desert Warfare* (1954), by General Sir Frank Messervy, who had followed most of his career in the British Indian Army, including as a commander of units in East and North Africa, and Burma, noted: 'The enemy is often, by force of circumstances, highly experienced in operations in the peculiar type of country and climates... The belief must not be allowed to spread that the enemy is superior in any way.'[3]

Containment reflected the degree to which strategy was very much given a spatial rationale; and this was the case for each of the competing blocs. They propounded supposedly universal values and ideologies, but plotted each in terms of specific locations. This process was most graphically displayed in the fortifications along the borders between the blocks, most prominently the Berlin Wall constructed by the East Germans in 1961, but also for example in Korea.

Both the Americans and the Soviets treated colonialism and imperialism as old fashioned and redundant. Each, however, found themselves committed across the world to a wide-ranging and unfixed competition, one, moreover, in which it was difficult to arrive at lasting compromise. The 'Third World', itself a geographical plotting of a highly porous construct, became, for both blocs, a range of commitment, at once opportunity and problem, not least in terms of the burdens of containment or, indeed, supporting counter-insurgency combat. The buildup of the Soviet navy to become the second largest in the world very much transformed the possibilities for American containment of the Soviet Union.[4]

At the same time, conflict brought the specificities of fighting over particular sites, such as Heartbreak Ridge in Korea in late 1951, and Plei Me and Khe Sanh in Vietnam in 1965 and 1968 respectively, as well as the need for routes along which supplies could be moved, most prominently the Ho Chi Minh Trail in the Vietnam War. This route was a key element at the operational level in that struggle, but also one of major strategic significance as providing the prime way to link North Vietnam with the Viet Cong and thus give both a degree of flexibility lacking if they could only operate across the narrow DMZ (Demilitarized Zone) between North and South Vietnam. This route was a classic outflanking, one that took benefit from the politics of using the territory of weak neutral states: Laos and Cambodia.

More generally, the ability to exploit physical and human environments was important to the ability of insurgency forces to sustain their presence[5] and thus seek to win or at least sustain a struggle in which the will to do so was important. Therefore, limiting the flow of munitions to insurgents proved important in suppressing both Communist insurrections in Greece, Malaya and the Philippines, as well as Western-backed opposition to Communist rule in Eastern Europe, Tibet and Cuba. So also in 2020–2 with Ethiopia benefiting in its struggle with opponents in the rebellious Tigray region from the support of neighbouring Sudan and Eritrea, thus cutting supply lines. Moreover, Eritrean forces joined in on the government side.

On a long-standing pattern, controlling rural geography in the shape of agricultural production was also important in lessening chances for insurgents, as with anti-Francoists in Spain in the late 1940s, or those against British rule in the West Indies in the 1790s, and against Ottoman rule in Anatolia in the 1600s. Famine via blockade was also used by Nigeria in suppressing Biafran separatism in 1967–70 and in Ethiopia in 1983 and 2020–2.

In the extensive province of Dhofar, the westernmost area of the Sultanate of Oman, a left-wing insurgency backed by neighbouring South Yemen was overcome in the mid-1970s in part by a similar control over food supplies. In addition, the human geography was altered in 1974 with the construction of Hornbeam, a line of positions providing an anchor for the British-backed Omani forces, and the movement out of the civilian population between Hornbeam and the frontier of pro-insurgent South Yemeni, thus leaving the insurgents without cover and assistance. Conversely, Communist victory in the Chinese Civil War in 1949 was followed by the provision of support to the Communist and nationalist Viet Minh against the French in neighbouring Vietnam, notably in the Le Hong Phong II offensive in late 1950. The French were finally defeated in 1954.

There was also the particular geographies created, first, by the synergy of guerrilla and conventional warfare, as successfully used by the Viet Minh against the French in Vietnam in 1946–54, and, secondly, by the Communist powers 'leapfrogging' containment in order to take a role in confrontation and conflict in the Third World, notably in Africa. As far as the first was concerned that created a geography linked to the supposed stages of revolutionary war, each of which was characterised by a different presence in society and the environment, moving from marginal to central areas. Thus, in 1965, the last stage appeared in play with the deployment of large Communist forces in South Vietnam, and the same was to be attempted in 1968, 1972 and, finally successfully, in 1975.

In contrast, the Americans focused there initially on defending coastal areas that were strongholds of South Vietnamese power and essential for American deployment, but gradually, having built up an impressive logistical infrastructure, they moved into the Central Highlands. The Americans were able to advance into parts of South Vietnam that had been outside the control of Saigon and to inflict serious blows on the Viet Cong in the Mekong Delta. The geography of the campaigning zone was transformed by the extensive American use of the helicopter, which provided both mobility and firepower, and lessened the need for movement on land by means of convoys that could be ambushed. Yet the volume of supplies required ensured that convoys provided the major means of movement.

The very contrasting physical environment of the Six Days War in 1967, notably the Sinai Desert in which the Israelis defeated the Egyptians, was such that, once air superiority had been rapidly gained by Israel, tanks were the key element. The Egyptian armoured vehicles were vulnerable to Israeli aircraft even though the latter were using ordnance and guidance systems that were 'dumb' and thus very different from what were to follow by the Gulf Wars of 1991 and 2003.

The Sinai, however, in turn, became a problem for the Israelis in 1973, when a surprise Egyptian attack overcame the obstacles of the Suez Canal and the defending Bar Lev Line, and the Israeli forces were without cover in the flat desert to the east. In contrast, the Israeli forces facing the contemporaneous Syrian attack in the Yom Kippur War benefited from a hilly terrain that provided more defensive sites and a better opportunity for counterattacks.[6] The loss of clear Israeli air superiority to Soviet-supplied Egyptian ground-to-air missiles in the early stages of the Sinai fighting in 1973, was part of the resetting of the vertical geography of the battlespace, one also seen with the Viet Minh's anti-aircraft fire at Dien Bien Phu in 1954, and with the Soviet-supplied missiles used by the MPLA against the Portuguese in Angola in 1973–4.

The shrinking of distance, particularly by, and for, major powers, was not only a matter of the deployment and support of forces, land, sea and air, but also, subsequently, of the reduced time-distance between sensor and shooter. A global confrontation in which war was always an immediate prospect, the Cold War ensured the need for more in-time and comprehensive information about opposing deployments than hitherto, and notably due to the possibility that attacks would be launched by air and rocket from sites very distant from the frontier, including submarines. This need for information, which produced geographies of Intelligence gathering and sharing,[7] was a key aspect of the extent to which the activities of forces across the world were covered at home; and by politicians, military leaders, and the civilian population.

As a consequence, and in the aftermath of both the Soviet Union and the United States having experienced traumatic surprise attacks in 1941, at the hands of Germany and Japan respectively, the requirements for reconnaissance increased, and, in this, both requirements and technology interacted. Thus, the range of aircraft increased greatly with the introduction of jet aircraft. The American Boeing RB-47 Stratojet, a version of the high-speed and high-altitude B-47E bomber, first flown in 1953, had a range of about 4,000 miles. The availability and capability of Soviet jet fighters, however, threatened these flights, as did improvements to ground-based anti-aircraft fire. As a result, the U-2 was introduced by the Americans, with its first flight in 1955. Able to fly at more than 80,000 feet and to provide accurate pictures, the U-2 provided much long-range intelligence for strategic intentions and target selection.[8]

Aircraft as a source of information were supplemented by satellites projected into orbit by rockets after the first satellite, the Soviet Sputnik 1, was launched in 1957. Orbiting satellites offered the potential for obtaining material, for transmitting it speedily by means of the radio dispatch of images, and for the creation of a global telecommunications system. Satellites were too high to be shot down, as a U-2 aircraft, en-route from Peshawar in Pakistan to Bodø in Norway, had been brought down over Sverdlorsk by a Soviet surface-to-air missile in 1960. The Corona programme of American reconnaissance satellites produced and operated by the CIA began in 1959, although it was only in 1960 that, with Discoverer 13, the first pictures were received. Discoverer 14, also in 1960, was the first fully-successful mission. It provided sixteen pounds of film, and extensive coverage of the Soviet Union.

The overlap between photography and mapping was increasingly pronounced. Satellites offered the possibility of frequent overflights and, thus, of more data. Regular satellite images provided the opportunity to map change on the ground, including the construction of missile sites. In 1960, the National Reconnaissance Office was created as a secret agency designed to coordinate American spy satellites. It became possible to map the entire world at small scale, while, in 1961, the National Photographic Interpretation Center was established by the Americans in order to perform photographic analysis as part of the CIA's Directorate of Science and Technology.[9] Photoreconnaissance operated at a number of levels, in marked contrast to the situation in the First World War.

Photoreconnaissance was also crucial to the American Army Map Service (AMS) which, as a result, delivered large numbers of maps to American forces in the Vietnam War, and as part of a major expansion in the accumulation of spatial information. The Americans enhanced their reconnaissance capability with the Lockheed SR-71 Blackbird, which could fly at Mach 3 and outrun any missile. Moreover, drones brought back high-resolution photographs from Vietnam. That war saw the establishment in 1972 of the Defense Mapping Agency (DMA).

The use of such material encouraged secrecy about cartographic applications, which was an important aspect of a more general secrecy that was seen, in particular, with the deliberate distortion of maps, not least by altering positions, but also by omitting information. This process was particularly apparent with the Eastern bloc during the Cold War, but was not only seen there. For example, the American government omitted federal military sites, such as the North American Aerospace Command, from maps, and also degraded GPS radio signals for non-military uses, while British and other maps also disguised facilities. The use of maps to help targeting was therefore linked to the more general process of camouflage, with the distortion of maps a key element of camouflage. Geography was both weaponized, and also an aspect of the anti-weaponry that sought to counter advantages. The former was certainly so in the extension of information coverage.

Faced, as a result in particular of aerial surveillance, by a vast amount of data, the military was also necessarily active in addressing improved systems for data compilation and usage, which became a key element in the response to geographical data. The need to analyse vast amounts of information provided a major spur in the development of computer systems and then, more significantly, in their improvement. Computer systems, in turn, proved especially significant in new cartographic techniques, in large part, not least in image correlation and aerial triangulation, so as to produce digital terrain maps. The military profited greatly from the use of digital technology for mapping and for the application of cartographic information. The United States proved much more adept than the Soviet Union in developing computer capacity. This contrast was of growing significance by the 1980s and helped encourage a sense that the Soviet Union was becoming obsolescent and needed to reform, a process that led to its dissolution.[10]

Satellite information came to serve as the basis for enhanced weaponry. The US Department of Defense developed a Global Positioning System (GPS) that depended on satellites, the first of which was launched in 1978. Automatic aiming and firing techniques rested on accurate surveying. Far more accurate than in the Second World War, 'smart' weaponry, such as guided bombs and missiles, make use of precise mapping in order to follow predetermined courses to targets actualized for the weapon as a grid reference, thus increasing accuracy and counteracting the financial commitment involved. Cruise missiles use digital terrain models of the intended flight path: the flight profiles of cruise missiles reflected terrain contour matching that characterized the landscape and could be scrutinized by missile sensor systems managed by a computer guidance programme.[11] The Soviet Union sought to match the GPS system with its own Global Navigation Satellite System, which, in 1996, reached its full design specification of twenty-four satellites. All spatial information was potentially of military value, and, indeed, weaponisable.

The Korean War of 1950–3 led to the production of about ten million map sheets by the US Army Corps of Engineers. In contrast, in the

1991 First Gulf War with Iraq, the American DMA alone produced over 100 million maps, including 12,000 new map products, for its forces and, benefiting from digital photography, the Americans used cruise missiles and aircraft with great accuracy and effect against Iraq.[12] This encouraged air-power commentators to emphasize a geography of comprehensive targeting: 'air power's speed and range allow it to strike targets across the entire depth and breadth of an enemy country.'[13] Precise positioning devices, indeed, interacted with American satellites to offer an effective GPS that was employed with success by Allied (the American-led coalition) tanks in their combat with Iraqi counterparts, a situation dramatically different to those previous conflicts in which tanks had played a major role. In addition, satellite information helped in the rapid production of photo-maps. Geographical Information System software provides instantaneous two- and three-dimensional views of battlefields.

At the same time, the geography of the Allied plan was simple and, based on skilful terrain analysis, a reprise of the standard fix and flank: while the Iraqis were attacked on the coast on the direct route to Kuwait City, their right (on the coalition forces' left) was outmanoeuvred by a rapid American advance to the west. This advance put tremendous pressure on the Iraqis, as the outflanking American forces turned to attack them and destroyed much of the Iraqi army which, by having to turn from prepared defensive positions, was forced into the vulnerability of movement.

The speed and range of advanced-capability militaries were not restricted to satellites and air attack. More generally, aerial movement and supply capabilities further transformed the situation, as front lines were thereby dissolved and were perceived as dissolved, or at least as a matter of zones and gradations, rather than lines. Already, in confronting the Algerian insurrection launched in 1954, the French had complemented static garrisons by pursuit groups, often moved by helicopter, which were stepped up in 1959 in response to the arrival of significant numbers of large helicopters, hitting the insurgents hard. In 2001, the Americans used helicopters to lift troops into combat from ships in the Arabian Sea to Kandahar in Afghanistan, a distance of 450 miles. This deployment provided both range and speed.

Alongside this high-specification spatially-based knowledge and technology, came the reality of more ordinary maps used for struggles at the local level, not least, but not only, by states that lacked this cutting-edge capability. Different, but sometimes related to this, the limited mapping of much of the world for most of the twentieth century, and notably its first two-thirds, could be a factor. Thus, in 1963–6, the maps used by the British military in their 'Confrontation' (low-level conflict) with Indonesia in Borneo were largely blank for the Indonesian side of the frontier with the former British territories (by 1963 part of Malaysia) that the British were protecting.

Conflicts in defence of British imperial interests led to the production of topographic maps by Field Survey Squadrons, as in Kenya in the 1950s, in response to the Mau Mau uprising; in Malaya, also in the 1950s in the 'Emergency' against Communist insurgents; and in Borneo during the 'Confrontation'. Similarly, the French were active in map-making in Algeria in 1956–62 as they resisted insurrection, and the Portuguese in their African colonies. However, when the British drove the Argentinian invaders from the Falkland Islands in 1982, they suffered from a lack of adequate mapping, including no digital coverage.

Newly-independent states rapidly established their own mapping agencies, in many cases building on previous imperial bodies. For example, the Egyptian Military Directorate was founded in 1954. In most states, military mapping was, and is, highly confidential, for example that of India on its borders with China and Pakistan. Maps in the Indian Army are prepared by the Survey Department which comes under the General Staff. As an aspect of conflict as broadly conceived, maps are also used to assert claims, as with the frontiers of South Asia, notably in the case of China, India and Pakistan, and to rename and remake landscapes. Thus, Arab villages were taken out of some Israeli maps.

The mapping of insurgency and counterinsurgency struggles, and indeed of terrorism and counterterrorism, were problematic, an issue that continues to this day, as, in this warfare, the notion of control over territory is challenged by forces that cannot be readily described in terms of conventional military units. They seek to operate from within the civilian population, and do so not only for cover and sustenance, but also in order to deny their opponents any unchallenged control over populated areas. This is conflict that is psychological and political, as much as more narrowly military. A soldier sent into Greece in 1944, as part of the British force designed to end the incipient civil war, recalled:

'The enemy was just the same as any other Greeks as far as we knew, they didn't have any uniform as such.... It was a situation that was quite completely different to the way we had been used to fighting... As an average infantryman, one of the first questions that you ask is "Which way is the front?" so that you know if the worst comes to the worst which way you can go to get out of the bloody place. In this sort of situation, which is a typical urban "battlefront", it's all around you.'[14]

It is difficult often to understand, let alone map a situation of shared insurgency and counter-insurgency presence, one, as with Soviet forces in Afghanistan in 1979–89, in which military or police patrols move relatively unhindered, or suffer occasional sniping and ambushes, and have to consider mines; but, otherwise, control little beyond the ground they stand on. Moreover, the situation can vary greatly between daylight and night-time. Furthermore, this situation included the standard geography of insurgency, that of particular areas being frequently or always rebellious, with the more wide-ranging challenge from terrorism.[15] There were also the psychological ideas of space, the mental mapping that reflected varied strategic geographies. Thus, in states that had military coups, the location of barracks, presidential palaces, and radio stations, took on particular significance.

The geographies of war were also at issue in the depiction of past, current, and possibly future conflict. Thus, there was a major difference between Communist mapping, which presented people's warfare, such as 'struggles for national liberation' and class struggle, and the non-Communist emphasis, instead, on homogenous blocs of territory. *Történelmi atlasz* (1961), the atlas for Hungarian secondary school pupils, presented maps for the Hussite rebellion (1419–34), the Peasants' War in Germany (1524–5), and the Paris Commune (1871), while the *Školní Atlas Československých Dejin* (1959) had maps of the 1680 and 1775 Bohemian uprisings. In the map of the Paris Commune in the Albanian *Atlas Histork* (1974), the dramatic arrows of the Communards advancing from Paris had a greater visual impact than those of their more numerous and successful opponents, but the latter did not fit the narrative. Anti-Communist atlases, such as Iwo Pogonowski's *Poland. A Historical Atlas* (1987), were very different in their themes, as in the battles depicted, for example victories over the Russians at Orsha (1514) and over the Moldavians at Obertyn (1531).[16] So also with the emphasis on the role of the Poles in blocking the advance of the Red Army on Warsaw in 1920.

The Cold War looks toward the present situation. There is repeated discussion today of how cyberwarfare, and the related electronic assault forces and internet attacks, will provide a global-range capability that can swamp conventional defences. As a consequence, the integration of space, cyber and intelligence is presented as crucial to military utility in the land, maritime and air domains.[17] While this point is true of force-output, that, however, does not equate with outcome which, instead, will continue to be culturally dependent on the human environment, which was the position during the Cold War.

This chapter, like the book as a whole, seeks to show a wide range of conflict zones in which there were physical and human constraints, as well as the means by which such constraints were overcome. The latter included improved mobility, as with helicopters in Vietnam, or sophisticated orbiting spy satellites, and surveillance systems that enabled missiles to be detonated at their targets with pin-point accuracy. Technological development has been a catalyst for computer development, which was required for the complex analysis of the enormous amount of data received. Thus, modern warfare is highly complex and technologically eminently sophisticated, although more conventional military operations did not cease. They still occurred in locations where political and economic conditions meant that highly-technical operations were not possible or where conflict occurred at an essentially local level.

Chapter 14

From 2001 into the Future

Most conflicts today occur as forms of civil war and thus within countries, for example Afghanistan, Ethiopia, Iraq, Mali, Sudan and Syria. As a consequence, the nature of war is particularly complex, not least because of overlapping with other forms of violence and politics, including coups. This nature is not one readily, let alone necessarily, addressed in terms of cutting-edge capability, whether weaponry or with reference to information availability and cartographic methods; and there is scant sign that this situation is changing. Moreover, as warfare, both past and contemporary, amply indicates, and as is argued in this book, an understanding of place simply as a physical phenomenon, while it can be very necessary and useful at the strategic, operational and tactical levels of war, is less helpful in enforcing will, the true goal of conflict. Indeed, in some respects, by creating a deceptive sense that other peoples, societies and lands are readily 'knowable', mapping is to a degree misleading. It is more appropriate, instead, to understand the complexities, ambiguities and nuances of human geography, including the ambiguities of capabilities, the precariousness of results, and the degree to which the shared nature of any military situation throws the focus on to political understanding and skill.

One aspect of this complexity can be a confusion over goals. This is an aspect closely linked to the nexus of the strategic level of war and human geography, as opposed to the rival nexus of the tactical level and physical geography. This situation was notably so in the case of Afghanistan from 2001 to 2021, with the Western (principally American) interventionist goals the very different ones of eliminating al-Qaeda as part of the 'American War on Terror,' removing the Taliban regime that provided al-Qaeda with shelter, establishing democracy in Afghanistan, ensuring stability, eliminating drug-production, and improving the economy. Such a combination, in part clashing, even contradictory, and also changeable, was/

is typical of the way in which priorities accumulate, in part as a constituency and coalition of support is sought, both domestically and internationally.

Yet, linked to this, as was frequently argued at the time, insufficient effort was made to stabilize Afghanistan in a way fitted to Afghan society, practices of power, and concepts of honour. Instead, a global perspective took precedence over that of the locality and specific.[1] As an instance of the degree to which human geography readily affects strategy, it is clear that, without an understanding of local culture, religion, language and custom, and the adoption of policies accordingly, lasting peace at the closure of operations was unlikely to pertain. The overlap of conflict and politics, or overt and covert, was a matter not only of engaging in Afghanistan, but, more generally, of a challenge posed to conventional assumptions about warfare, not least by Russia.[2]

Meanwhile, physical and human images and terms of conflict overlapped and competed, and especially so in the political sphere. Thus, in 2003, the United States focused on Iraq, a definite and defiant target with regular armed forces, rather than on the more intangible struggle with al-Qaeda terrorism and the Taliban pursued in Afghanistan from 2001. Iraq was presented in, and by, the United States in terms of 'drying up the swamp': eliminating a state allegedly supporting terrorism, as well as, more specifically, destroying Iraq's supposed capability in weapons of mass destruction. The reference to the swamp was an echo of the use by Americans, such as Ronald Reagan and Pat Buchanan, of the phrase 'drain the swamp' to refer to what they disliked, most frequently the federal bureaucracy, a phrase later frequently used by Donald Trump.

In practice, the Saddam Hussein regime, while doubtless noxious and, as Iran, Kuwait and Israel could testify, regionally threatening, did not support al-Qaeda, but the American terror narrative proved a way to link national security to conflict with a particular hostile state. More generally, 'the War on Terror' that began in 2001 had a geography that was all-encompassing. This was seen in a worldwide anxiety of scanning for threats, as in defences and defence procedures in every airport and passenger jet, and widespread surveillance systems, barriers and protective features, such as toughened glass. The all-encompassing character was also seen in linking the 'Home Front' to abroad, and in the merger of military, intelligence, and policing functions and tasks. Yet 'the War on Terror' was also highly specific to particular geographical areas.

Great power tensions, indeed confrontations, suggest that warfare may take a different form and, as a result, that there may be contrasting geographical assumptions. This possibility came to the fore anew in the mid-2010s, first when greater tension between China and Japan over the East China Sea, led to the possibility of a confrontation between China and Japan's leading ally, the United States, and, secondly, when the crisis between Russia and Ukraine in 2014, notably over Crimea, escalated to include the possibility of Russian expansionism at the expense of Estonia, Latvia and/or Lithuania, with the danger that such activity might lead to conflict with NATO, a crisis that recurred in 2022.

In each case, the range of weaponry was a major element, notably in defining geographies of menace. Thus, the range of Russian and Chinese missiles became centrally linked to ideas of area-denial for other forces. Control over particular parts of territory, on land (as with the Russians in the Kaliningrad enclave, and with the Russians and NATO for the Suwalki Gap between the enclave and Belarus through which NATO would reinforce the Baltic Republics[3]) and sea (as with the Chinese man-made or enhanced islands in the South China Sea), became more significant as a result of their serving as the bases of these missiles. This significance underlined the importance of strategically-located tiny places to the world powers, including, for the United States, Diego Garcia, Guam, and Incirlik airbase in Turkey, and, for Britain, Akrotiri in Cyprus. Bases for aircraft, rockets and listening stations were all involved. In some respects, these places were the equivalent to the naval bases and coaling stations of former years, although Intelligence facilities can be more significant. In November 2020, however, Diego Garcia was mentioned as a possible base if the Americans established a new numbered fleet for the Indian Ocean, which was to be called the First Fleet.

The allocation of naval tasks is a reminder of the fluidity of geopolitical construction. For example, in place of the earlier focus on the Asia-Pacific, the term Indo-Pacific became more significant from 2007 when the Japanese Prime Minister, Shinzo Abe, gave a speech to the Indian Parliament entitled 'The Confluence of Two Seas,' in which he argued that:

'The Pacific and the Indian Oceans are now bringing about a dynamic coupling as seas of freedom and of prosperity. A "broader Asia" that broke away from geographical boundaries is now beginning to take on a distinct form... By Japan and India coming together in this way, this "broader Asia" will evolve into an immense network spanning the entirety of the Pacific Ocean, incorporating the United States of America and Australia.'

The American government recognised this in 2018 by changing the name of United States Pacific Command to Indo-Pacific Command, Jim Mattis, the Defense Secretary, referring to a 'recognition of the increasing connectivity between the Indian and Pacific oceans'. The idea of a new First Fleet was a reflection of this, one designed to reduce the pressure on the Seventh Fleet, which operates out of Japan, covering from the International Dateline to the Indo-Pakistan border.

The technological situation was also changing rapidly. In 2018, Russia deployed its nuclear-capable, 500 kilometre (300 miles) range, Iskander missiles to the Kaliningrad enclave. The lethality of such missiles was a factor alongside their range, as with the Chinese test firing of a nuclear-capable DF-21D 'carrier-killer' anti-ship ballistic missile into the South China Sea in August 2020. The other missile then tested, the Chinese DF-26B, can carry nuclear or conventional warheads and has a range of 4,000 kilometres, thus making it capable of hitting American forces on the Pacific base of Guam. Access-denial weaponry was the key theme, with Russia trying to deny the Baltic to NATO and Swedish forces, and to threaten, as well as harass, NATO activity in the Black Sea. China did the same to the Americans in the western Pacific, and, more specifically, the waters round Taiwan. Access-denial at the least increases the risk inherent in deployment, which is another, but different, form of denial.

In addition, hypersonic weapons, in which Russia led the way, offered an ability to get inside opponents' command-and-control system times, thus providing another type of range capability. In December 2019, Russia claimed to have deployed Avangard hypersonic glide vehicles able to travel twenty times the speed of sound at a continental range and to deliver both nuclear and conventional payloads. In October 2020, the Tsirkon missile, which had been revealed by Russia the previous year, was successfully tested: a ship- or submarine-launched, hypersonic cruise missile, able to travel at up to eight times the speed of sound, with a range of 600 miles, that could be armed with a conventional or nuclear warhead, covered over 280 miles in 4.5 minutes in order to destroy a target in the

Barents Sea. For this and other weapons, nevertheless, the uncertainty of performance in wartime conditions, notably exposure to defence mechanisms that themselves improve, was part of the unpredictability of weapons' capabilities, usage and impact. Moreover, although hypersonic weapons may be fast and not hindered by physical geographic features, the potential targets are geographic, and these smart weapons depend on spatial information. So also with local geographical features affecting the blast, blast wave and radioactivity of atomic bombs.

Confrontation with China created a greater test for the United States than Russia. The notion of space as an index of political determination was underlined in August 2020 when Mark Esper, the American Defense Secretary, announced, of the South China Sea, 'We're not going to cede this region, an inch of ground if you will, to another country.' The idea of the Pacific as an American lake was part of the psychological equation, as was the legacy and validation of America's role in the Second World War in the Pacific. Such ideas, however, and the strategic culture bound up in them, were challenged by the increased range of land-based strategic and intermediate weapon systems. This led to American naval interest, expressed by Rear Admiral Robert Gaucher in 2020, in unmanned systems in order to get inside the Chinese 'denied areas',[4] and to reduce the cost of doing so.

Turning to more general politics, the various definitions possible for stability came into play, as did their implications for political geography. On the one hand, there is only an occasional creation of new states with the instability they can reflect or help cause; but, more common, is a position of instability related to shared power in a situation of rivalry and often violence. That instability can vary from competing claims between states, as in the Mediterranean and South and East China Seas at present, to internal instability. From that latter perspective, many states may not be failed, but are certainly failing, with ethno-nationalism a problem, and in very differing ways, for states as varied as Britain, Spain, Ethiopia and South Africa.

Separately, the geography of conflict operates at a number of levels, as with the Iranian quest from the 2000s to create an 'area of influence' or a 'corridor' to the Mediterranean to extend its control, via Iraq and Syria, to southern Lebanon, where its ally, Hezbollah, is in power as part of a more general practice of proxy warfare.[5] Hezbollah also underlines the potential role of non-state groups, not least when armed with long-range missiles, and, as Israel can testify, the military challenge such groups can pose. The crisis in the sub-Saharan *sahel* is different in its geopolitics, but also indicates the military significance of such groups.

These issues see the interplay of zones of concern with the specificities of particular routes and bases through, and from, which power is deployed, as with French bases in sub-Saharan Africa from which force is articulated in the struggle with *jihadists* in the *sahel*, or Russian bases in Syria. In 2020, Britain announced a £23.8 million investment in a logistics hub in the port of Duqm, in part to support more British army training in Oman, but also as a possible base for the new British aircraft carriers. Oman sees this as a way to increase its security with regard to Iran by having significant American and British forces based in and around them. Ben Wallace, the British Defence Secretary, said that there would be a shift to 'forward-deploy' British military forces to protect British interest and those of allies.[6] That meant a particular focus on the Middle East, Indian Ocean and Far East, which was in line with the emphasis on the navy in the November 2020 statement on an increase in military expenditure, a statement that suggested the permanent basing of one of Britain's two aircraft carriers in the region.

Such a form of deployment is very public and deliberately prominent. In contrast, submarines rely on stealth. As a result, they are a hidden component in military geography. Yet, for political purposes they can be brought to the fore, as in December 2020 when an American submarine with a formidable cruise warfare armament surfaced at the entrance to the Persian Gulf in a clear warning to Iran that was much reported in the media.

The same year, Russia and Sudan negotiated an agreement for Port Sudan on the Red Sea to become a Russian base, which would provide a defended setting for refueling and repairs, as well as enable the monitoring of American naval moves. Also in the region, and possibly in line with what has been referred to as a Neo-Ottomanist foreign policy, Turkey opened a base in Mogadishu, Somalia in 2017. In contrast, the United Arab Emirates withdrew its training forces from Mogadishu in 2018, and, by late 2020 appeared to be heavily over-extended militarily, notably in Yemen, and keen to retract. Geopolitical interest and commitments do not need to be permanent.

So also with the role of bases in the American confrontation with China, a confrontation that poses issues for local powers whose support is sought, or, as with Palau and the United States in 2020, that seek to use the confrontation to attract investment. The Pentagon annual report to Congress on China's military modernization programme, released in September 2020, noted that China had only one overseas base, in Djibouti, which extended its reach into the wider Middle East, but that China wished to have bases also in Myanmar, Thailand, Singapore, Indonesia, Pakistan, Sri Lanka, the United Arab Emirates, Kenya, the Seychelles, Tanzania, Angola, and Tajikistan. The report stated that this would permit the People's Liberation Army (PLA): 'to project and sustain military power at greater distances... A global PLA military logistics network could interfere with US military operations and provide flexibility to support offensive operations against the United States.'[7]

The impression was of a global span, and China's initiatives, notably the land and sea corridors of the Belt and Road Initiative, certainly have both strategic and commercial implications in terms of a heartland power dominating what Halford Mackinder had termed the world island.[8] However, in practice, there was a particular focus in Chinese strategic geography, notably on the south-west Pacific and the Indian Ocean,[9] while the Atlantic, although an area of interest to China, particularly with Angola, Equatorial Guinea, and the West Indies, was less of a primary combat zone.

More generally, alongside the rhetoric of world-wide ideological applicability and more specific political and commercial interests, the interplay of weapons technology and political possibilities, notably the role of local and subregional views and realities,[10] in moulding strategic geography was readily apparent. Thus, in 2018, in response to concern about Russia, the Americans re-established the Second Fleet, which represented a renewed American defence commitment to the North Atlantic Ocean.[11]

So also with oil and gas pipelines. These reflect both historical and current initiatives and events. In the first case, Israel built a 158-mile Eilat-Ashkelon pipeline to parallel the Suez Canal, while the Trans-Arabian pipeline from the Gulf to Lebanon was disrupted in 1967 when the Syrian part in the Golan Heights was captured by Israel in the Six Days' War. At the current moment, but as a continuance of a major issue of the 1980s, Russia's Nord Stream 2 plan to expand the capacity of the undersea gas pipeline to Germany is a matter of acute geopolitical controversy, not least as likely to create a strategic relationship of German dependency on Russia and, therefore, vulnerability both for Germany and for NATO as a whole. American policymakers are particularly anxious on this point. The Ukraine crisis of 2021–2 underlined its significance.

Meanwhile, the mapping of confrontation and conflict was affected by the new possibilities created by developing technology, and notably so with cyber-warfare. In the context of real-time mapping in response to the closure of the gaps between surveillance, decision and firing, the prospect of such mapping being affected by attacks on communication systems, whether satellites or computers, was one that threatened to plunge opponents into a cartographic void. Thus, ironically, the very enhanced capability that appeared to stem from cartographic improvement and application also threatened to create a vulnerability that was far greater in type than that posed by attacks on air reconnaissance assets in the two world wars and the Cold War.

The dynamic character of reconnaissance was further demonstrated by the role of drones, and subsequently micro-drones, in an enhanced reconnaissance capability, as well as the relevant effectiveness of cyber-warfare. Mini-drones capable of entering buildings are part of the miniaturization of a combined firepower and mobility capability. More generally, drone technology has expanded, for example with naval drones, such as the MQ-9B Sea Guardian sold by America to Taiwan in 2020, underwater drones, and aerial refueling drones, such as the American MQ-25 Stingray.[12]

Moreover, drones have been shown to be highly effective in conflict. Alongside artillery and missiles, the drones and missiles provided to Azerbaijan by Turkey ensured that in terms of the weaponry used the conflict with Armenia was different to previous clashes between the two sides, notably in 1994 and, on a smaller scale, 2016. In 2020, drones were successfully used by the Azeris against tanks in large part because the Armenians lacked adequate counter-drone weaponry. The Azeris also employed Israeli-made missiles that loiter above the battlefield until they can identify a target. In 2021, Ethiopia used Chinese and Turkish drones against Tigray rebels.

Not only states have used drones. In 2020, the Taliban allegedly used a weaponized drone against Afghan forces, taking on their earlier use of surveillance drones. Earlier, Islamic State had, from 2013, employed drones, including to drop munitions in Iraq and Syria.[13] Other non-state actors that have drone capabilities included the Houthi in Yemen, Hamas, Hezbollah, the PKK Kurds, Boko Haram, the Maute movement in the Philippines, and Palestinian Islamic Jihad.

A sense of the future geography of war is obviously one that evades precision, and there is therefore a temptation to address the subject predominantly in terms of developments in technology. In particular, these lend themselves to the themes of geography overcome, or, if a less triumphalist account is adopted, reshaped. To ignore that perspective would be foolish in the extreme, not least as developments in miniaturized reconnaissance, robotics and Artificial Intelligence, all suggest very significant and rapid changes, reaching to the most immediate and individual of tactical levels, and in some cases bringing down the cost of weapon systems.

Furthermore, the particular environments, and therefore geographies, of land, sea, submarine, air, space, and cyber, are all ones that are subject to technological change, as are the interactions between them and the possibility of using these interactions in order to gain or lose advantage. In 2020, the US military signed contracts to assess technical and cost challenges for building a 7,500 mph rocket able to blast 80 tonnes of cargo into space and land it anywhere in the world within about a hour. Whereas, to reinforce Bagram airbase in Afghanistan took a C-17 Globemaster, with its maximum speed of 590 mph, up to 15 hours, 7,000 miles from Cape Canaveral for a rocket was designed to take an hour. Moreover, under the 1967 Outer Space Treaty, over-flight via orbit did not require arrangements with foreign governments. Cost, precision, and the safe arrival of cargo were all factors. However, while the existing system was not cost-free, C-17s costing $218 million each and C-5 Galaxies over $100 million, this was far more feasible than the proposed new system, even though the Falcon 9, a partly reusable rocket that can carry 22 tonnes of cargo and can land in a powered controlled descent, has been developed.

As during the Cold War, notably, but not only, with rocketry and atomic weaponry, the need for a first-strike to destroy the opposing threat will encourage an active defence that may well be proactive, in the sense of attacking potentially hostile platforms, including satelites. This brings together questions of nomenclature, law (international and domestic), ethics, technology and doctrine, and the issue can be seen in the American response to a North Korea that deploys access-denial as well as strategic strike weaponry. The range of geographies at play is seen with both powers and types of weaponry.

Thus, test-fired by North Korea in 2017, the 74-foot long Hwasong-15 intercontinental ballistic missile has a range of over 8,000 miles and can possibly reach New York and Washington, and, if the range may probably be less with a nuclear warhead, calculations of range, a key element now of strategic geography, have to include the element of uncertainty over new systems. At the tactical level, the missile's mobile transporter-erector-launcher, a massive flatbed truck, makes it harder to detect and destroy. Yet a target is provided by the need for a storage and assembly area for the missiles, one constructed close to Pyongyang's main airport and including underground storage areas and rail links to nearby factories producing missile components. In 2020, reinforcement work was carried out on the Okryu Bridge in Pyongyang, presumably so that it was able to carry the transporters. In 2021, North Korea issued renewed public threats by its leader Kim Il-Jung about its determination to be able to attack the United States, including by submarine-launched missiles.

At the same time, technology is deployed, and doctrine and training focused by powers, in response to a range of tasks, and with variations in the related planned distance of effectiveness. Thus, anti-missile preparedness takes a variety of forms, both symmetrical and asymmetrical. For example, in 2020, in Exercise Noble Fury, the US Marines tested the concept of 'expeditionary advanced base operations', covert arrivals, by means of tilt-rotor aircraft, at Pacific islands, the rapid firing from them of long-range missiles at Chinese warships and missile sites, and then departure. This was an aspect of a 2018 refocus by the Pentagon on China and Russia as military rivals, and, on the part of the Marines, a subsequent move to lighter weapon systems and the abandonment of heavier artillery and tanks.

Furthermore, in 2020, in part as an aspect of American preparedness, but more particularly linked to home-defence, Taiwan purchased, for $1.8 billion, 135 precision land-based attack missiles with a striking range of over 270 kilometres manufactured by Boeing, 11 truck-based rocket launchers, and related equipment and training. This was presented as a credible combat capability but also an asymmetrical one able to respond to Chinese advances in conventional equipment.

Amidst all these possibilities, notably of lethality at great range, and the active research, development and implementation being employed to profit from them, it may appear foolish to insist on such crucial geographical military factors, as the continuing significance of the dichotomy of nearness and distance, the tensions of accuracy, the constraints of logistics, and the issues involved in reconciling movement and firepower. Leaving aside these overall points, however, come the continued specific requirements of operating in particular physical and human environments, and the pronounced 'frictions' these environments and requirements continue to impose. Human society does not bend easily to the requirements of systems and machines, and the geography of conflict will continue to have to respond to the resulting issues and tensions of this society.

The impact of climate change is an especially potent illustration of the folly of assuming that the essential narrative is that of a successively greater control by mankind of both physical and human geography. Indeed, growing historical interest in the relationship between climate change and conflict[14] encourages, as well as reflects, consideration of the present and future in this respect, and notably so with reference to pressures on resources. More specifically, there is currently a need to respond to the new possibilities and problems created by the rapid melting of the Arctic ice, which very much transforms the possibility for naval operations, and thus leads to new issues for geopolitics, strategy, and force structures. China is one of the powers interested in using Arctic routes. Separately, the environmental consequences of war have attracted greater academic and public interest, as in the map of war space as a multiple of the biosphere, an index of potential destruction, in the *New State of War and Peace* (1991).[15] These consequences are an element in 'critical geopolitics,' as well as a matter of concern to some armed forces.

The non-linear nature of change is very differently indicated by that of force-space ratios. In the twentieth century, there was an emphasis on very large militaries based on the practice of conscription, the idea of the nation under armies, and the need for large numbers, both to man continuous front lines and to occupy territories. Since the end of the Cold War, however, partly as a result of the cost of trained manpower, but largely due to investment in technology, troop numbers have fallen greatly, and that despite there being, in most states, more military manpower available than ever before as a consequence of a major and continuous rise in the world's population to consistently unprecedented numbers.

As a result of the fall in troop numbers, not only has the force-space ratio declined in terms of territory but also with reference to the percentage of the population, much of which now lives in an urban environment, with the particular challenges that poses for maintaining order and suppressing disorder.[16] Indeed, the geographies of control and insurgency will be transformed as a result of this issue. By 2012, over half of the world's population lived in cities; while the global population was then seven billion as compared to one in about 1804, two in 1927, and three in 1960. Thus, in Brazil, it is Sao Paolo and Rio de Janeiro, and not Amazonia, that is the central area of risk; and, in Pakistan, Karachi, and not the mountainous fringe of Waziristan. By 2020, the population was 7.8 billion and it was projected to grow to 9.9 billion by 2050 and 10.9 by 2100, with much of the predicted growth in Africa.

Aside from the terrain issues of cities for particular weapons such as tanks,[17] differing force-space ratios have major implications in terms of what is practical, and that issue risks a reversion to the tendency of seeking to fight in a means that is convenient, rather than one that is more likely to fulfil goals. Thus, the emphasis in terms of planning, doctrine, procurement and training, is generally on rapid advances and short battles; and not on the problems posed by having to sustain an occupation, although less so than prior to the problems following the conquest of Iraq in 2003. The need in the case of some states, notably Western ones, to avoid casualties can also ensure that tactics can eat strategy, or, at least, that that becomes a risk. The likely geography of future warfare is unclear, but, for the major states, the emphasis is likely to be on a swift resolution, although Russia failed to ensure this in Ukraine in 2022.

Most conflict, however, is unlikely to match this military, political and fiscal requirement. Instead, struggles within states are likely to have a lengthy, if not intractable, character, not least given the difficulties of ensuring consent and, separately, the overlaps of policing, law and order, politics and military activity. The use in October 2020, in Bishkek, the capital of Kyrgyzstan, of water cannon, stun grenades and tear gas in an unsuccessful attempt to suppress protestors in what the President called a coup, with the protestors seizing the state broadcaster and storming the parliament, underlined the difficulties of assessing civil conflicts. More generally, the increased employment in the West, from the Russian takeover of Crimea in 2014 onwards, of the concept of hybrid warfare, a concept that can be readily traced back to Communist ideas and practice,[18] captures the limitation of previous ideas about a clear contrast, between regular and irregular warfare, between inter-state and intra-state conflict, and between conflict and politics.

Ultimately, one way to consider assessing war is to do so in terms of continuums. One is between spheres of likely high-tech, short war, notably space, sea and air, and those that are not so, particularly highly populated areas. There is also the continuum between those situations, environments and weapon systems that conform to what governments and the military want from conflict, and those that are more intractable. Military history that presents war-winning 'magic bullets', of revolutionary change toward greater capability and success, fits into the former model. However, this approach does not match the human environment of the present-day world, nor, I would argue, that of the past. In particular, the scale and sophistication of material provided by geospatial intelligence systems have to be complemented by human terrain systems able to grasp the behavioural complexity, variety and inherently changeable character of the human environment.

Chapter 15

Conclusions

Survive. Move. Fight. That is the key adage for troops in hostile environments, notably, but not only, ice, jungle and desert. All these three military requirements are definitely handicapped by facets of physical geography, while, conversely, the infrastructure of human geography, from communication links to water supply, seeks to make the adaptation to environment easier. The sway of the environment, however, was more complex and allowed for more variations in practice than broad-brush interpretations might suggest.

War, moreover, is not a matter simply of responding to the environment, but, rather, of doing so in order to defeat an opponent, and in the context of their response, not least opposing and deadly efforts. The latter process is part of the human environment of war. This environment is very much one that is culturally conditioned. This is not least with respect to differing assumptions and norms about victory and defeat, struggle and suffering; assumptions and norms that refer both to how the phenomena are defined and how individuals relate to them. Indeed, this is an aspect of war as geography, of the need for planners to confront the variety of the world as it is; while historians, in contrast, look for variation across time.

A related difference emerges in military history, more particularly between accounts that focus on a single paradigm of capability and progress, leading for instance to autonomous swarms of drones in the near future, with a geography of use and threat accordingly; and those, in contrast, that emphasise a variety and diversity in both capability and progress. In addition, there is the geography of the standard coverage of war, whether in military academies or the world of print, in both of which the emphasis is on major states and on the human ability to overcome environmental challenges. There is also a frequent primitivisation of areas not seen as at the forefront of military development and practice, a process termed military Orientalism with regard to Asia, but also more generally apparent with past military observers.[1] This primitivisation indeed was scarcely unique to the West, being seen for example also with Chinese attitudes toward their neighbours. There and elsewhere, the concept of the 'barbarian' was frequently, but inaccurately, used to suggest a primitive character in war-making and much else.

In every case, however, rather than assuming that military progress was set in the core of civilisations and empires, it is pertinent to note that warfare on the periphery represented a melding, both long-standing and more recent, of practices, and, in some cases, could influence the core. This was the case in Western Europe in the late eighteenth century which was influenced by light warfare/small war practices in North America and in the Balkans, and also with the influence of steppe warfare in China.

A variant on primitivisation is to assume that powers in the past were obliged to operate as if modern, and that, if they failed to do so, they were in some form deficient. For example, in geopolitical terms, Ottoman naval power was relatively confined, largely to the Mediterranean, the Red Sea, and the Persian Gulf. However, it is not appropriate in considering the sixteenth, seventeenth and eighteenth centuries to think primarily in later geopolitical terms, and notably of an attempt to 'break through to the oceans', as if the Ottomans were the Soviet Union of the twentieth century, an empire anyway that did not last for so long.

And so more generally. The perception of geographical elements in the past reflected a range of factors that in turn played out through a human geography that could adapt to, but also alter, elements of the physical geography. This was notably so with hybrid military systems, but, again, their development reflected cultural as well as functional parameters, and also possibilities as much as problems and therefore needs.

Another field of cultural assumption is the understanding and presentation of the meaning of control. For much of history, the geography of control was in reality a shared one in which rivals and others in effect shared a given area, or controlled different aspects of it.[2] There has been a tendency to underplay this reality.

Cultural suppositions of a different type arise in considering geography in the form of limits of military capability and power. In practice, possible limits of capability and power can be seen as much, if not more, a product of policy and related debate, as of the geography of military strategy understood in terms of the constraints of environment and distance on successful operations. These constraints very much push operational aspects of military activity to the fore, but, in practice, different political and military strategies would probably have led (and lead) to very different situations. These situations would have affected the possibility of opposition to incorporation or conquest, or of rebellion, the likelihood of support within the areas that rebelled, and the prospect for a reconciliation short of revolution.

Thus, a different politics and strategy could have led to a contrasting human geography of war, and therefore to contrasting needs to adapt to (and even understand) the physical geography. This issue cuts to the quick of the discussion of inherent geographical limits to military capability and political power because it removes this discussion from the realm of mechanistic theories of the empire, state or stage, of the form 'thus far is appropriate,' rather like a machine cutting out, or a rubber band losing its stretch. That is not an appropriate analysis. This point can be seen with religious as well as political authority, as contingency emerges in each. Thus, the Hussite movement in Bohemia, which, in 1420–31, defeated a series of crusades, benefited from a mastery of terrain, notably the use of hills, superior command, and the use of handgunners and field fortifications; but also, crucially, from the breakdown of Catholic authority and the religious zeal of the Hussites.

Turning to today, there is a risk that as we appear to have 'conquered' nature to a large extent, from distance and disease in campaigning, to weather forecasting and the mastery of geographical information, so, as a result, less attention has been paid to the role of geography in warfare. Geography, indeed, may be less and less of an obstacle or advantage to deployed forces in the future as technologies are developed that counter terrain features and vast distances. Militaries often speak of warfighting domains, namely land, sea, air, space and cyberspace. Seizing and holding ground usually makes land the most important in a conflict, but capabilities brought to combat by the other four and especially the last two in recent years, may well make land, and hence the physical geography bound up in it, less of a factor in planning and executing campaigns.[3]

At the same time, although, due to technological innovation, many physical constraints have been overcome, the complex nature of the human element of geography is such that it will continue to be influential long into the future. Geography matters in the sense not only of winning or losing but also of shaping the battlefield and the theatre of operations.

It also helps determine, or, at the least, interacts with, the degree of warfare (low or high intensity, the level of warfare (tactical, operational and strategic), and the speed of combat, as well as the domains of land, sea, air, space, and cyberspace. In addition, the significance of geography, both physical and human, rests on the very varied way in which its impact can be experienced, countered and considered, with this variety in perception in part an aspect of human geography. This is a geography, moreover, that while greatly affected by change, has not been shelved or necessarily lessened by technology. To underrate the dynamic character of geography in the history, present, and future, of war is mistaken, but, in doing so, geography has always to be understood as more than a series of physical factors.

Notes

Chapter 1

1. K.Roy, *Military Thought of Asia. From the Bronze Age to the Information Age* (Abingdon, 2021), esp. p. 263.
2. M. Livingstone (ed.), *The Battle of Brunanburh: A Casebook* (Exeter, 2011); M. Larnach, 'The Battle of the Gates of Trajan, 986: A Reassessment', *JMH*, 84 (2020), pp. 25–31.
3. W.A. Griswold and D.W. Linebaugh (eds),*The Saratoga Campaign: Uncovering an Embattled Landscape* (Lebanon, NH, 2016); M.S. Fulton, 'The Siege of Montfort and Mamluk Artillery Technology in 1271: Integrating the Archaeology and Topography with the Narrative Sources', *JMH*, 83 (2019), pp. 689–717; N.J Saunders, *Desert Insurgency. Archaeology, T.E. Lawrence, and the Arab Revolt* (Oxford, 2020).
4. A. Boltanski, Y. Lagedec and F. Mercier (eds), *La Bataille: Du fait d'armes au combat idéologique* (Rennes, 2015).
5. H.A. Winters, *Battling the Elements. Weather and Terrain in the conduct of War* (Baltimore, MD, 1998), p. 4.
6. A.J. Bousquet, *The Eye of War: Military Perception from the Telescope to the Drone* (Minneapolis, Minn., 2018).
7. See also the pieces, with a geopolitical emphasis, by myself and others in S. Conti (ed.), *Storia Militare della Geografia* (Rome, 2020)
8. B.W. Harvey and C. Fitzgerald (eds), *Edward Heron-Allen's Journal: The Great War: From Sussex Shore to Flanders Fields* (Lewes, 2002), pp. 253–5.

Chapter 2

1. J. Keegan, *The Face of Battle: A Study of Agincourt, Waterloo and the Somme* (1976).
2. D. Buchholtz, *The Battle of the Greasy Grass/Little Bighorn: Custer's Last Stand in Memory, History, and Popular Culture* (New York, 2012).
3. P. Doyle and M.R. Bennett, 'Military Geography: the Influence of Terrain in the Outcome of the Gallipoli Campaign, 1915', *Geographical Journal*, 165 (1999), pp. 12–36, and 'Terrain in Military History: an Introduction', in their (eds), *Fields of Battle: Terrain in Military History* (Oxford, 2002), pp. 1–17.
4. E. Rose, J. Elen and U. Lawrence (eds), *Military Aspects of Geology: Fortification, Excavation and Terrain Evaluation* (2019); Rose and J.D. Mather (eds), *Military Aspects of Hydrogeology* (2012); Rose and C.P. Nathanail (eds), *Geology and Warfare* (2000).
5. K. Roy, *Military Thought of Asia. From the Bronze Age to the Information Age* (Abingdon, 2021), p. 40.
6. J.A. Ciciarelli, 'The Geology of the Battle of Monte Cassino, 1944', in Doyle and Bennett (eds), *Fields of Battle*, pp. 325–43.

7. T.B. Smith, *The Union Assaults at Vicksburg: Grant Attacks Pemberton, May 17–22, 1863* (Lawrence, KS, 2020).
8. M. Ehrlich, 'The Battle of 'Ain al-Mallāha, 19 June 1157', *JMH*, 83 (2019), pp. 34, 41.
9. M. Wood, *A Soldier's Story. Neville 'Timber' Wood's War, from Dunkirk to D-Day* (2020), p. 221.
10. R.L. DiNardo, 'The Limits of Technology: The Invasion of Serbia, 1915', *JMH*, 79 (2015), p. 986.
11. G. Hanlon, *Italy 1636: Cemetery of Armies* (Oxford, 2016).
12. Pownall to Ismay, 26 Ap. 1944, LH, Ismay, 4/26/2.
13. Brigadier-General James Cholmondeley, Chester, Cheshire Record Office, DCH/X/9a, 48.
14. J. Black, *Culloden and the '45* (Stroud, 1990), p. 139.
15. Report by General Stanley Savige on operations of the 3rd Australian Division in the Salamanca area of New Guinea, 1943, AWM. 3 DRL/6643, 3/12.
16. Dill to Field Marshal Montgomery-Massingberd, former Chief of the Imperial General Staff, 18 Nov. 1939, LH., Montgomery-Massingberd papers, 10/14.
17. J. Hussey, 'The Flanders Battleground and the Weather in 1917', in P.H. Liddle (ed.), *Passchendaele in Perspective: The Third Battle of Ypres* (1997), pp. 140–58.
18. C. Boutin, 'Adversary and Ally: The Role of Weather in the Life and Career of George Washington', *JMH*, 81 (2017), p. 715.
19. P.R. Kemmerly, 'Environment and the Course of Battle: Flooding at Shiloh (6–7 April, 1862)', *JMH*, 79 (2015), pp. 1079–82.
20. C.B. Faught, *Allenby* (2020), p. 87; J. Russell, *Theirs The Strife. The Forgotten Battles of British Second Army and Armeegruppe Blumentritt, April 1945* (Warwick, 2020), p. 26.
21. J.R. McNeill, 'The Ecological Basis of Warfare in the Caribbean, 1700–1804', in M. Ultee (ed.), *Adapting to Conditions: War and Society in the Eighteenth Century* (Tuscaloosa, Al., 1986), pp. 26–42.
22. P. Van Pul, *In Flanders' Flooded Fields: Before Ypres there was Yser* (Barnsley, 2006).
23. J.I. Israel, *Conflicts of Empires: Spain, the Low Countries and the Struggle for World Supremacy, 1585–1713* (1997), pp. 45–62.
24. J. Abel, *Guibert: Father of Napoleon's Grande Armée* (Norman, Ok., 2016).
25. I.F.W. Beckett, 'How Wars End: Victorian Colonial Conflicts', *JMH*, 82 (2018), pp. 29–44.
26. Hamilton, British Adjutant General, report on Saxon military exercises, LH, Hamilton papers 4/2/9, p. 60.
27. J.J. Abbatiello, *Anti Submarine Warfare in World War I: British Naval Aviation and the Defeat of the U-Boats* (Abingdon, 2006), pp. 11–12.
28. B.A. Friedman, *On Tactics: A Theory of Victory in Battle* (Annapolis, MD, 2017).
29. L.H. Alanbrooke papers 6/2/37.
30. J. Buckley, *Monty's Men. The British Army and the Liberation of Europe, 1944–5* (New Haven, Conn., 2013), esp. pp. 15–17.
31. A. Gordon, *The Rules of the Game. Jutland and British Naval Command* (1996).
32. I owe this point on rivers to Stephen Morillo.

Chapter 3
1. Odeleben, *A Circumstantial Narrative of the Campaign in Saxony, in the year 1813*, I, 265–6; M. Leggiere, *Napoleon and the Struggle for Germany: The Franco-Prussian War of 1813, II: The Defeat of Napoleon* (Cambridge, 2015), p. 180.

2. P. McNicholls, *Journey Through the Wilderness. Garnet Wolseley's Canadian Red River Expedition of 1870*, (Warwick, 2019), p. 164.

3. I.F.W. Beckett (ed.), *Wolseley and Ashanti: The Asante War Journal and Correspondence of Major General Sir Garnet Wolseley, 1873–1874* (Stroud, 2009).

4. Henry, 3rd Viscount Palmerston, Prime Minister, to John, Earl Russell, Foreign Secretary, 2 Oct. 1862, G.P. Gooch (ed.), *The Later Correspondence of Lord John Russell, 1840–1878* (1925), II, 326–7.

5. A.F. Chew, *Fighting the Russians in Winter: Three Case Studies* (Fort Leavenworth, KS, 1981).

6. L. White, 'Strategic Geography and the Spanish Habsburg Monarchy's Failure to Recover Portugal, 1640–1668', *Journal of Military History*, 71 (2007), pp. 373–409.

7. M.T. Ducey, 'Village, Nation, and Constitution: Insurgent Politics in Papantla, Veracruz, 1810–1821', *Hispanic American Historical Review*, 79 (1999), pp. 471–2, 476.

8. J. Black, *Logistics: The Key to Victory* (Barnsley, 2021).

9. A. Goldsworthy, *Hadrian's Wall* (New York, 2018).

10. D. Graff, 'Dou Jiande's Dilemma: Logistics, Strategy, and State Formation in Seventh-Century China', in H. van de Ven (ed.), *Warfare in Chinese History* (Leiden, 2000), pp. 82–4.

11. R. Matthee, 'Was Safavid Iran an Empire?', *Journal of the Economic and Social History of the Orient*, 53 (2010), p. 261.

12. J. Holland, *Sicily '43* (2020), pp. 498–9.

13. J. Black, *Strategy and the Second World War* (2021).

14. Julius Caesar, 'The Spanish War', in A.G. Way (trans.), *Caesar, Alexandrian, African and Spanish Wars* (1955), p. 8.

15. Vegetius, *Epitoma Rei Militaris*, II, 5, translated in A.L.F. Rivet and C. Smith, *The Place Names of Roman Britain* (1979), p. 148.

16. Blamey to John Curtin, Australian Prime Minister, 4 Dec. 1942, AWM. 3 DRL/6643, 2/11.

17. T.M. El-Geziry and I.G. Bryden, 'The circulation pattern in the Mediterranean Seas: issues for modeller consideration', *Journal of Operational Oceanography*, 3,2 (2010), pp. 39–46.

18. M. Partridge, *Military Planning for the Defense of the United Kingdom, 1814–1870* (New York, 1989).

19. R. Muir, *New School Atlas* (1911), p. xvii.

20. J. Black, *Logistics: The Key to Victory* (Barnsley, 2021).

21. D. Lee, 'The Survival of France: Logistics and Strategy in the 1709 Flanders Campaign', *JMH*, 84 (2020), pp. 1021–50.

22. LH. Alanbrooke, 6/2/37.

23. D. Krüger and V. Bausch (eds), *Fulda Gap: Battlefield of the Cold War Alliances* (Lanham, MD., 2018).

24. D.P. Marston, *Phoenix from the Ashes: The Indian Army in the Burma Campaign* (Westport, Conn., 2014).

25. G. Parker, *Global Crisis: War, Climate Change and Catastrophe in the Seventeenth Century* (New Haven, Conn., 2013).

26. D. McMahon, 'Geomancy and Walled Fortifications in Late Eighteenth Century China', *JMH*, 76 (2012), pp. 373–93.

27. N. Tackett, 'The Great Wall and Conceptualizations of the Border under the Northern Song', *Journal of Song-Yuan Studies*, 38 (2008), pp. 99–138.

28. K. Cathers, '"Markings on the Land" and Early Medieval Warfare in the British Isles', in Doyle and Bennett, *Fields of Battle*, p. 10.

29. A. Holland, *Conflict and Society in the Anglo-Saxon Landscape* (DPhil., Oxford, 2020).

30. R.D. Kaplan, *The Revenge of Geography. What the Map Tells Us About Coming Conflicts and the Battle Against Fate* (New York 2012); see, more perceptively, P. Dibb, 'The return of Geography', in R.W. Glenn (ed.), *New Directions in Strategic Thinking* (Canberra, 2018), pp. 91–104.

31. A. Mombauer, *Helmuth von Moltke and the Origins of the First World War* (Cambridge, 2001); D. Showalter, J.A. Robinson and J.P. Robinson, *The German Failure in Belgium, August 1914: How Faulty Reconnaissance Exposed the Weakness of the Schlieffen Plan* (Jefferson, NC., 2019).

Chapter 4

1. E. Reich, *Atlas*, p. iii.

2. J. Black, *Plotting Power: Strategy in the Eighteenth Century* (Bloomington, Ind., 2017) and *Military Strategy. A Global History* (New Haven, Conn., 2020).

3. J.R. Hayworth, *Revolutionary France's War of Conquest in the Rhineland: Conquering the Natural Frontier, 1792 to 1797* (Cambridge, 2019).

4. T.J. Halsall, 'Geology and Warfare in England and Wales 1450–1650', in Doyle and Bennett, *Fields of Battle*, pp. 19–31.

5. P. Wilson, *The Thirty Years War: Europe's Tragedy* (2009).

6. J. Lynch, *Caudillos in Spanish America, 1800–1850* (Oxford, 1992); T. Anna, *Forging Mexico, 1821–1835* (Lincoln, NB, 1998).

7. E. Luttwak, *The Grand Strategy of the Roman Empire from the First Century AD to the Third* (Baltimore, MD, 1976); J.P. LeDonne, *The Grand Strategy of the Russian Empire, 1650–1831* (Oxford, 2004). See the maps in F.P. Pucha, 'Distribution of Regular Army Troops before the Civil War', *Military Affairs*, 16 (1952), pp. 172–3. See also R. Wooster, 'Military Strategy in the Southwest, 1848–1860', *Military History of Texas and the Southwest*, 15,2 (1979), pp. 5–15.

8. See, eg. P. Thonemann, 'A man, a plan: a canard', review of Luttwak, *Roman Empire*, *Times Literary Supplement*, issue 5924, 14 Oct. 2016, pp. 25–6.

9. U. Baram and L. Carroll (eds), *A Historical Archaeology of the Ottoman Empire: Breaking New Ground* (New York, 2000); A.C.S. Peacock (ed.), *The Frontiers of the Ottoman World* (Oxford, 2009).

10. H.O. Rekavadi et al, 'The Enigma of the "Red Snake": Revealing One of the World's Greatest Frontier Walls', *Current World Archaeology*, 27 (Feb./Mar. 2004), pp. 12–22.

11. N. Tackett, 'The Great Wall and Conceptualizations of the Border under the Northern Song', *Journal of Song-Yuan Studies*, 38 (2008), pp. 99–138; A. Waldron, *The Great Wall of China: From History to Myth* (Cambridge, 1990).

12. B.S. Bachrach and D.S. Bachrach, *Warfare in Medieval Europe c.400–c.1453* (2017), pp. 67–9.

13. M. Khodarkovsky, *Russia's Steppe Frontier: The Making of a Colonial Empire, 1500–1800* (Bloomington, Ind., 2002).

14. D.J. Wyatt (ed.), *Battlefronts Real and Imagined: War, Border, and Identity in the Chinese Middle Period* (Basingstoke, 2008).

15. R.J. Barendse, *The Arabian Seas. The Indian Ocean World of the Seventeenth Century* (Armonk, New York, 2002), p. 454.

16. F. Maurice, *On the Uses of the Study of War* (1927), p. x.
17. R.N.E. Blake, 'Airfield Country: Terrain, Land-Use and the Air Defence of Britain, 1939–1945,' in Doyle and Bennett (eds), *Fields of Battle*, pp. 365–83.
18. D. Omissi, *Air Power and Colonial Control: The Royal Air Force, 1919–1939* (Manchester, 1990).
19. G. Till (ed.), *The Development of British Naval Thinking: Essays in Memory of Bryan Ranft* (Abingdon, 2006).
20. K. Kotani, 'Japan's Southward Advance and the Imperial Japanese Army and Navy in 1941: Strategy of "Autarky" and "Regional Strategy"', *NIDS 2008 International Forum on War History: Proceedings* (Tokyo, 2009).
21. A.C.S. Peacock (ed.), *The Frontiers of the Ottoman World* (Oxford, 2009); M. Stein, *Guarding the Frontier: Ottoman Border Forts in Europe* (2007).
22. President and Council at Madras to Court of Directors of East India Company, 31 July 1760, BL. IO. H/Misc./96, p. 56.
23. P. Nath, *Climate of Conquest: War, Environment, and Empire in Mughal North India* (Delhi, 2019).
24. NAS. GD. 248/50/1/10.
25. A.W. Mitchell, *The Grand Strategy of the Habsburg Empire* (Princeton, NJ, 2018).
26. C. Ripodi, 'Grand Strategy and the Graveyard of Assumptions: Britain and Afghanistan, 1839–1919', *Journal of Strategic Studies*, 33 (2010), pp. 701–25.
27. J.H. Rose, 'Sir Hudson Lowe and the beginnings of the Campaign of 1815', *English Historical Review*, 16 (1901), pp. 517–27.
28. E. Farruggia, '"A farm too far." Maps at Waterloo', S. Conti (ed.), *Storia Militare della Geografia* (Rome, 2020), pp. 267–84.

Chapter 5

1. H.J. Mackinder, 'The Geographical Pivot of History', *Geographical Journal*, 23 (1904), pp. 421–37.
2. The light-gauge rails restricted the weight and volume of cargo that could be carried.
3. S. Badsey, *Doctrine and Reform in the British Cavalry, 1880–1918* (Aldershot, 2008).
4. Liddell Hart to Brian Melland, 29 May 1961, LH, Liddell Hart papers, 4/31.
5. Manchester, John Rylands Library, Auchinleck Papers, nos. 1155, 1143.
6. T. May, *The Mongol Art of War: Chinggis Khan and the Mongol Military System* (Yardley, Penn., 2007); C.F. Sverdrup, *The Mongol Conquests: The Military Operations of Genghis Khan and Sübe'etei* (Solihull, 2017).
7. S. Tibble, *The Crusader Armies, 1099–1187* (New Haven, Conn., 2018).
8. M. Axworthy, *Sword of Persia: Nader Shah, from Tribal Warrior to Conquering Tyrant* (2006).
9. Rawlinson to Montgomery-Massingberd, 21 Sept. 1922, LH. MM. 8/27.
10. S.P. Huntington, *The Clash of Civilisations and the Remaking of World Order* (New York 1996).
11. C.R. Po, 'Conceptualising the Blue Frontier: The Great Qing and the Maritime World in the Long Eighteenth Century', (PhD., Heidelberg, 2015), and 'Mapping maritime power and control: a study of the late eighteenth century Qisheng yanhai tu', *Late Imperial China*, 37,2 (2016), pp. 93–136.
12. Graham to Fitzroy, Lord Raglan, commander of the British expeditionary force, 8 May 1854, BL. Add. 79696 fol. 129.

13. Stirling to Graham, 27 Nov. 1854, BL. Add. 79696 fol. 163.
14. Y. Suzuki, 'Anglo-Russian War-Scare and British Occupation of Kŏmundo, 1885–7: The Initial Phase of Globalisation of International Affairs Between Great Powers', *Journal of Imperial and Commonwealth History*, 47 (2019), pp. 1100–1124.
15. A. Rath, *The Crimean War in Imperial Context, 1854–1856* (Basingstoke, 2015).
16. NA. FO. 371/56753 fol. 26.
17. D. Felix, *Kennan and the Cold War: An Unauthorized Biography* (Piscataway, NJ., 2015).
18. M.W. Lewis and K. Wigen, *The Myth of Continents: A Critique of Metageography* (Berkeley, Calif., 1997).
19. J. Black, *Geopolitics and the Quest for Dominance* (Bloomington, Ind., 2016).
20. G. Sloan, 'Haldane's Mackindergarten: a radical experiment in British military education?', *War in History*, 19 (2012), pp. 322–52; P. Grant, 'Edward Ward, Halford Mackinder and the army administration course at the London School of Economics, 1907–1914', in M. Locicero, R. Mahoney and S. Mitchell (eds), *A Military Transformed: Adaptation and Innovation in the British Military, 1792–1945* (Solihull, 2014), pp. 97–109.
21. *Hansard Parliamentary Debates*, 3rd series, vol. 234, cols 1564–5.
22. A. Roksund, *The Jeune École: The Strategy of the Weak* (Leiden, 2007).
23. D.A. Yerxa, *Admirals and Empire. The United States Navy and the Caribbean, 1898–1945* (Columbia, S.C., 1991), p. 253.
24. S. Schulten, *The Geographical Imagination of America, 1880–1950* (Chicago, Ill., 2001).
25. R.E. Harrison, 'One World, One War', *Fortune* (Mar. 1943).
26. R. Woodward, *Military Geographies* (Oxford, 2004). A more sophisticated approach is offered in C. Flint, *Geopolitical Constructs: The Mulberry Harbours, the Second World War, and the Making of a Militarised Transatlantic* (Lanham, MD., 2016).
27. J. Black, *Logistics: The Key to Victory* (Barnsley, 2021).
28. R. Drews, *Militarism and the Indo-Europeanising of Europe* (Abingdon, 2017).
29. J.J. Gommans, *The Rise of the Indo-Afghan Empire, c. 1710–1780* (Leiden, 1995).
30. R. Law, 'Horses, Firearms, and Political Power in Pre-Colonial West Africa', *Past and Present*, 72 (1976), p. 120; P. Kelekna, *The Horse in Human History* (Cambridge, 2009).
31. V.H. Lien, *The Mongol Navy: Kublai Khan's Invasions in Dai Viet and Champa* (Singapore, 2017), pp. 16–19.
32. P. Hämäläinen, *The Comanche Empire* (New Haven, Conn., 2008).
33. J. Tracy, *Emperor Charles V, Impresario of War: Campaign Strategy, International Finance, and Domestic Politics* (Cambridge, 2002), p. 38.
34. D. Veevers, *The Origins of the British Empire in Asia, 1600–1750* (Cambridge, 2020).
35. A.C.S. Peacock (ed.), *The Frontiers of the Ottoman World* (2009).
36. K. Barkey, *Bandits and Bureaucrats: The Ottoman Route to State Centralization* (Ithaca, NY, 1994) and *Empire of Difference: The Ottomans in Comparative Perspective* (Cambridge, Mass., 2008).
37. J.C. Heesterman, 'Warrior, Peasant and Brahmin', *Modern Asian Studies*, 29 (1995), pp. 637–54.
38. Y. Dai, *The White Lotus War: Rebellion and Suppression in Late Imperial China* (Seattle, Wa., 2019).
39. Popham to Viscount Melville, 23 Nov. 1807, BL. Loan 57/108 fol. 19.

40. D. Kolff, *Naukar, Rajput and Sepoy: The Ethnohistory of the Military Labour Market in Hindustan, 1450–1850* (Cambridge, 1990).
41. C.J. Rogers, 'Medieval Strategy and the Economics of Conquest', *JMH*, 82 (2018), p. 737.
42. For example, R. Johnson, *The Great War and the Middle East: A Strategic Study* (Oxford, 2016).
43. A. Lambert, *Seapower States: Maritime Culture, Continental Empires, and the Conflict that Made the Modern World* (New Haven, Conn., 2018).
44. R. Gildea and I. Tames (eds), *Fighters Across Frontiers. Transnational Resistance in Europe, 1936–48* (Manchester, 2020).

Chapter 6
1. J. Black, *The Power of Knowledge. How Information and Technology Made the Modern World* (New Haven, Conn., 2015).
2. P. O'Brien, '*L'Embastillement de Paris:* The Fortification of Paris during the July Monarchy', *French Historical Studies*, 9 (1975), pp. 63–82.
3. F.C. Schneid, 'A Well-Coordinated Affair: Franco-Piedmontese War Planning in 1859', *JMH*, 76 (2012), pp. 395–425.
4. G. Wawro, *The Austro-Prussian War* (Cambridge, 1996).
5. G. Wawro, *The Franco-Prussian War* (Cambridge, 2003).
6. R.A. Doughty, 'French strategy in 1914: Joffre's own', *JMH,* 67 (2003), p. 453 and *Pyrrhic Victory: French Strategy and Operations in the Great War* (Cambridge, Mass., 2009); J.C. Arnold, 'French tactical doctrine, 1870–1914', *Military Affairs*, 42 (1978), p. 64.
7. Cockburn memorandum, 9 June 1845, BL. Add. 40458 fol. 57.
8. J. Goldrick, *After Jutland: The Naval War in Northern European Waters, June 1916–November 1918* (Annapolis, MD., 2018).
9. D. Edgerton, 'Controlling Resources: Coal, Iron Ore and Oil in the Second World War', in M. Geyer and A. Tooze (eds), *The Cambridge History of the Second World War. III: Total War: Economy, Society and Culture* (Cambridge, 2015), pp. 122–48; A. Toprani, *Oil and the Great Powers: Britain and Germany, 1914 to 1945* (Oxford, 2019).
10. Graham to Fitzroy, Lord Raglan, Master-General of the Ordnance, 10 Jan. 1854, BL. Add. 79696 fol. 87.
11. D. McNab, B.W. Hodgins and D.S. Standen, '"Black with Canoes": Aboriginal Resistance and the Canoe: Diplomacy, Trade and Warfare in the Meeting Grounds of Northeastern North America, 1600–1821', in G. Raudzens (ed.), *Technology, Disease and Colonial Conquests, Sixteenth to Eighteenth Centuries* (Leiden, 2001), pp. 237–92.
12. D. Morgan-Owen and L. Halewood (eds), *Economic Warfare and the Sea: Grand Strategies for Maritime Powers, 1650–1945* (Liverpool, 2020). For qualification of technological 'revolutions', Morgan-Owen, 'Continuity and Change: Strategy and Technology in the Royal Navy, 1890–1918', *English Historical Review*, 135 (2020), pp. 892–930.
13. A. Taylor, *The Maori Warrior* (Laie, Ha., 1998); N.B. Dukas, *A Military History of Sovereign Hawai'i* (Honolulu, Ha., 2004), pp. 2–26.
14. M. Ford, *Weapon of Choice: Small Arms and the Culture of Military Innovation* (Oxford, 2017).

234 The Geographies of War

15. Birdwood to General Sir John Maxwell, 8 June 1915, AWM., 3 DRL. 3376, 11/4.
16. C. Phillips, *Civilian Specialists at War. Britain's Transport Experts and the First World War* (2020), pp. 323–35, 365–6.
17. J.P. Duffy, *Target America. Hitler's Plan to Attack the United States* (Westport, Conn., 2004).
18. N. Friedman, *Network-Centric Warfare: How Navies Learned to Fight Smarter through Three World Wars* (Annapolis, Md., 2009).
19. For such claims, G. Rocess, 'The World Has Just Witnessed a "Pearl Harbor Moment" in Armenia', https://glennrocess.medium.com/the-world-has-just-witnessed-a-pearl-harbor-moment-in-armenia-953f0ad3f31d, accessed 12 Nov. 2020.
20. D. Edgerton, 'Innovation, Technology, or History. What is the History of Technology About?', *Technology and Culture*, 51 (2010), pp. 680–97.
21. M.E. Latham, *Modernisation as Ideology: American Social Science and 'Nation Building' in the Kennedy Era* (Chapel Hill, North Carolina, 2000) and *The Right Kind of Revolution: Modernisation, Development, and U.S. Foreign Policy from the Cold War to the Present* (Ithaca, NY., 2011); N. Gilman, *Mandarins of the Future: Modernization Theory in Cold War America* (Baltimore, MD., 2003); D.C. Engerman, 'American Knowledge and Global Power', *Diplomatic History*, 31 (2007), pp. 599–622.
22. G.A. Gaddis, *No Sure Victory: Measuring U.S. Army Effectiveness and Progress in the Vietnam War* (New York, 2011).
23. For a critique, J.C.D. Clark, 'Secularisation and Modernisation: The Failure of a "Grand Narrative"', *Historical Journal*, 55 (2012), pp. 161–94.
24. J.D. Chambers, and G.E. Mingay, *The Agricultural Revolution* (1966).
25. M. Roberts, *The Military Revolution, 1560–1660* (Belfast, 1956).
26. M.G.S. Hodgson, *The Venture of Islam* (Chicago, Ill., 1974); D.E. Streusand, *Islamic Gunpowder Empires: Ottomans, Safavids, and Mughals* (Philadelphia, Penn., 2011).
27. G. Parker, 'In Defense of *The Military Revolution*', in C.J. Rogers (ed.), *The Military Revolution Debate* (Boulder, Colorado, 1995), p. 355.
28. T. Stiefel, *The Intellectual Revolution in Twelfth-Century Europe* (London, 1985); D.C. Lindberg and M.H. Shank (eds), *The Cambridge History of Science, Vol 2, Medieval Science* (Cambridge, 2011).
29. P. Porter, *Military Orientalism: Eastern War Through Western Eyes* (London, 2009); K. Roy, *Military Thought of Asia. From the Bronze Age to the Information Age* (Abingdon, 2021); J, Black, *War in the World: A Comparative History, 1450–1600* (Basingstoke, 2011) and *Beyond the Military Revolution: War in the Seventeenth-Century World* (Basingstoke, 2011).
30. J. Gommans, *The Rise of the Indo-Afghan Empire, c. 1710–1780* (Leiden, 1995); P.C. Perdue, *China Marches West: The Qing Conquest of Central Eurasia* (Cambridge, Mass., 2005).
31. J. Black, *War in the Eighteenth-Century World* (Basingstoke, 2013).
32. A. Goldsworthy, *Cannae: Hannibal's Greatest Victory* (London, 2001); Y. Mosig and I. Belhassen, 'Revision and reconstruction in the Punic Wars: Cannae revisited', *International Journal of the Humanities*, 4,2 (2006), pp. 103–10.

Chapter 7
1. Mansel to Black, email, 13 Dec. 2020. Mansel is a biographer of Louis.
2. Torcy to Bolingbroke, 28 July 1712, NA. SP. 78/154.
3. T. Smollett, *Humphry Clinker* (1771), letter 35.

4. 3rd Earl of Malmesbury (ed.), *Diaries and Correspondence of James Harris, First Earl of Malmesbury* (4 vols, 1844), II, 304–6.

5. Macpherson to Shelburne, 6 Dec. 1782, BL. Bowood papers, 56.

6. A. Packwood, *How Churchill Waged War: The Most Challenging Decisions of the Second World War* (Havertown, Penn., 2018).

7. B.L. Hart, 'Strategy and the American War', *Quarterly Review* (July 1929), pp. 125–8; J.F.C. Fuller, *The Conduct of War 1789–1961* (1961), p. 102.

8. With reference to the Condamine expedition of 1738–44, Thomas, 9th Earl of Kinnoull, British envoy in Lisbon, to William Pitt, Secretary of State in the Southern Department, 16 Ap. 1760, NA. SP. 89/52 fols 65–6.

9. See, more generally, N. Ginsburger, *"La guerre, la plus terrible des érosions"*, *Cultures de guerre et géographes universitaires Allemagne-France-États-Unis, 1914–1921* (Paris Ouest Nanterre-La Defense, PhD., 2010).

10. M. Heffernan, 'Geography, Cartography and Military Intelligence: The Royal Geographical Society and the First World War', *Transactions of the Institute of British Geographers*, 21 (1996), pp. 504–33.

11. F.S. Grandinetti, 'Armin Kohl Lobeck, 1886–1958', *Geographers: Biobibliographical Studies*, 22 (2003), pp. 112–31.

12. T.J. Barnes, 'Geographical Intelligence: American Geographers and Research and Analysis in the Office of Strategic Services, 1941–1945', *Journal of Historical Geography*, 32 (2006), pp. 149–68.

13. T.R. Smith and L.D. Black, 'German Geography: War Work and Present Status', *Geographical Review*, 36 (1946), pp. 398–408; P.F. Rose and D. Willig, 'Specialist Maps Prepared by German Military Geologists for Operation Sealion: The Invasion of England Scheduled for September 1940', *Cartographic Journal*, 41 (2004), pp. 13–35; Rose and J.C. Clatworthy, 'Specialist Maps of the Geological Section, Inter-Service Topographical Department: Aids to British Military Planning during World War II', *Ibid.*, 44 (2007), pp. 13–43.

Chapter 8

1. I. Lazier and S. Gal (eds), *Les Alpes de Jean de Beins. Des cartes aux paysages, 1604–1634* (Grenoble, 2017).

2. T. Harper, *Atlas. A World of Maps from The British Library* (2018), pp. 204–5.

3. M.H. Edney and M.S. Pedley (eds), *The History of Cartography. IV. History in the European Enlightenment* (2 vols, Chicago, Ill., 2020) I, 949–1017.

4. R. Sconfienza, 'L'atlante di Daniele Minutoli. Carte e relazioni militari per il Re di Sardegna'. Re Spanish military mapping, V. Manfrie, 'Ingenieros y cartografía al compás de la guerra de la Cuádruple Alianza', in S. Conti (ed.), *Storia Militare della Geografia* (Rome, 2020), pp. 93–105, 65–86.

5. G. Whittington and A.J.S. Gibson, *The Military Survey of Scotland, 1747–1755: A Critique* (Norwich, 1986).

6. M. Troude, *Le baron Bacier d'Albe, maréchal de camp* (Saint-Pol-sur Ternoise, 1954); N. Dion and N. Gastaldi, 'La "Carte Générale du Théâtre de la Guerre en Italie et dans Les Alpes…" de Bacler d'Albe (1798) et sa Numérisation', *Cartes et Géomatique*, 238 (Dec. 2018), pp. 99–112.

7. J.B. Harley and Y. O'Donoghue, 'The Origins of the Ordnance Survey', in W.A. Seymour (eds.), *A History of the Ordnance Survey* (Folkestone, 1980), pp. 1–20.

8. P. Boulanger, *La Géographie Militaire Française, 1871–1939* (Paris, 2002).

9. R. Oliver, 'The Baker Committee of 1892', *Sheetlines*, 100 (Aug. 2014), pp. 11–22; T. Nicolson, 'The Ordnance Survey and smaller scale military maps of Britain, 1854–1914', *Cartographic Journal*, 25 (1988), pp. 109–27.
10. J.W. Smith, *To Master the Boundless Sea: The U.S. Navy, the Marine Environment, and the Cartography of Empire* (Chapel Hill, NC, 2018).
11. M. Altić, 'Military Cartography of WWII: The British Geographical Section of the General Staff and the US Army Map Service and their Production of the Topographic Map Series of the Balkans, 1939–1945', *Cartographic Journal*, 56,4 (2019), pp. 295–320.

Chapter 9
1. I.K. Steele, *Warpaths: Invasions of North America* (New York, 1994).
2. Montresor to Amherst, 18 Oct. 1760, NA. WO. 34/83 fols 120–1.
3. H.C. Rice and A.S.K. Brown (eds), *The American Campaigns of Rochambeau's Army* (Princeton, NJ, 1972); J.B. Harley, B.B. Petchenik and L.W. Towner, *Mapping the American Revolutionary War* (Chicago, Ill., 1978).
4. P.D. Chase (ed.), *The Papers of George Washington: Revolutionary War Series*, vol. 10 (Charlottesville, Va, 2000), p. 507.
5. J. Black, *The War of 1812 in the Age of Napoleon* (Norman, Ok., 2009).
6. F.P. Prucha, 'Distribution of Regular Army Troops before the Civil War', *Military Affairs*, 16 (1952), pp. 172–3.
7. F.P Prucha, 'The Settler and the Army in Frontier Minnesota', *Minnesota History*, 29 (1948), p. 233; R. Wooster, 'Military Strategy in the Southwest, 1848–1860', *Military History of Texas and the Southwest*, 15, 2 (1979), pp. 5–15.
8. With an emphasis on logistics, W.E. Grabau, *Ninety-Eight Days. A Geographer's View of the Vicksburg Campaign* (Knoxville, Tenn., 2000); R.K. Krick, *Civil War Weather in Virginia* (Tuscaloosa, Al., 2007). See, more generally, L.M. Brady, *War Upon the Land: Military Strategy and the Transformation of Southern Landscapes during the American Civil War* (Athens, Ga, 2012); J. Browning and T. Silver, *An Environmental History of the Civil War* (Chapel Hill, NC., 2020).
9. B.H. Reid, *The American Civil War and the Wars of the Industrial Revolution* (1999), p. 41.
10. J. Ehlen and R.J. Abrahart, 'Effective use of Terrain in the American Civil War: The Battle of Fredericksburg, December 1862', in Doyle and Bennett (eds), *Fields of Battle*, pp. 63–97; A.H. Petty, *The Battle of the Wilderness in Myth and Memory* (Baton Rouge, La., 2019).
11. C. Nelson, *Mapping the Civil War* (Washington, DC, 1992).
12. E.J. Hess, *Civil War Logistics: A Study of Military Transportation* (Baton Rouge, La., 2017).
13. D. Canfield, 'Opportunity Lost: Combined Operations and the Development of Union Military Strategy, April 1861–April 1862', *JMH*, 79 (2015), pp. 687–9.
14. E.J. Hess, *Fighting for Atlanta: Tactics, Terrain, and Trenches in the Civil War* (Chapel Hill, NC., 2018)
15. H. George, *The Relations of Geography and History* (5th edn, Oxford, 1924), p. 295.
16. W.H. Goetzmann, *Army Exploration in the American West, 1803–63* (New Haven, Conn., 1959); F. Schubert, *Vanguard of Expansion: Army Engineers in the Trans-Mississippi West, 1819–1879* (Washington, 1980); A. G. Traas, *From the Golden Gate to Mexico City: The U.S. Topographical Engineers in the Mexican War, 1846–*

1848 (Washington, 1993); M. Warhus, 'Cartographic Encounters: An Exhibition of Native American Maps from Central Mexico to the Arctic', special issue of *Mapline*, 7 (Sept. 1993), pp. 15–16.

17. J. Knetsch, J. Missall and M.L. Missall, *History of the Third Seminole War, 1849–1858* (Havertown, Penn., 2018); T.T. Petersen, *The Military Conquest of the Prairie: Native American Resistance, Evasion, and Survival, 1865–1890* (Eastbourne, 2016).

Chapter 10

1. C. Callwell, *Small Wars: Their Principles and Practice* (3rd edn, 1906), p. 39.
2. I.F.W. Beckett, 'The Road from Kandahar: The Politics of Retention and Withdrawal in Afghanistan, 1880–81', *JMH*, 78 (2014), pp. 1263–94.
3. D. Whittingham, *Charles E. Callwell and the British Way in Warfare* (Cambridge, 2020), pp. 113–58
4. J.B. Harley, 'Maps, Knowledge and Power', in D. Cosgrove and S. Daniels (eds), *The Iconography of Landscape* (Cambridge, 1988), pp. 277–312; J.K. Noyes, *Colonial Space: Spatiality in the Discourse of German South West Africa, 1884–1915* (Chur, 1992); A. Godlewska and N. Smith (eds), *Geography and Empire* (Oxford, 1994).
5. Dalhousie to General Sir Charles Napier, Commander-in-Chief in India, 24 Dec. 1849, BL. Add. 49016 fol. 57.
6. C. Farah, *The Sultan's Yemen. Nineteenth-Century Challenges to Ottoman Rule* (2002).
7. J.P. LeDonne, *The Grand Strategy of the Russian Empire, 1650–1831* (Oxford, 2004).
8. D. McMahon, 'New Order on the Hunan Miao Frontier, 1796–1812', *Journal of Colonialism and Colonial History*, 9 (2008), pp. 1–26.
9. Lister to Secretary to Governor of Bengal, 2 Feb. 1850, BL. Add. 49016 fol. 88; P.K. Pau, *Indo-Burma Frontier and the Making of the Chin Hills. Empire and Resistance* (Abingdon, 2020).
10. Pearson to his parents, 14 May 1858, BL. IO. MSS. Eur. C231, p. 161.
11. BL. Add. 49357.
12. M.H. Edney, *Mapping an Empire: The Geographical Construction of British India, 1765–1843* (Chicago, Ill., 1997).
13. M.M. Evans, 'Maps and Decisions: Buller South and North of the Tugela, 1899–1900', in Doyle and Bennett (eds), *Fields of Battle*, pp. 137–41. See also A.C. Jewitt, *Maps for Empire: The First 2000 Numbered War Office Maps, 1881–1905* (London, 1992).
14. M. Heffernan, 'The Cartography of the Fourth Estate: Mapping the New Imperialism in British and French Newspapers, 1875–1925', in J.R. Akerman, *The Imperial Map. Cartography and the Mastery of Empire* (Chicago, Ill., 2009), pp. 261–99.
15. A.R. McGinnis, 'When Courage Was Not Enough: Plains Indians at War with the United States Army', *JMH*, 76 (2012), p. 473.
16. User agency is ably emphasised in G. Macola, *The Gun in Central Africa: A History of Technology and Politics* (Athens, OH, 2016).
17. J. Sharman, *Empires of the Weak: The Real Story of European Expansion and the Creation of the New World* (Princeton, NJ, 2019).
18. F. Schneid, 'A Well-Coordinated Affair: Franco-Piedmontese War Planning in 1859', *JMH*, 76 (2012), pp. 395–425 and the *French-Piedmontese Campaign of 1859* (Rome, 2014), pp. 43–59.

19. J. Black, *The Age of Total War, 1860–1945* (Westport, Conn., 2006) and *War in the Nineteenth Century* (Cambridge, 2009).

20. J. Black, *Eighteenth-Century Europe* (2nd edn, Basingstoke, 1999) and *Kings, Nobles and Commoners. States and Societies in Early Modern Europe. A Revisionist History* (London, 2004).

21. Bull to General Amherst, 15 Ap. 1761, NA, Colonial Office papers, 5/61 fol. 277.

22. Warren, Reminiscences, BL. IO. MSS. Eur. C 607, pp. 188–91.

23. D. Porch, *The Conquest of Morocco* (2nd edn, New York, 2005).

24. Roberts to George, Duke of Cambridge, Commander-in-Chief of the Forces, 9 July 1885, LH, Hamilton papers, 1/3/3, II, 265; Cavan to Major-General Sir Frederick Maurice, 6 Feb. 1924, LH, Maurice papers, 3/5/150; T.R. Moreman, *The Army in India and the Development of Frontier Warfare, 1849–1947* (1998).

25. W. Slim, 'Higher Command in War', Kermit Roosevelt Memorial Lecture, 1952, in *Military Review* (May 1990).

26. General, Lord Rawlinson, to Major-General Sir Archibald Montgomery-Massingberd, 8 Nov. 1922, LH. MM. 8/27.

27. NA. WO. 33/2764, p. 257.

28. D. Omissi, *Air Power and Colonial Control: The Royal Air Force 1919–1939* (Manchester, 1990); R. Newton, *The RAF and Tribal Control: Airpower and Irregular Warfare between the World Wars* (Lawrence, KS, 2019).

29. Layton to First Sea Lord, Admiral Sir Andrew Cunningham, 13 Sept. 1944, BL. Add. 74796.

30. Mountbatten to Layton, 15 Sept. 1944, BL. Add. 74796.

Chapter 11
1. W.C. Sweeney, *Military Intelligence: A New Weapon in War* (New York, 1924).

2. D. Showalter, J.P. Robinson, and J.A. Robinson, *The German Failure in Belgium, August 1914* (Jefferson, NC, 2019).

3. BL. Add. 50344, pp. 131–3.

4. BL. Add. 49703 fols 137–18.

5. C. Bell, *Churchill and the Dardanelles* (Oxford, 2017).

6. P. Doyle and M. Bennett, *Fields of Battle. Terrain in Military History* (Oxford, 2002), pp. 143–256.

7. T.J. Finnegan, *Shooting the Front: Allied Aerial Reconnaissance in the First World War* (Stroud, 2011); J. Streckfuss, *Eyes All Over the Sky: Aerial Reconnaissance in the First World War* (Oxford, 2016); T. Morton, *From Kites to Cold War: The Evolution of Manned Airborne Reconnaissance* (Annapolis, Md., 2019).

8. Exeter, Devon Record Office (DRO), 5277 M/F/3/29, 5277M/F3/29.

9. DRO. 5277 M/F3/30.

10. C. Phillips, *Civilian Specialists at War: Britain's Transport Experts and the First World War* (2020).

11. F. Saffroy, '14–18: L'Émergence de la Carte Combinée', *Cartes et Géomatique*, 223 (Mar. 2015), pp. 35–49; P. Chausseaud and P. Doyle, *Grasping Gallipoli - Terrain, Maps and Failure at the Dardanelles, 1915* (Staplehurst, 2005).

12. A. Siotto, 'Mapping the First World War: The Empowering Development of Mapmaking during the First World War in the British Army', *JMH*, 82 (2018), pp. 45–66.

13. E.P.F. Rose, 'Water Supply Maps for the Western Front (Belgium and Northern France) Developed by British, German and American Military Geologists during World War I: Pioneering Studies in Hydrogeology from Trench Warfare', *Cartographic Journal*, 46 (2009), pp. 76–103.

14. A. Roden, *Trains to the Trenches* (2014); M.J.B. and J.S. Farebrother, *Allied Railways of the Western Front – Narrow Gauge in the Arras Sector: Before, During and After the First World War* (Barnsley, 2015).

15. M. Leonard, *Beneath the Killing Fields: Exploring the Subterranean Landscapes of the Western Front* (Barnsley, 2016).

16. P. Collier, 'Innovative Military Mapping Using Aerial Photography in the First World War: Sinai, Palestine and Mesopotamia, 1914–1919', *Cartographic Journal*, 31 (1994), pp. 100–104; N.J. Saunders, *Desert Insurgency. Archaeology, T.E. Lawrence, and the Arab Revolt* (Oxford, 2020), eg., p. 89.

17. P. Chausseaud, *Mapping the First World War. The Great War through maps from 1914 to 1918* (2013); '14/18: la guerre en cartes', *Cartes et Géomatique*, 223 (Mar. 2015).

18. N. Lloyd, *Passchendaele: The Lost Victory of World War I* (New York, 2017).

19. H. Clout, *After the Ruins: Restoring the Countryside of Northern France after the Great War* (Exeter, 1996).

20. Polish-Russian conflict: NA. WO. 106/6238, p. 19. Spanish Civil War, NA. WO. 105/1588, pp. 2–7, 106/1578, pp. 1–7.

21. C.J. Esdaile, *The Spanish Civil War. A Military History* (Abingdon, 2019).

22. W. Mitchell, *Winged Defense* (New York, 1925), pp. 3–4.

23. C. Morris, *The Origins of American Strategic Bombing Theory* (Annapolis, Md., 2017).

24. G.H. Bennett, *The Royal Navy in the Age of Austerity, 1919–22: Naval and Foreign Policy under Lloyd George* (2016).

25. I. Lefort, *La Lettre et l'esprit. Géographie scolaire et géographie savant en France, 1870–1970* (Paris, 1992).

Chapter 12

1. War Cabinet Minutes, 4, 12 Feb. 1941, Canberra, National Archives of Australia, A5954, 805/1, pp. 562, 572.

2. Strategic review for regional commanders, 16 Aug. 1941, AWM. 3 DRL/6643, 1/27.

3. A. Jackson, *Persian Gulf Command: A History of the Second World War in Iran and Iraq* (New Haven, Conn., 2018).

4. A. Toprani, 'The First War for Oil: The Caucasus, German Strategy, and the Turning Point of the War on the Eastern Front, 1942', *JMH*, 80 (2016), pp. 815–54; J. Black, *Strategy and the Second World War: How the War was Won and Lost* (2021).

5. D.M. Glantz, *Soviet Operational and Tactical Combat in Manchuria, 1945: 'August Storm'* (2003).

6. M.R. Matheny, *Carrying the War to the Enemy: American Operational Art to 1945* (Norman, Ok., 2011).

7. J. Holland (ed.), *An Englishman at War. The Wartime Diaries of Stanley Christopherson* (2014), p. 510.

8. C.J. Dick, *From Victory to Stalemate: The Western Front, Summer 1944* and *From Defeat to Victory: The Eastern Front, Summer 1944*, both Lawrence, KS, 2016.

9. Auchinleck, memorandum, 18 Oct. 1941, AWM. 3 DRL/6643, 1/27.

10. B. Willems, 'Defiant Breakwaters or Desperate Blunders? A Revision of the German Late-War Fortress Strategy', *Journal of Slavic Military Studies*, 28 (2015), pp. 353–78.
11. C.B. Smith, *Evidence in Camera* (1957), p. 6.
12. T. Downing, *Spies in the Sky. The Secret Battle for Aerial Intelligence During World War II* (2011).
13. J. Black, *The Second World War in 100 Maps* (2020), pp. 34–5.
14. F. Saffroy, '"La limite de la zone des patrouilles": dimensions et representations de la guerre des côtes', http://rgh.univ-lorraine.fr/articles/view/84/La_limite_de_la_zone_des_patrouilles_dimensions_et_representations_de_la_guerre_des_cotes , accessed 17 Jan. 2021.
15. P. Chausseaud and R. Happer, *D-Day: the story of D-Day through maps* (2014).
16. M.K. Bokovoy, *Peasants and Communists: Politics and Ideology in the Yugoslav Countryside, 1941–1953* (Pittsburgh, Penn., 1998); P.B. Minehan, *Civil War and World War in Europe: Spain, Yugoslavia, and Greece, 1936–1946* (Basingstoke, 2006).
17. J.W. Smith, *To Master the Boundless Sea: The U.S. Navy, the Marine Environment, and the Cartography of Empire* (Chapel Hill, NC, 2018).
18. E. Mawdsley, *The War for the Seas: A Maritime history of the Second World War* (New Haven, Conn., 2019).
19. J. Black, *100 Maps*, pp. 156–7.
20. S. Badsey, 'Terrain as a Factor in the Battle of Normandy, 1944', in Doyle and Bennett (eds), *Fields of Battle*, pp. 345–63.
21. J. Black, *100 Maps*, pp. 82–3.
22. *Ibid.*, pp. 142–3.
23. *Ibid.*, pp. 12–13.
24. G. Goodall (ed.), *The War in Maps*, pp. 6, 14. For a modern mapping, J. Lopez, N. Aubin, V. Bernard and N. Guillerat, *World War II Infographics* (2019).
25. T. Robertson, R.B. Tucker, N.B. Breyfogle and P.R. Mansoor (eds), *Nature at War: American Environments and World War II* (Cambridge, 2020).
26. R. Hammond, *Strangling the Axis. The Fight for Control of the Mediterranean during the Second World War* (Cambridge, 2020), p. 173.

Chapter 13
1. *The National Defense Program: Unification and Strategy: Hearings before the U.S. House of Representatives Committee on the Armed Services*, 81st Congress, 1st session, October 1949 (Washington, DC., 1949), p. 521.
2. E. Hatzivassiliou, 'Cold War Pressures, Regional Strategies, and Relative Decline: British Military and Strategic Planning for Cyprus, 1950–1960', *JMH*, 73 (2009), pp. 1143–66.
3. *Warfare in Undeveloped Countries* (1954), p. iii.
4. N. Polmar, T.A. Brooks and G.E. Fedoroff, *Admiral Gorshkov: The Man Who Challenged the U.S. Navy* (Annapolis, MD, 2019).
5. A.T. Weldemichad, 'The Eritrean Long March: The Strategic Withdrawal of the Eritrean Liberation Front, 1978–1979', *JMH*, 73, (2009), p. 1268.
6. D. Rodman, 'A Tale of Two Fronts: Israeli Military Performance during the Early Days of the 1973 Yom Kippur War', *JMH*, 82 (2018), p. 211.
7. J. Ferris, *Behind the Enigma. The Authorised History of GCHQ, Britain's Secret Cyber-Intelligence Agency* (2020), pp. 324–89.

8. T. Huntington, 'U-2', *American Heritage of Invention and Technology*, 22, no. 3 (2007), pp. 40–9.

9. D.A. Day, J.M. Logsdon and B. Latell (eds), *Eye in the Sky: The Story of the CORONA Spy Satellites* (Washington, 2011); R.L. Perry, *A History of Satellite Reconnaissance*, ed. By J.D. Outzen (Chantilly, 2012).

10. J. Cloud, 'American Cartographic Transformations during the Cold War', *Cartography and Geographic Information Science*, 29 (2002), pp. 261–82.

11. M. Monmonier, *Technological Transition in Cartography* (Madison, Wis., 1985); K.P. Werrell, *The Evolution of the Cruise Missile* (Maxwell Air Force Base, Al., 1985).

12. K.C. Clarke, 'Maps and Mapping Technologies of the Persian Gulf War', *Cartography and Geographic Information Systems*, 19 (1992), pp. 84.

13. P.S. Meilinger, *10 Propositions Regarding Air Power* (Maxwell AFB, Alabama, 1995), p. 37.

14. P. Hart, *The Heat of Battle: The 16th Battalion Durham Light Infantry: The Italian Campaign, 1943–1945* (Barnsley, 1999), pp. 201–2.

15. W.M. Waddell, *In the Year of the Tiger: The War for Cochinchina 1945–1951* (Norman, Ok., 2018).

16. I. Pogonowski, *Poland. A Historical Atlas* (2nd edn, New York, 1988), p. 100.

17. N. Carter, 30 Sept. 2020, speech 'Future Defence. The Integrated Operating Concept', at Policy Exchange, London.

Chapter 14

1. B. Bailey and R. Immerman (eds), *Understanding the U.S. Wars in Iraq and Afghanistan* (New York, 2015).

2. C. Tripodi, *The Unknown Enemy. Counterinsurgency and the Illusion of Control* (Cambridge, 2021), pp. 206–7.

3. L. Scholtz, 'The Suwalki Gap Dilemma: A Strategic and Operational Analysis', *Militaire Spectator*, 189 (2020), pp. 540–53.

4. *Times*, 11 Sept. 2020.

5. E. Berman and D.A. Lake, *Proxy Wars: Suppressing Violence through Local Agents* (Ithaca, NY, 2019); T.L. Groh, *Proxy War: the least bad option* (Stanford, Calif., 2019); A Krieg and J.-M. Rickli, *Surrogate Warfare: the Transformation of War in the twenty-first century* (Washington, DC, 2019).

6. BBC News, 12 Sept. 2020.

7. *Times*, 3 Sept. 2020.

8. J.D.T. Ward, *China's Vision of Victory* (Arlington, Va, 2019), pp. 54–87.

9. M. McDevitt, *China as a Twenty-First-Century Naval Power. Theory, Practice, and Implications* (Annapolis, MD., 2020).

10. D.S. Markey, *China's Western Horizon: Beijing and the New Geopolitics of Eurasia* (Oxford, 2020).

11. Navy Office of Information, 'CNO Announces Establishment of U.S. 2nd Fleet', *America's Navy*, 5 May 2018, www.navy.mil

12. M.J. Boyle, *The Drone Age. How Drone Technology Will Change War and Peace* (Oxford, 2020).

13. T.H. Tønnessen, 'Islamic State and Technology – A Literature Review', *Perspectives on Terrorism*, 11, 6 (Dec. 2017), pp. 101–11; K. Chavez and O. Swed, 'Off the Shelf: The Violent Nonstate Actor Drone Threat', *Air and Space Power Journal*, fall 2020,

pp. 29–41; E. Archambault and Y. Veilleux-Lepage, 'Drone Imagery in Islamic State propaganda: flying like a state', *International Affairs*, 96 (2020), pp. 955–73.

14. D. Zhang et al, 'Climate Change and War Frequency in Eastern China over the Last Millennium', *Human Ecology*, 35 (2007), pp. 403–33; R. Tol and S. Wagner, 'Climate change and violent conflict in Europe over the last millennium', *Climatic Change*, 99 (2010), pp. 65–79; G. Parker, *Global Crisis: Climate Change and Catastrophe in the Seventeenth Century* (New Haven, Conn., 2013); J. Connor, 'Climate, Environment, and Australian Frontier Wars: New South Wales, 1788–1841', *JMH*, 81 (2017), pp. 985–1006.

15. M. Kidron and D. Smith, *The New State of War and Peace* (1991), pp. 54–5.

16. A. Wahlman, *Storming the City: U.S. Military Performance in Urban Warfare from World War II to Vietnam* (Denton, Tx., 2015).

17. J. Black, *Tank Warfare* (Bloomington, Ind., 2020), pp. 216–17.

18. O. Jonsson, *The Russian Understanding of War: Blurring the Lines between War and Peace* (Washington, DC., 2019).

Chapter 15

1. P. Porter, *Military Orientalism: Eastern War Through Western Eyes* (2009); L. Wolff, *Inventing Eastern Europe: The Map of Civilisation on the Mind of the Enlightenment* (Stanford, Calif., 1994); R. Hall, *The Balkan Wars, 1912–1913: Prelude to the First World War* (2000), p. 134.

2. P. Hämäläinen, *The Comanche Empire* (New Haven, Conn., 2008), p. 135.

3. *Doctrine of the Armed Forces of the United States* (Washington, 2017).

Selected Further Reading

Black, J., *Geopolitics and the Quest for Dominance* (Bloomington, Ind., 2016).

Boulanger, P. (ed.), *Géographie et guerre, de la géographie militaire au Geospatial Intelligence en France, XVIIIe-XXI siècles* (Paris, 2016).

Bousquet, A.J., *The Eye of War: Military Perception from the Telescope to the Drone* (Minneapolis, Minn., 2018).

Boyle, M.J., *The Drone Age. How Drone Technology Will Change War and Peace* (Oxford, 2020).

Cartes et Géomatique, 223 (Mar. 2015), special issue on '14/18: la guerre en cartes'.

Chasseaud, P., *Artillery's Astrologers: A History of British Survey and Mapping on the Western Front 1914–1918* (Lewes, 1999).

Chasseaud, P., *Mapping the First World War. The Great War through maps from 1914 to 1918* (London, 2013).

Chasseaud, P., *Mapping the Second World War* (2015).

Chasseaud, P. and Doyle, P., *Grasping Gallipoli-Terrain, Maps and Failure at the Dardanelles, 1915* (Staplehurst, 2004).

Chasseaud, P. and Happer, R., *D-Day:the story of D-Day through maps* (London, 2014).

Conti, Simonetta (ed.), *Storia Militare della Geografia* (Rome, 2020).

Doyle, P. and Bennett M. (eds), *Fields of Battle. Terrain in Military History* (Oxford, 2002).

Flint, C. (ed.), *The Geography of War and Peace. From Death Camps to Diplomats* (Oxford, 2005).

Flint, C., *Geopolitical Constructs: The Mulberry Harbours, the Second World War, and the Making of a Militarized Transatlantic* (Lanham, MD., 2016).

Ginsburger, N., *'La guerre, la plus terrible des érosions', Cultures de guerre et géographes universitaires Allemagne-France-États-Unis, 1914–1921* (Paris, 2010).

Hämäläinen, P., *The Comanche Empire* (New Haven, Conn., 2008).

Macola, G., *The Gun in Central Africa: A History of Technology and Politics* (Athens, Oh., 2016).

Monmonier, M., *Rhumb Lines and Map Wars – A Social History of the Mercator Projection* (Chicago, Ill., 2004).

O'Sullivan, P., *Terrain and Tactics* (London, 1991).

O'Sullivan, P. and J.W. Miller, *The Geography of Warfare* (London 1983).

O'Sullivan, P., *The Geography of War in the Post-Cold War World* (London, 2001).

Palka, E. and F. Galgano, *The Scope of Military Geography: Across the Spectrum from Peacetime to War* (London, 2000).

Palka, E. and F. Galgano (eds), *Modern Military Geography* (London, 2010).

Peltier, L.C., *Bibliography of Military Geography* (London, 1962).

Peltier, L.C. and G.E. Pearcy, *Military Geography* (Princeton NJ, 1955).

Pilkey, O. and Dixon, K.L., *The Corps and the Shore* (Washington, 1996).

Porter, P., *Military Orientalism: Eastern War Through Western Eyes* (London, 2009).

Toprani, A., *Oil and the Great Powers: Britain and Germany, 1914 to 1945* (Oxford, 2019)

Woodward, R., *Military Geographies* (Oxford, 2004).

Index